CHRONICLES OF TERROR
VOL. **8**

CHRONICLES OF TERROR
VOL. 8
Polish soldiers in Soviet captivity

On the Kola Peninsula, we were told clearly: "This land is your grave."

From the testimony of Walenty Kasprzyk, who was sent for forced labor to the Far North.

WITNESSES OF TOTALITARIANISM SPEAK OUT

Chronicles of Terror is an innovative project spanning historical research, popularization efforts, and memory culture. We are building the largest collection of civilian accounts of life in occupied Europe.

Our database features the accounts of Polish citizens who suffered at the hands of two totalitarian regimes – German and Soviet – during World War II. These testimonies reflect the experience of thousands of Polish victims of totalitarian crimes and of their families and loved ones.

Scattered and locked up in different archives for many years, the accounts are currently reaching a wide audience, allowing people to discover local and family history, and inspiring scholars, journalists and makers of culture. Thanks to their translation into English, they are entering international circulation, spreading information about the double occupation of Poland around the globe, and preserving the memory of victims of totalitarianism.

Testimonies from different parts of Poland will be published in successive volumes as part of this book series.

More testimonies can be found at:

ChroniclesofTerror.pl
ZapisyTerroru.pl

TABLE OF CONTENTS

In September 1939, the Soviet troops entering Grodno met with heavy resistance. The Polish Army troops, supported by selfless civilian volunteers (especially scouts) – defended the city for two days, despite being vastly outnumbered by the Red Army. Pages 12 and 13: panoramic view of Grodno, 1931.

Photo. National Digital Archives

EDITOR'S NOTE

The present book series derives directly from the bilingual online database of testimonies *Chronicles of Terror* (ZapisyTerroru.pl, ChroniclesofTerror.pl), containing accounts of Polish citizens who suffered at the hands of two totalitarian regimes – German and Soviet – during World War II. The series and database feature depositions taken by the Main Commission for the Investigation of German Crimes in Poland as well as accounts of Poles who left the Soviet Union along with Anders' Army, the latter collected since 1943 in the Middle East. Thanks to our cooperation with the Polish Institute of National Remembrance (Instytut Pamięci Narodowej, IPN) and the Hoover Institution in the United States, for the first time all of these documents can reach a broad audience. We are creating one of the largest databases of civilian testimonies from Nazi-occupied Europe.

The Main Commission for the Investigation of German Crimes in Poland was established on 29 March 1945, before World War II had come to an end (the relevant decree, however, was not issued until 10 November that same year). Its tasks included collecting and publishing materials documenting Nazi German crimes, and conducting research. At the same time, the Commission conducted investigations under the Polish Code of Criminal Procedure, and its members had to be qualified judges or prosecutors, while its proceedings had the status of judicial activities.[1] 1946 saw the appearance of the first issue of *Biuletyn Głównej Komisji Badania Zbrodni*

1 *Dekret z 10.11.1945 r.*, "Dziennik Ustaw" 1945, no. 51, item 293. On the beginnings of the Commission's activity see: M. Motas, *Główna Komisja Badania Zbrodni Niemieckich w Polsce i jej oddziały terenowe w 1945 roku. Wybór dokumentów*, Warszawa 1995.

Niemieckich w Polsce [Bulletin of the Main Commission for the Investigation of German Crimes], listing topics of interest to the Commission, including the operation of concentration camps, death camps, and labor camps, the extermination of Polish Jews, crimes committed in Warsaw (before, during, and after the Warsaw Uprising), and the fate of Soviet prisoners of war. Yet already in 1948 the authorities began to dismantle the elaborate structure of the Commission's regional branches. By the end of 1949, all of the local branches had been abolished with the exception of the one in Kraków (which continued to function until 1953).[2] The word "German" in the name was also replaced with the word "Hitlerite." It was not until after the end of Stalinism that the Main Commission and its bulletin once again became an important forum for research on the German occupation of Poland. From the 1960s on, the Commission was headed by Czesław Pilichowski, a historian and political scientist. In the 1970s, Franciszek Ryszka, author of the classic monograph *Państwo stanu wyjątkowego: rzecz o systemie państwa i prawa Trzeciej Rzeszy* [State of Emergency: On the Political and Legal System of the Third Reich], became editor-in-chief of the bulletin.

Of the materials gathered by the Main Commission those produced in connection with proceedings before the Supreme National Tribunal and various courts and prosecutor's offices hold a particular value. It is among these that we find an enormous body of thousands of witness testimonies documenting German crimes. Altogether, by the end of the 1970s, a total of some 11,000 investigations and nearly 6,000 discovery proceedings had been carried out in Poland, with 105,000 witness depositions taken.[3] After the war, these served to sentence many German war criminals, including Amon Göth, Arthur Greiser, Rudolf Höss, or Ludwig Fischer.

Regardless of the public interest in the bulletin and other Main Commission publications in the past, today the material is for the most part known only to a narrow circle of specialists. In building the *Chronicles of Terror* digital archive, we set ourselves the ambitious goal of making it available in full for the first time to all those interested, not only scholars dealing with Poland's recent history.

A similar premise was adopted with regard to the testimonies of Poles who left the Soviet Union with Anders' Army. The bulk of this collection

2 Ł. Jasiński, "Główna Komisja Badania Zbrodni Niemieckich/Hitlerowskich w Polsce. Narzędzie rozliczeń i propagandy", in: *Rozliczanie totalitarnej przeszłości: instytucje i ulice*, ed. A. Paczkowski, Warszawa 2017, p. 54.

3 P. Lewandowski, "Główna Komisja Badania Zbrodni Przeciwko Narodowi Polskiemu w Polsce (1945–1999)", *Piotrkowskie Zeszyty Historyczne* 2015, vol. 16, p. 163.

consists of some 18,000 questionnaires and accounts collected pursuant to orders issued by the Commander of the Polish Armed Forces in the East on 21 December 1942.[4] We are talking about a total of some 30,000 testimonies of different kinds.[5] Most of them were deposited by victims of Stalinist terror as early as 1943. They concern arrests by the NKVD, tortures used during investigations, deportations, and life in the GULAG. In these accounts, we find shattering descriptions of several weeks of traveling in cattle cars, backbreaking labor, constant hunger, and often of the death of loved ones.

These materials were deposited immediately after the war in the California-based Hoover Institution due to fears that they would be seized by the communist authorities. Until 1970 they remained essentially unavailable to the outside world.[6] It was not until the 1990s that they became available in Poland in the form of microfilms at the Archive of Modern Records in Warsaw. In this case, too, it was mostly historians doing research on twentieth-century Polish history who consulted them.

Due to the size of both of the abovementioned archival collections and on account of the fact that the Main Commission documents are scattered across the whole Institute of National Remembrance Archive, we have adopted a strategy of gradually publishing the effects of our work in our testimonies database. We are bringing to light witness accounts from across a range of archival units, transcribing them and translating them into English, editing both language versions, and making them available online along with digitized copies of the original documents. The website also features images, articles developing the historical context of the events, as well as a variety of tools facilitating searching the collection.

Thanks to the present book series readers can encounter selected testimonies from the digital archive. The thematic headings of forthcoming volumes will reflect successive work done within the framework of the project. By compiling selections of testimonies, we are keenly aware of the nature of the undertaking, which is addressed to a whole range of audiences. One of our aims is to deliver high-quality source materials for scholars in Poland and abroad; we are also hoping to revive memory within families and local communities and to inspire cultural creators and all those interested in the history of World War II and the double occupation of Poland. Readers

---

4 W. Stępniak, *Archiwalia polskie w zbiorach Instytutu Hoovera Uniwersytetu Stanforda*, Warszawa 1997, p. 180.

5 M. Wieliczko, "Biuro Dokumentów Wojska Polskiego na Obczyźnie w latach 1941–1946", *Annales Universitatis Mariae Curie-Skłodowska* 2006, vol. 61, p. 199.

6 W. Stępniak, op. cit., p. 180.

wanting to get a broader glimpse of a specific topic through the lens of individual testimonies are encouraged to explore the ChroniclesofTerror.pl website.

The *Chronicles of Terror* series draws directly on the online database. It therefore follows the editorial guidelines of the digital archive. Neither the online database nor this volume pretend to be a critical edition of the archival sources. This kind of undertaking would require many years of work by a large research team.

Our intention is to redact the material as little as possible. We make minimum editorial changes, allowing the archival documents to speak for themselves. We leave it up to the reader to carry out their own analysis and arrive at their own interpretation, although it must be emphasized that the documents cannot be read uncritically. We encourage all those interested to visit the online database, which features scans of the original documents in addition to the Polish transcriptions and English translations of the testimonies.

Taking care to stay as close to the original as possible, we only corrected grammar and spelling mistakes as well as slips of the pen (*lapsus calami*). Linguistic modernization was applied sparingly so as not to alter the character of the sources. Editorial annotations were kept to a minimum and were placed in square brackets rather than footnotes. All proper names (surnames, place names) were kept in the language of the original (only obvious spelling mistakes were corrected). In cases where only a fragment of a given account has been published in the book, we marked the ellipses with suspension points in square brackets. The present volume is supplemented with a glossary of basic terms relating to deportations of POWs to the USSR.

In September 1939, the Red Army soldiers entering the territory of the Second Polish Republic, murdered approximately 1,500 civilians and soldiers. One of their victims among high-ranking officers was the commander of the "Grodno" Operational Group, General **Józef Olszyna-Wilczyński** (in the photograph: fifth from the left, with participants of the Zułów–Wilno cross-country skiing race, 1938).

Photo. National Digital Archives

THE EPILOGUE TO SEPTEMBER 1939 – POLISH SOLDIERS IN SOVIET CAPTIVITY

The aggression against Poland in September 1939 sealed the pact concluded by Nazi Germany and the Soviet Union on 23 August of the same year. The guarantee of Soviet collaboration effectively removed any obstacles for Adolf Hitler to order the attack on Poland. Since 1 September, Polish soldiers were engaged in combat with superior German forces, delaying the Wehrmacht's march on Warsaw. In line with the orders of the Commander-in-Chief, Marshal Edward Rydz-Śmigły, the Polish president, government, state administration and units with combat capabilities headed for the border with neutral Romania in order to create a new defense area there, awaiting military support from allies – the United Kingdom and France.

Consequently, when on the morning of 17 September Vladimir Potemkin, Deputy People's Commissar of Foreign Affairs of the USSR, served Wacław Grzybowski, the Polish ambassador to Moscow, with the Soviet note to the Polish government, the latter refused to accept it. The text, edited in cooperation with the Germans, read that "the Polish state and government had effectively ceased to exist." Given that Poland's president, government and commander-in-chief had not yet left the country, and the Polish army could still count on half its initial number, the document was a mere propaganda tool meant to justify the Red Army's entry into Poland without a declaration of war.

Once information about the USSR's breach of the 1932 non-aggression pact reached the headquarters of the Commander-in-Chief, Marshal Rydz-Śmigły gave an order "not to engage with the Soviets." Nevertheless, Polish units stationed near the eastern border adopted differing attitudes when faced with Red Army troops. Soldiers from Border Protection Corps and "Polesie" Independent Operational Group fought heavy battles in the Wołyń and Polesie area. Civilian and military defenders of Lwów, Grodno and Wilno also distinguished themselves in combat. Most Polish troops, however, ultimately surrendered in the face of superior enemy forces and dwindling hopes for any help from the allies. A telling symbol of collaboration between the two totalitarian states was a joint German-Soviet military parade in Brześć on the Bug River on 22 September, and the German-Soviet Boundary and Friendship Treaty signed six days later. The Red Army's invasion precipitated Poland's downfall.

As a result of military operations, almost 240,000 soldiers, including around 10,000 officers, were taken prisoner in the USSR.[1] Most were detained near Brześć, Włodzimierz Wołyński and Dubno. On 19 September, the Political Bureau of VKP(b)'s Central Committee decided that all POWs would remain at the disposal of the NKVD. To this end, People's Commissar for the Interior, Lavrentiy Beria, appointed the Prisoner of War Command. Transit camps were established in border towns with broad-gauge railway stations. Shepetovka, Volochysk, Yarmolyntsi, Kamenets-Podolskyi, Orzechowo, Radashkovichy, Stołpce, Timkovichi and Zhytkavichy became the first rallying points for Polish soldiers. Then, they were to be transpor ted to one of NKVD's special camps for POWs in Ostashkov, Kozelsk, Starobelsk, Yukhnovo, Putyvl´, Yuzha (Vyazniki) or Oranki. Most camps, like the ones in Ostashkov and Kozelsk, were established in former monasteries that had been taken over by the state following the 1917 Bolshevik revolution. The camps were not fit to accommodate such a vast number of POWs, a fact reported by their commandants from the very outset. Rooms were damp and dirty, often also unheated. Food and water were lacking. Buildings were overcrowded, so prisoners had to sleep on bare floors. In Ostashkov, the average area per prisoner was 0.5 square meter.

Initially, the Bolshevik party executive planned to send all imprisoned Polish soldiers to camps, irrespective of their rank. Yet owing to the large number of POWs, privates from Eastern voivodeships of the Second Polish

---

1 *Katyń. Dokumenty zbrodni*, vol. 1: *Jeńcy nie wypowiedzianej wojny*, collective work, Warsaw 1995, p. 18; A. Głowacki, "Poland between the Soviet Union and Germany, 1939-1941" in *White Spots. Black Spots. Difficult Matters in Polish-Russian relations, 1918-2008*, ed. A. D. Rotfeld and A. V. Torkunov, Pittsburgh 2015.

Republic were released in early October. Officers, civil servants, members of the police force, Border Protection Corps, Border Guards, prison warders, intelligence and counterintelligence agents remained at the disposal of the NKVD. Between 7 and 18 October, the Soviets released 42,500 privates and non-commissioned officers.

Not all privates were that lucky, though. Soldiers from the German-occupied part of Poland remained in NKVD custody. They were provisionally gathered in the Kozelsk and Putyvl′ camps, while the Soviet Union began negotiating the exchange of POWs with the Third Reich. As a result of mutual agreements, in October and November 1939 the Soviets handed over 42,292 people to the Germans. These included Jews and declared communists, who – fearing Nazi repressions – pleaded to remain in the USSR. Most such requests were denied. As a result of a similar operation, the Germans sent 13,757 soldiers to the USSR.[2]

Another group of prisoners was sent to forced labor: either to build a road connecting Novograd-Volynskyi and Lwów or to work in the mines and steelworks of the People's Commissariat of Ferrous Metallurgy in the Donets Basin, Zaporozhye and Krivoy Rog. On 25 September, Beria issued an order concerning the construction of a road between Novograd-Volynskyi and Lwów, also referred to as "NKVD construction camp no. 1." Around 25,000 Polish POWs (privates) were designated to work there, and a camp to house them was established in Równe, with a few outposts along the route of the construction. In early October, another decision was issued to transfer around 11,000 POWs to work in state-owned industrial enterprises. Three labor camps were created for them: in Krivoy Rog, Olenovka (Karakuba) and Zaporozhye.

Once most privates and non-commissioned officers were released home, handed over to the Germans or sent to forced labor, the initial structure of NKVD's POW camps changed. Starobelsk became the first camp for officers, where most officers and reserve officers were held. In late November, a total of 3,907 people were detained there. The Kozelsk camp was second: as at 1 December it held 4,596 officers, civil servants and priests. The Ostashkov camp was designated for police officers, gendarmes, members of the Border Protection Corps, Border Guards, prison warders as well as intelligence and counterintelligence agents. As at 2 December, 6,364 people were held there.[3] The structure of the camps remained relatively unchanged until spring 1940.

2 *Katyń. Dokumenty zbrodni*, vol. 1, p. 27.

3 Ibid., pp. 29–32.

NKVD investigations were ongoing until the late January 1940. Political police aimed to uncover "counterrevolutionary element," a term used to designate members of the intelligence, police officers, prison warders, soldiers from Border Protection Corps as well as political and social activists and members of pre-war Polish organizations. Through establishing a network of agents and interrogations, the Soviets intended to gauge the sentiment among POWs, and see if they would collaborate. However, reports delivered to Beria were clear: Polish officers presented a clear anti-Soviet stance and any attempts at establishing cooperation ended in a fiasco. Since then, the highest Soviet executive deliberated on what to do with the Polish officers. Releasing them home, like privates, was out of the question for fear they would go on to organize armed Polish resistance on Soviet-occupied areas.

The fate of Polish officers was sealed on 5 March 1940. The Political Bureau of VKP(b) headed by Joseph Stalin accepted Beria's solution for 14,700 Polish POWs and more than 11,000 detainees, whose cases were to be "reviewed in a special procedure, and the supreme penalty, execution by firing squad, should be administered."[4] In the language of the Soviet security services, this equaled the murder of at least 21,857 Polish citizens – in cold blood, with a shot to the back of the head. Prisoners from Ostashkov were murdered in Tver, those from Starobelsk in Kharkov, and those from Kozelsk directly above death pits in a forest near Katyn.

"SURVEY CAMPAIGN"

This volume is the first book in the *Chronicles of Terror* publishing series, devoted entirely to the fate of Polish soldiers in Soviet captivity in the years 1939–1941. It is divided into four sections presenting selected testimonies of Polish POWs and internees who joined the Anders' Army and in 1943, in the Middle East, responded to a questionnaire prepared by the Historical Office and Documentation Office of the Polish Armed Forces in the East. Both institutions aimed to document the fate and experiences of Polish citizens under Soviet occupation: in camps, prisons, forced labor camps and exile.

Chapters one and two present the testimonies of soldiers who, as POWs, were sent to forced labor camps established in former Eastern voivodeships of the Second Polish Republic and in Ukraine. Chapters three and four describe the fate of Poles interned in the Baltic states, from where, in the summer of 1940, they were deported to camps in the heart of Russia

4 L. Beria's note to J. Stalin of 5 March 1940 in *Katyń. Dokumenty zbrodni*, vol. 1, pp. 469–475.

and in the Far North. These testimonies represent a fascinating document of the Polish citizens' personal confrontations with the totalitarian Stalinist regime: from 17 September 1939 to the "amnesty" of August 1941. They were written down by people of various social backgrounds, education and military rank. They do not include the accounts of officers murdered in the spring of 1940. Despite its immense historical value, this vast body of material has so far been rather poorly researched. This is why we have decided to make it available in the *Chronicles of Terror* publishing series. Most testimonies contained in this volume have not been published before.

The Independent Historical Office of the Command of the Polish Armed Forces of the Soviet Union was established pursuant to an order issued by General Władysław Anders, directly after the conclusion of the Polish-Soviet agreement of 30 July 1941 (the Sikorski-Mayski Agreement). A group of officers noted the need to gather materials and historical mementoes, and equip the emerging army with a unit modelled on the pre-war Military Historical Office. The Independent Historical Office was headed by Lieutenant Dr. Walerian Charkiewicz, and its organization and operations were regulated by the order of 17 December 1941. Thus began the collection and organization of historical materials related to the establishment of the Polish Armed Forces in the Soviet Union as well as the process of collecting accounts of the fate of Polish citizens in the USSR.

Following the Polish Army's evacuation from the USSR to Iran, where in September 1942 it joined troops stationed in the Middle East, the resulting operational unit was referred to as Polish Armed Forces in the East. In his order of 15 April 1943, General Anders founded the army's Documentation Office, into which the Historical Office was incorporated. The office was not only meant to serve as an archive institution, but also as a unit working with the collected material with a view to using it to counteract Soviet propaganda. Without a doubt, the greatest endeavor pursued by both institutions – the Historical Office and then the Documentation Office – was collecting testimonies from POWs, internees, camp inmates and deportees who managed to join the Anders' Army. This task was divided into several stages, but period documents mostly refer to it jointly as the "survey campaign."

The survey campaign is said to have begun in the spring of 1942, after the army had left for Iran. The project gained momentum in early 1943. Former POWs and camp inmates arriving at the Polish Army's rallying points were among the first to complete the questionnaires. In the discussed period, several templates of questionnaires and surveys were circulated among Poles. The most frequent one was the "questionnaire of a former POW – internee – prisoner – *'lagernik'* – deportee in USSR," with considerable importance also attached to the "plebiscite survey," which collected information about fictional plebiscites carried out in October 1939 in Polish areas occupied by the Red Army. Apart from these two flagship projects, there were also detailed surveys, such as the "Jewish survey," the survey on Kolyma, or the "women's survey." Although the questionnaires differed in terms of their form, the fundamental questions remained the same. The most important data included full name, age, profession, marital status as well as the circumstances of arrest/deportation. These were followed by a series of questions about the camp, prison or other detention site: its name, location, appearance, daily routine, food, work quotas, attitudes of the NKVD, medical assistance, contacts with home and family and circumstances of release. Sometimes responses were entered directly on the form and limited to briefly stating personal data and detention sites, such as "Ukhta forced labor camp", "Sevpechlag", "a kolkhoz in Kazakhstan." Sometimes the questions were formulated in a way that suggested a longer written statement, a memoir of sorts, such as "Biography", "An account of my time in Russia", "My life in Russia." Many of the answers display great literary and journalistic value.

These surveys, questionnaires and testimonies are currently held at the Hoover Institution Library & Archives in Stanford, California. The documents were transported to the United States so as to avoid their capture by Communists, which could have resulted in repressions against the respondents and their families. The Hoover Institution was selected since – as a private entity – it was free from direct political pressures. In his correspondence with the Institution, General Anders expressed the desire to send the materials already in the summer of 1946. Consequently, they were transferred in two batches: the first one was sent from Italy in the late 1946, and the second in November 1947 from Foxley, England, where the Documentation Office was relocated. In order to further protect the archive documents against undesirable surveillance at the hands of foreign intelligence, General Anders was named the "sole keeper" of the entire collection, which was thus transformed into a private deposit.

In 1993, the Head Office of State Archives entered into an agreement with the Hoover Institution, as a result of which the documents – in the form of microfilms – were handed over to the Central Archives of Modern Records. They were also digitized and published by the National Digital Archives on the szukajwarchiwach.pl website, which – apart from the Anders Collection of documents – also provides access to other archive documentation owned by the Hoover Institution Library & Archives. Since 17 September 2017, the *Chronicles of Terror* website has been systematically publishing testimonies of those who survived Soviet hell.

FORCED LABOR CAMPS FOR POWS

According to international conventions – the Hague Convention (IV) and the Geneva Convention of 1929 as well as customary law of armed conflict – prisoners of war (POWs) are soldiers of the warring side who were taken captive. Although the Soviet Union never formally declared war on Poland, the Red Army entered Polish territory and Polish soldiers were attacked, disarmed and taken prisoner. While the Soviet Union only expressed its readiness to abide by the above conventions after the Soviet-German War broke out, on 1 July 1941, the term "prisoners of war" was universally employed in Soviet documents already from the outset of the Polish September Campaign. Nevertheless, Polish soldiers were treated in breach of the spirit of international agreements, more like criminals than rightful members of the armed forces of one of the warring sides, e.g. by being shifted to political police jurisdiction – the NKVD.

The above conventions also regulate the use of POW labor. POWs cannot be forced to perform work associated with military operations or wartime economy and should be ensured proper and secure conditions. They may only perform work on their own account, work for their own camp or paid voluntary work. Forced labor camps for POWs operated in stark contradiction to these values. From the ideological standpoint, each of the Polish soldiers held against their will represented a threat to Soviet rule, a "socially dangerous element" – but from the economic standpoint, they represented the potential of a free labor force. Consequently, a substantial part of this volume is devoted to forced labor of POWs in Soviet captivity.

Some of the soldiers who were released home in October 1939 – privates and non-commissioned officers – were sent to forced labor in the aforementioned enterprises owned by the People's Commissariat of Ferrous Metallurgy and the so-called Równe camp (in other words: NKVD construction camp no. 1). The Równe camp was established on 25 September, and POWs held there were to be used in the construction of a paved road connecting Novograd-Volynskyi and Lwów. The first stage of work supervised by the NKVD was planned to end on 15 December 1939, and the asphalt road surface was meant to be installed in the spring, by 15 April. Poles sent to the construction camp were assured that they would be released once the first stage was over. However, the Soviets wanted to use the POWs' slave labor to the maximum and – once the stretch to Lwów was finished, the route was extended westwards, until Przemyśl and the border with the Third Reich. In October 1940, the same POWs were sent to modernize the Proskurov–Tarnopol–Lwów–Jaworów road leading to the USSR's western border and to construction sites of military air bases, e.g. in Brody, Czerlany, Olszanica, Stawki and Berezowice – the newly established sites were jointly referred to as the Lwów camp.

The largest branches of the Równe camp created along the road under construction included Równe, Brody, Jaryczów Stary, Żytyń, Zahorce Wielkie, Sapożyn, Olesko, Warkowicze and Werba Dubieńska. In total, more than 90 forced labor camps for POWs of varying sizes were established on lands annexed by the USSR.[5] The work was extremely hard and mostly involved earthworks and transport of crushed stone to pave the road. Owing to the priority nature of the endeavor, POWs had to work irrespective of weather conditions. They later recalled that "there often were no tools to work with, and if one failed to meet the work quota [...], he would get 400 grams of bread and watery soup. [...] Sundays and Saturdays were not work-free. After arriving from work in the evening and eating combined lunch and dinner, which invariably failed to satisfy the hunger, there was no opportunity to rest, because political instructors would call on us to attend communist talks and convince us how good life was in their country."[6] The camps were characterized by a large number of fugitives. According to NKVD reports, between September 1939 and August 1940, more than 1,400 people escaped from various stretches of the Równe camp. This was largely facilitated by going to work without NKVD's escort on some stretches, and the fact that inmates – apart from NKVD Convoy Troops – were supervised by camp guards, 70% of whom were inmates too. This was also influenced by the proximity of German-occupied territory – more than half of Polish POWs hailed from these areas.

The investment projects planned for 1941 were not completed. Work was interrupted by Germany's sudden attack against its ally.

A hasty and chaotic evacuation began, during which POWs were rushed on foot or transported in crowded freight cars to the east. During the march, they were beaten by NKVD soldiers convoying them, who also set dogs upon them. Those who grew weak were either shot dead on the spot or stabbed to death with bayonets. The number of POWs murdered along the way is estimated at 428.[7] One of the survivors, Jan Golonka, recalled: "This march from 23 June to 17 July 1941 represented a single terrible streak of torture. We made 40–50 kilometers a day; there were days when we did not receive any food and were not allowed to collect water, we were lucky if someone managed to collect a tiny bit of foul-smelling water from a puddle. When people sometimes wanted to give us something along the way,

---

5 P. Żaroń, *Obozy jeńców polskich w ZSRR w latach 1939–1941*, Warszawa–London 1994, pp. 104–106.

6 Henryk Gansiniec's account – Collection of the Hoover Institution Library & Archives at the disposal of the Central Archives of Modern Records, Władysław Anders Collection. Reports, 800/1/0/-/47, account no. 570.

7 *Katyń. Dokumenty zbrodni*, vol. 1, p. 28.

As a result of the September Campaign, more than one million Polish soldiers and members of uniformed services found themselves in German and Soviet captivity. Most were placed in German Oflag or Stalag camps or in Soviet POW camps supervised by the NKVD. In the photograph: farewell to chief of staff of the Border Protection Guards high command, Lieutenant Colonel **Witold Kirszenstein**, in an officers' mess in Warsaw, 1932.

Photo. National Digital Archives

the NKVD soldiers escorting us did not allow them, saying: 'They shot at our people, and you are giving them water!', explaining to the bystanders that we were German. Along the way, we were joined by others, so the column kept getting bigger. Those unable to walk were beaten with rifle butts, and whoever collapsed and fainted, was gone."[8] This thread resurfaces in a number of testimonies presented in the volume. The evacuation destination was the camp in Starobelsk: subsequent larger and smaller groups of evacuated Polish POWs reached it in July 1941, totaling more than 12,000 people.

A considerable group of POWs – privates and non-commissioned officers from Starobelsk, Putyvl′and Kozelsk who had not been released home in October 1939 – were handed over by the NKVD to the People's Commissariat of Ferrous Metallurgy. These soldiers were sent to one of the three aforementioned camps in Krivoy Rog, Olenovka (Karakuba) and Zaporozhye. The Commissariat of Metallurgy was to provide them with adequate clothing, food and accommodation, and POWs were meant to work in state-owned industrial enterprises: mines and steelworks. Living conditions and safety of work were dramatically low, a fact confirmed even by NKVD officers supervising the camps. POW testimonies paint a picture of their reality: "Mud around the barracks was up to our ankles, the barracks were not well heated during winter, we were responsible for keeping them in order. Sanitary conditions were terrible, there were plenty of lice. We would hand over underwear for washing in private and in secret. We had to beg to be allowed to bathe."[9] POWs were sent to work in industrial enterprises and mines without any prior check-up of their professional skills or health situation. There were situations when heads of such enterprises notified their superiors that they did not want forced laborers from Poland who were unprepared and generated additional costs. Consequently, they were treated as "provisional workforce" and sent to perform the worst types of work. As a result, the material situation of POWs deteriorated so badly that when one of the canteens refused to give them breakfast on 20 December, they declared a strike. The negative atmosphere was strengthened by letters from home, mentioning that other Polish Army privates had already been released. In the Soviet Union of the 1930s and 1940s, organized refusal to go to work to protect one's rights was an unprecedented act. In most workplaces, POWs came into contact with Soviet citizens hired as laborers. Therefore, NKVD officers decided that the strike would have to be quickly

8 Jan Golonka's account – Collection of the Hoover Institution Library & Archives at the disposal of the Central Archives of Modern Records, Władysław Anders Collection. Reports, 800/1/0/-/47, account no. 517.

9 Czesław Kościelny's account – Collection of the Hoover Institution Library & Archives at the disposal of the Central Archives of Modern Records, Władysław Anders Collection. Reports, 800/1/0/-/48, account no. 2035.

stifled to serve as an example. Repressions ensued: the camp regime was toughened and "ringleaders" were identified and arrested. What is more, POWs were to be transferred to the Northern Railway Camp (Sevzheldorlag) that formed part of the Gulag, so that the situation would not repeat.

The Northern Railway Camp was a set of *lagers* situated mainly within today's Arkhangelsk Oblast and Komi Republic. In line with Beria's order of 14 May 1940, Sevzheldorlag inmates were to work on the construction site of a 728-kilometer stretch of the North Pechora Trunk Line leading from Kotlas to Vorkuta. This was another strategic investment of the USSR overseen by the NKVD and built, among others, using the labor of Polish POWs. First transports were already sent north on 15 May, and the Eastern Ukrainian camps subordinated to the Commissariat of Metallurgy were disbanded on 9 June. In Sevzheldorlag, POWs were treated equally with Gulag inmates. They were stripped of any personal belongings and lodged in shelters, dugouts and provisional barracks. They were refused warmer clothes and shoes, and the working hours, whether in the forest or doing earthworks, were prolonged at will. Already at the outset, many POWs were beaten up and robbed by criminals and inmates holding posts at the camp. Without a trial or sentence, Polish citizens were forced to confront the reality of living in Soviet lagers.

Work was hard, food was poor, and medical care was at the lowest possible level. Consequently, mortality rates skyrocketed in early 1941, and more than 80% POWs suffered from acute forms of scurvy. Given the general wasting of the body, they were not able to work well enough to receive full food rations, the so-called third pot. The vast majority of Poles failed to meet the inflated work quotas and only received the so-called first pot. Making food ratios dependent on meeting work quotas was another element of the thought-out system of exploiting prisoners and sentencing them to a slow death. For inmates in the Far North, "amnesty" meant that they could leave the Gulag hell behind and save their lives. In early July, more than 7,700 people from Sevzheldorlag were transported to the POW camp in Yuzha.

INTERNEES IN THE BALTIC STATES

Separate chapters are devoted to the fates of Polish soldiers who – faced with the Red Army's intrusion into Poland – decided to cross the border with neutral Lithuania or Latvia. There, they were interned in line with the provisions of international law, thus avoiding contact with the Soviets until June 1940, when the Baltic states lost their independence after power was seized by Communist parties controlled by Moscow.

The first Polish soldiers crossed the border with Lithuania on 18 September 1939. In early October, their number already amounted to around 13,000.[10] The Lithuanian authorities treated the internees in line with international treaties. As participants of military operations who had found themselves in a neutral state, they had to be disarmed and subjected to control, so as not to compromise the neutrality of their host country. The first internment camps were organized ad hoc, but their structure was already stabilized in the winter of 1939/40. Polish soldiers and officers were quartered in Kalvarija, Rokiškis (in April 1940, the camp was transferred to the Kaunas barracks), Palanga, Kulautuva (transferred to Kaunas in March 1940), Birštonas (transferred to Vilkaviškis in January 1940), Ukmergė and Kaunas, where Forts V and VI were converted for this purpose. The camps in Palanga, Kulautuva and Birštonas were located in Lithuanian holiday and spa towns. The internees were quartered in holiday homes that had been provisionally adapted for winter. The camps in Kalvarija, Vilkaviškis and Ukmergė were located in military barracks. The soldiers held there enjoyed the best conditions. Camps established in Kaunas' Forts V and VI were maximum security camps, designated for fugitives, those failing to abide by camp discipline or regarded as particularly hostile towards Lithuania by Lithuanian authorities.

The camp regime was not too strict. The camp guards were Lithuanian soldiers, who displayed proper, at times even friendly behavior. Internees were allowed to move freely across the camps and granted leave passes. In some locations, they were even allowed to move around the entire town. In Ukmergė, for instance, one could meet a number of uniformed Polish soldiers in the streets, shops and restaurants. Visits of family members were permitted. Internees received food in the camps. Some camps even had their own canteens. Decent sanitary conditions were provided, as a result of which there were no outbreaks of contagious diseases or epidemics. Sending correspondence was possible (also outside Lithuania), but subject to Lithuanian censorship. A number of charity and social organizations provided assistance to Polish soldiers. These included the International Red Cross, YMCA as well as local Lithuanian and Polish charitable associations.

Lithuanian authorities tried to organize cultural life by providing internees with Lithuanian press and books. Radio sets were also installed, and film screenings were held. The internees organized themselves too. Libraries, where one could also find Polish books, operated in all camps.

10 J. Pięta, W. Roman, M. Szczurowski, *Polacy internowani na Litwie 1939–1940*, Warszawa 1997, p. 27.

A cultural and educational section, financed from donations, existed in Palanga. One of its projects was a choir that gave concerts both for Polish soldiers and for inhabitants of the town. Kalvarija, on the other hand, had a theatre group called "Nasz Teatr." Apart from these endeavors, self-education groups sprang up in almost all camps, teaching foreign languages and other courses. Magazines devoted to camp life, culture and classified ads were published, such as the "Kalwariat" or "Podchorąży." All of the above actions boosted the internees' morale. One of the most important initiatives were "information bulletins" published in Palanga since September, which compiled and commented on radio announcements. One of its editors was Lieutenant Walerian Charkiewicz, historian and graduate of the University of Wilno who went on to organize the Independent Historical Office of the Polish Armed Forces in the USSR and served as its first director.

Despite the high tensions in Polish-Lithuanian relations before the war – caused by the conflict over Wilno Region and leading to diplomatic ties being severed off until March 1938 – Lithuanian authorities treated Polish soldiers in a friendly manner. Tolerable housing conditions, the provision of food and medical care as well as freedom to pursue cultural and educational activities were secured by the Lithuanian authorities. Here one should recall that apart from the soldiers, Lithuania accepted 35,000 civilian refugees, which required considerable financial and administrative efforts from the small state. Descriptions of conflict situations conveyed in memoirs and testimonies prove that the Lithuanian administration and representatives of Polish internees were able to find a consensus on the most important matters.

The situation in Latvia developed in a similar manner. Until the end of September 1939, around 1,500 Polish soldiers crossed the border with Latvia. They were disarmed and moved to an interim camp in Daugavpils, and then transferred to one of four internment camps: in Ulbroka, Liepāja, Lilaste or Litene. Latvian authorities treated Poles properly. Like in Lithuanian camps, in Latvia the internees were also quartered in military buildings, suitable for the oncoming winter. Camp regulations and daily routines were developed. Food and sanitary conditions were good. Internees could participate in language and specialist courses as well as subscribe to press and listen to Latvian radio. Interest groups and organizations could function freely inside camps. Correspondence was censored. Passes were issued, but compared to Lithuania, where the number of internees was much higher, the authorities were stricter about leaving camps. The Red Cross and members of the local Polish community provided clothes and necessity goods. Internees were able to voluntarily take up work on agricultural farms in the vicinity of the camps – a possibility some of them used.

In view of the political events unfolding in the summer of 1940, the further fate of the Polish soldiers remained unknown. According to German-Soviet arrangements, Lithuania and Latvia formed part of the Soviet sphere of influence. Ever since the Wilno Region was handed over to Lithuania by the USSR, both countries were joined in a military alliance, and official Red Army bases were established on Lithuanian territory. Soviet-Latvian relations were similar. On 5 October 1939 a Mutual Assistance Treaty was signed, and 25,000 Soviet soldiers were deployed to Latvia. On 30 May 1940 the Lithuanian government received an ultimatum from Moscow, calling for the dismissal of two ministers, a snap election and the entry of additional Red Army troops. On 15 June, Lithuania agreed to the demands and power in the country was seized by a puppet communist government. A similar ultimatum was delivered to Latvia on 16 June and accepted the following day. Lithuania and Latvia were officially incorporated into the USSR as Soviet republics on 21 July and 5 August, respectively. The Baltic states lost their neutrality and became subordinate to Moscow.

According to NKVD data, 4,376 Polish soldiers and officers were held in Lithuania and 913 in Latvia in mid-1940.[11] On 6 July, Beria decided that the internees be transported to camps in Kozelsk (referred to as "Kozelsk II" in Soviet documents) and Yukhnovo. The former was designated for officers and police officers, the latter for privates and non-commissioned officers. The transport to Kozelsk arrived in mid-July: 2,357 internees were quartered in buildings not long ago occupied by their colleagues, murdered in the Katyn forest. The NKVD did not manage to erase the traces of Polish POWs, and newly arrived soldiers would find, e.g., inscriptions on walls. On 14 and 16 July, transports carrying a total of 2,023 detainees arrived in the Yukhnovo camp. After the internees were transferred to NKVD custody, their situation took a significant turn for the worse. Like the POWs before them, they too were subjected to surveillance and propaganda. A special NKVD unit active in the camp aimed to establish a network of agents, carried out investigations meant to uncover "anti-Soviet organizations" and filled in the internees' files and biographies. Officers and police officers kept in Kozelsk were subjected to particularly intense investigation. From the moment they arrived in the camp until the end of July 1941, the NKVD arrested several dozen Polish officers and transferred them to prisons, accusing them of membership in clandestine "counterrevolutionary" groups. One of them was General Wacław Przeździecki. The internees were provided with Soviet newspapers, magazines and books. Soviet radio messages and shows were broadcast from speakers placed in the day room and in some barracks. Board games, chess, draughts and dominoes

11 *Katyń. Dokumenty zbrodni*, vol. 3: *Losy ocalałych*, collective work, Warszawa 2001, pp. 12–14.

could be rented. There were also instruments in the day room – a piano and some guitars. A music band was also organized. All of the above forms of activity were subject to strict supervision of employees of the political department of the camp's headquarters. In Kozelsk, "Communist propaganda was apparent at almost every step. Suffice it for three internees to stand on the square, and a political instructor would appear right away, starting a conversation on the situation in Russia and speaking critically of the conditions in Poland. They organized information talks (a review of recent developments), emphasizing their good relations with the Germans and complaining about England. They would come to dormitories, taking up various subjects, but always propagating communism. They spoke about Poland as if it was non-existent."[12] The Soviets also sounded out the possibility of forming a Polish military unit that could fight alongside the Red Army. Both official Soviet reports and Polish testimonies concurred in one thing: the Poles hardly ever agreed to collaborate or succumbed to communist propaganda.

Consequently, the authorities had to decide what to do about the Polish internees. This time around, instead of murdering them, the Soviets intended to use them for torturous labor. On 8 April, Beria ordered that the internees be transported to Murmansk Oblast on the Kola Peninsula. An interim NKVD camp on the Ponoy River was established on 15 May. Internees, isolated from other categories of camp inmates, were to build a military airline base. The first transport, mostly composed of police officers from the Kozelsk camp, started its journey to the north on 16 May. After the detainees arrived in Murmansk by train, they were jammed onto "Stalingrad" and "Klara Zetkin" ships, and spent several more days heading east to their final destination. They were brought to a rocky, tundral shore of the Ponoy River, in the place where it flows into the White Sea. A total of 4,000 Polish internees were transferred there until the end of June. Awaiting them was a rocky wilderness, not suited in the slightest to accommodate such a large number of prisoners. Provisions and water were lacking – after all remains of snow had been melted, inmates transported bucketloads of saline drinking water from the river's mouth. The daily food ration amounted to 300–400 grams of bread, a bowl of soup or hot water and a portion of fish. The "lucky ones" were quartered in tents. Others slept outdoors, directly on the ground. Work was carried out around the clock, with inmates taking turns to sleep. This was possible because of the polar day – the sun basically did not set. Days were scorching, but at night temperatures dropped

12 Marian Janicki's account – Collection of the Hoover Institution Library & Archives at the disposal of the Central Archives of Modern Records, Władysław Anders Collection. Reports, 800/1/0/-/48, account no. 2027.

to just a few degrees. Internees unloaded construction materials and transported them to the main camp located on a 200-meter elevation. Then, some of them were engaged to build a road leading to the planned airport situated 12 kilometers away, while others built that same airport. Work lasted 12–14 hours, excluding the time required for the column of workers to arrive at the location. Since there were no means of transport, inmates carried the building materials and provisions on their backs, 3–4 times a day. There were not too many guards (NKVD soldiers), since there was nowhere to run anyway. One of the soldiers transported to Ponoy, Jan Pytlak, stated that "[a]s for food and the housing and working conditions on the Kola Peninsula, they were insupportable for everyone during the six months we spent there; it was a place of perdition for each of us Poles."[13]

After the German-Soviet war broke out, communication with the Kola Peninsula was broken off. On 11 and 15 July, Poles and other inmates were convoyed off from Ponoy to Arkhangelsk on "Aldan" and "Uzbekistan" vessels. Their food ration for the journey amounted to a few boiled potatoes, a herring and 10 grams of pork fat. When they got to the city, they were placed in an interim camp, and left without food or water for two days. As a result of loud protests of Polish soldiers, camp authorities finally gave them food and hot soup. The scene was observed in disbelief by Soviet forced labor camp inmates. A week later, on 22 July, the internees left Arkhangelsk by train to Suzdal and Yuzha (Vyazniki), where they were soon able to join the newly emerging Polish Armed Forces in the Soviet Union. They were extremely exhausted physically and their mental state was poor. The emergence of a Polish Army meant that they could be saved.

Internees from the Kozelsk and Yukhnovo camps who did not make it north were convoyed off to the camp in Gryazovets after 22 June. Although they were quartered in all available rooms, some still had to sleep outside. Pursuant to an agreement signed by the Polish and Soviet governments on 30 June 1941 the Soviet Union agreed to restore diplomatic ties and grant "amnesty" to all Polish citizens deprived of liberty. The amnesty decree issued by the USSR Supreme Soviet on 12 August concerned, above all, POWs and internees. As at 31 July, POW and internment camps in Gryazovets, Suzdal, Yuzha and Starobelsk held a total of 25,184 people who would later form the core of the Polish Army formed in the USSR. Apart from them, there were at least 380,000 Polish citizens in *lagers*, prisons and exile.[14]

---

13 Jan Pytlak's account – Collection of the Hoover Institution Library & Archives at the disposal of the Central Archives of Modern Records, Władysław Anders Collection. Reports, 800/1/0/-/48, account no. 1784.

14 *Katyń. Dokumenty zbrodni*, vol. 3: *Losy ocalałych...*, p. 29.

THE ANDERS' ARMY

The Third Reich's aggression against USSR on 22 June 1941 radically changed the international balance of power. Poland and the Soviet Union found themselves fighting on the same side as members of the anti-Nazi coalition, which resulted in the need to renegotiate the mutual relationship between both sides. Consequently, despite having stated that "the Polish state had effectively ceased to exist" in the note handed to ambassador Grzybowski on 17 September 1939, the Soviet Union agreed to negotiate with the Polish government-in-exile with the intermediation of the UK. Following an agreement signed on 30 July 1941 by the Prime Minister of Poland, General Władysław Sikorski, and USSR's ambassador to the UK, Ivan Mayski, diplomatic ties between both countries were reinstated, and the Soviet side was obliged to provide assistance in the creation of a Polish army in Soviet territory that would be controlled by the legal government in London. For Polish citizens under Soviet occupation, the additional protocol to the agreement proved the most important: it stipulated "amnesty" (i.e. release from POW camps, *lagers*, prisons and special estates) for all Polish citizens held there – prisoners of war, internees, political prisoners and deportees.

The Polish Armed Forces in the USSR were headed by General Władysław Anders, until recently imprisoned in the Lubyanka prison in Moscow. On 23 August 1941, delegations of Polish servicemen arrived in Gryazovets, Suzdal, Yuzha (Vyazniki) and Starobelsk to open conscription boards to the Polish Army on behalf of the Polish government. In the course of the first few days, almost 25,000 former POWs and internees were mobilized. One of them recalled these days in the Yuzha camp in the following words: "There was a parade, the old brothers-in-arms did not forget their trade, and marched before the tribune with such vigor as if they had just secured a most beautiful victory [...] with an appearance so solemn that, without knowing who we were, one might have taken us for guard units rather than people deprived of everything, harried by more than two years of camps, prisons and exile into the unknown, people who had no right to live. People, who – according to Hitler and Stalin's norms – were to disappear from the face of the earth."[15]

The Anders' Army was formed, above all, from POWs and internees, who had suffered a cruel fate following the defeat of September 1939. They were hungry, tired and ragged, but they still rushed to join the emerging

---

15 Antoni Pyzel's account – Collection of the Hoover Institution Library & Archives at the disposal of the Central Archives of Modern Records, Władysław Anders Collection. Reports, 800/1/0/-/48, account no. 2338.

Polish Army – not only in hope to save themselves, but, most of all, determined to again put on the Polish uniform and continue the fight that began on 1 September 1939.

Bartosz Gralicki

REFERAT HISTORYCZNY
POL. SIŁ ZBR. w ZSRR

O B Ó Z

W

Do niewoli sow
bowli,gdzie się znajd
wojennym 104,w którym
wego.Wiadomość o wkro
Polski nadeszła do Tr
przedsięwziąć żadnych
gdyż komendant otrzyma
kiego stanowczy rozka
się na przyjęcie 300
generała trzykrotnie;
jest dobrze poinformow
transport rannych,kom
pracę przygotowawczą
zjawili się w Trembow
się komisarz,późniejs
~~mniałem/~~.Obecność teg
rabunku nie było.Komi
oficerów i zgromadzen
cza,którego roli podj
brutalne wiecowe prze
i d-two W.P.Zakończył
polskich generałów,do
przekleństwo głośno p
tłumaczenia tych słów
tórzył.Wówczas komisa
i tam powtórzył przem
Znalazło się kilka gł
Oficerów szpi
brano im latarki elek

Plutonowy rez Sat
Pawłowice pow Le
Jadwigi z domu S
powołany do 52: p p
pod Złoczowem. Wedr
dnia 18 września n
mogąc się dostać do
wieśniaków celem u
ukraińca który p
zmieszkania i odst
odzenia śledztwa, i o
skąd nas prowadzili
dniowym pobycie w K
do Równego i odstaw
Polski Kop. Tam z
W początku listopada
żąc uciec zmiero
z Warszawy. Dnia
Sosenek pod Równ
ni Drobiązką do
do Saporożyna i bite

b. jenca,-
1/ Dane osob
Kaczm S
2/ Data i ok
23/IX 193
Przynie z
3/ Nazwa obo
Karakuł
Z Kara
do
4/ Opis obozu
higiena)
pole wo
a gdy j
czanie
Chigien
5/ Skład jen
pozioma un
Skład je
1500 ...
6/ Życie w o
pracy,noc
i kultur
drogą
7/ Stosunek
propagand
8/ Pomoc lek
Pomoc le
9/ Czy i jak
10/ Kiedy
Zwolnio

CHRONICLES OF TERROR

FORCED LABOR CAMPS FOR POWS IN THE TERRITORY OF THE SECOND POLISH REPUBLIC

The Communist ideology and propaganda presented the Polish officers as an "counterrevolutionary element." This is why, pursuant to the VKP(b) Political Office's decision of 5 March 1940, the NKVD murdered nearly 22,000 Polish citizens with shots to the back of the head, in the course of the Katyn Massacre. In the photograph: officers and non-commissioned officers in front of the mess of the 1st Polish Light Cavalry Regiment, 1928.

Photo. National Digital Archives

MARIAN CZAPIŃSKI

Personal data (name, surname, rank, age, occupation and marital status):
Marian Czapiński, senior sergeant, 42 years old, regular non-commissioned officer, married.

Date and circumstances of arrest:

On 17 September 1939, when we were marching to the rallying point with the company reserve and its commander, Captain Hiller, on orders from a battalion commander of the "Kopyczyńce" Border Protection Corps near Chorostków, we came under machine gun fire from two Soviet armored cars, firing at us from a distance of 300–400 meters. The captain was heavily wounded in both legs with three shots.

Name of the camp, prison or forced labor site:

I was disarmed and sent first to Kamenets-Podolskyi, then to a POW camp in Kozelshchyna, Poltava Oblast, and next to an iron mine in Krivoy Rog, Dnipropetrovsk Oblast. From there I was transferred to Emilianów, located 7 kilometers from Równe, to build an asphalt road between Kiev, Lwów, and Przemyśl. Later I was moved to a camp in Tuligłowy, Mościska District, next to Pługów, Zborów, and finally to Skole, Stryj District, where there were stone quarries (a mine).

Description of the camp or prison (grounds, buildings, housing conditions, hygiene):

In Kamenets-Podolskyi I was placed in military barracks, since almost the whole Soviet garrison had entered Poland and the barracks were empty. Over 10,000 slaves were imprisoned there at the time, and they were sent in various directions from there. Food was bearable. We slept on the floors in both the rooms and corridors of the barracks.

The camp in Kozelshchyna comprised approx. 12,000 people, including 2,157 officers and about 4,000 policemen; the rest were non-commissioned officers and infantrymen. Officers and senior non-commissioned officers (from sergeant up) were placed in six big stables, which had formerly housed a pig farm, liquidated due to an epidemic of swine erysipelas. The dung hadn't been removed from these stables, but only sprinkled with a solution of chlorinated lime. We had to take it out ourselves, with no tools or implements at hand, and then cover the floor with yellow sand – we had to sleep on this for a month, that is, until some material to make pallets was delivered. As time went by we built a kitchen, as previously we were being issued small amounts of foodstuffs (in kind) and everyone had to cook for himself, although we were short of firewood and the temperatures were freezing.

First the policemen were deported, then non-commissioned officers and infantrymen were taken away in groups, and finally the officers were deported, probably to Starobelsk. To this day I haven't met any of the officers who were with me in that camp. I recall the following surnames: non-commissioned officer Dr. Lalak, from an Uhlan regiment, who had a peaked cap with a white brim; Captain Sylwester Trojanowski, from a battalion of the "Ostróg" Border Protection Corps; Szurlej from the Border Protection Corps; Cavalry Captain Komorowski (a world famous show jumping champion); Second Lieutenant Wróblewski, a pilot from the Warsaw air force regiment.

In that camp, once or twice a week we worked at a train station situated 2 kilometers from the camp, where we unloaded wagons with timber, and on other days we performed various tasks on the camp premises.

In the mines in Krivoy Rog we worked three shifts, eight hours each, at various jobs. We worked three days in a row and had the fourth day off; we were quartered in a building. In the rest of the camps, where we worked at road construction, we had to work from dawn to dusk, up to twelve hours a day. At first we had every second Sunday off, and later we had to work on all days, except for those when it was pouring with rain.

In the above-enumerated labor camps we were quartered in large tents, heated with iron stoves during winter, or in wooden barracks. There was an emergency room and a bathhouse with disinfectant facilities in each camp.

Social composition of POWs, prisoners, exiles (nationality, type of crimes, intellectual and moral standing, mutual relations, etc.):

In Kozelshchyna, Poltava Oblast – 12,000; in Krivoy Rog it depended on the size of the mine: in the one where I worked there were 54 people, and in Krivoy Rog there were generally over 12,000 prisoners; in Emilianów near Równe – 800; in Tuligłowy, Mościska District – 1,400; in Pługów – 400; in Zborów – approx. 600; in Skole, Stryj District – 900. In general, the moral standing of the Poles in all those camps was good, with single exceptions. National minorities usually cooperated with the Soviets, helping them determine the military ranks of soldiers and detect opponents of Communism; they often laughed at our misery and complained to the Soviets that they had been persecuted and mistreated back in Poland. However, there were also some members of the minorities who stuck with us and believed that this situation wouldn't last, as the war wasn't over yet and from time to time we received news that the Polish Army was being raised abroad and that Poland would be reborn.

Life in the camp or prison (daily routine, working conditions, quotas, wages, food, clothes, social and cultural life, etc.):

In the camp we worked from dawn to dusk, up to twelve hours a day. The work quotas were very high (for instance to dig a trench, 9 cubic meters). Those who met them received bearable and sufficient food. Those who didn't fill the quota received food from the so-called upper caldron, and if someone skipped work for some reason, for example due to illness, he received only watery soup and 400 or 600 grams of bread, depending on the camp commander. Five rubles per day were deducted from the monthly remuneration to cover food expenses. Various swindles, such as documenting work that had never been done, were carried out by our people so that we could meet the quotas. For filling the quota one could earn from eight to twelve rubles a day. New clothes were issued only to those who went to work, and only when their old garments were ragged. Mutual relations were good only among the Poles.

Cultural life was very poor, there were only communist propaganda books and magazines, which were rarely read. Sometimes an obligatory meeting was organized, and then a political commissar would read something out to the rest.

Attitude of the NKVD towards Poles (interrogation methods, torture and other forms of punishment, communist propaganda, information about Poland, etc.):

On the surface the NKVD authorities were rather kind, but they were secretly obtaining information from other prisoners, asking them what plans one had or what he had been doing back in Poland etc. Interrogations took place usually at night. Those who refused to talk were locked up in solitary confinement, where they had water poured on the floor or were divested of their clothes and starved, all to extort confessions. They wanted to turn everyone into their informer, who would tell them what the others thought of them and what views they held. For instance, on 17, 18, and 19 June 1941 in Skole, an investigation was carried out against me, and I was questioned as to why three people had been serving time for holding communist views in my region in 1936, at the time when I commanded a Border Protection Corps fort. I was indicted for counter-revolutionary activities and I was to be tried on such charges. It didn't happen only due to the outbreak of the German-Soviet War on 22 June 1941.

Medical assistance, hospitals, mortality rate (provide the names of the deceased):

Medical assistance was quite good, I don't recall any cases of death.

Was it at all possible to get in contact with one's home country and family?

I had contact with my family, that is my wife, by post, but not all her letters reached me.

When were you released and how did you manage to join the Polish Army?

I was released in Starobelsk, from where on 7 September 1941 I was sent in a military transport to Totskoye.

Khanaqin, 17 February 1942

Collection of the Hoover Institution Library & Archives at the disposal of the Central Archives of Modern Records, Władysław Anders Collection. Reports, 800/1/0/-/48, account no. 2012.

STANISŁAW KACZOROWSKI

Stanisław Kaczorowski, ensign, 27 years old, university of technology student, unmarried.

I was taken into Soviet custody on 28 September 1939, in Włodzimierz Wołyński, through which I was intending to get through towards Hungarian border.

POW camps which I was placed in were all on Polish grounds. They were: Olesko near Brody, Hoszcza near Równe, and Równe.

Olesko camp was situated in the historic Jan Sobieski's castle where three-level bunk beds had been set up in its memorial halls. The camp in Hoszcza had exceptionally good hygienic conditions, as it was situated in modern barracks of the Border Protection Corps Battalion. There was a bathroom with showers, water supply, electric lights, etc.

As the Border Protection Corps' barracks were taken over by a unit of Soviet tanks in February 1941, the camp was liquidated, and POWs were sent to other camps. I got into Równe camp. It was placed in wooden barracks built specifically for that purpose. All these camps were fenced with several rows of barbed wire and overseen by guards from elevated watch-houses.

The camps that I stayed in included mostly privates, a small percentage were non-commissioned officers and officers, who hid their rank from the camp's authorities. In terms of nationality, Poles were the larger part, and there were POWs of other nationalities too. Most of the Polish POWs took a negative attitude towards the Bolsheviks. But POWs of Jewish nationality cooperated with the Soviet authorities. They would usually take all the posts of warehousemen, office workers, store clerks, etc. Most of the Ukrainians and Belarusians believed the propaganda too, forming "Stakhanovite brigades." Apart from that, Ukrainians and Belarusians were keen on joining and were accepted into the guard, which recruited its voluntary members from among POWs.

While in the camps, we were working on building the asphalt road between Kiev and Lwów. We worked in groups (brigades) under command of brigadiers.

At 5.00 a.m. in the morning, an on-call person would wake up the camp by ringing a bell. Thin, watery soup would be brought in buckets from the kitchen. At 6.00 a.m., we marched out to work. We worked until 4.00 or 5.00 p.m., and in the period of the most intense work in summer 1940, even until 8.00 p.m. That way, we spent whole days, from dawn till dusk, on earthworks, crushing stones, carrying dirt in wheelbarrows, paving, etc.

Food would be delivered to the construction site, but only for those who worked beyond quotas. Often, there would be 6–8 kilometers to the work site. That distance had to be walked back and forth. After returning from work, we would receive dinner in the form of thick soup, in which sometimes a piece of meat could be found. A few hours later we would get supper, which was tea. The meals weren't all the same for everybody. They were divided into the so-called first, second, and third cauldron. The third cauldron was for the most efficient workers, the so-called Stakhanovites; the second cauldron was for average workers; and the first – for the worst workers. The cauldrons were different when it came to the amount of groats and potatoes.

In a visible spot in the camp, there was a board where percentage work results of all brigades were listed. The exceptionally resistant POWs who didn't want to work were condemned by being placed on a special list and often locked in a punishment cell to eat only bread and water.

A slogan often used by the Soviet authorities to keep up the pace of work at the road construction was: "finish the road, ride home." After some time, it only made us laugh. The bread portions that we received, depended on the cauldron: 400 grams, 600 to 800 grams, and 1,000 grams for the exceptional workers. Sugar, tobacco, matches, and soap would only be given if these items were in the warehouse, and because that happened rarely, there were long periods when they were missing. Lice were a disastrous plague. The infestation was caused by only occasional baths, lack of clean underwear, and overall dirt in the camps. The hardest working and living conditions occurred in the winter of 1939: lack of gloves, footwraps, torn uniforms and boots, and facing temperatures beyond minus 30 degrees [Celsius] causing numerous frostbites. Despite the freezing temperatures, we were forced to leave for work.

Due to bad nourishment, there were many cases of night blindness, which the camp doctors didn't have means to cure.

The outbreak of the Soviet-German war happened when I was in Równe. We were escorted to Zhytomyr on foot, from where we reached Starobelsk. I regained freedom there and joined the Polish army.

Encampment, 10 March 1943

Collection of the Hoover Institution Library & Archives at the disposal of the Central Archives of Modern Records, Władysław Anders Collection. Reports, 800/1/0/-/47, account no. 591.

MIECZYSŁAW JUSZCZYK

Mieczysław Juszczyk, reserve corporal, son of Władysław and Anna, born 15 August 1905 in Łódź, an official at the Social Insurance Institution in Łódź, Control and Investigation Department, married, one child (son).

On 24 August 1939, I was conscripted into the army based on a draft card to join the 1st Anti-aircraft Artillery Regiment in Warsaw, Rakowiecka Street, from where, after completing a battery under command of Lieutenant Szpigonowicz, I set out to a firing point in the village of Babice near Warsaw and stayed there until 2 September.

On 3 September 1939, we changed our staging post from Babice to Warsaw, Saska Kępa District. I was at the said post in Warsaw until 7 September, when the battery commander issued an order to close the post and leave to Brześć on the Bug River by train.

We stationed in Brześć for two days, then the equipment was loaded onto the train on 10 September. On the night of 10/11 September, the battery commander and Artillery Sergeant Lenarczyk set out into an unknown direction and I didn't see them until the disarmament. On 11 September 1939, in the morning, the deputy commander (I don't recall the surname, a reserve ensign) gathered us and announced that we were not going to use the railway because of the air raids by the German planes, following which, almost an hour later, he set off along with a part of the battery, ordering us to rally the remaining soldiers and lead them to the city park.

Having rallied about 30 people accordingly to the instructions, I headed to the given location, but nobody was there. In the meantime, a cadet artillery sergeant (I don't recall the surname) joined us, a forestry engineer from around Wilno, who took charge and led us to Kowel and Łuck, towards Dubno. In Kowel and Łuck, the cadet reported at the stage command and found out where we were supposed to go. We were directed to Dubno.

After arriving in Dubno on 19 September 1939 in the morning, we were defeated by Soviets who used light tanks. They escorted us to the barracks of one of the infantry regiments. We stayed there for three days without any food, and after that our group (of around 2,000 people) was led to the railway station, where we were loaded onto coal wagons. On that train, we arrived in Zdołbunów in the morning.

I learned from a Polish railwayman walking by that we were going to be taken across to the Soviet side to Shepetovka. After consideration, I decided to run and I fully succeeded. The above mentioned ensign and two gunners ran with me, but they wandered off on the way to Kowel. I bid farewell to the ensign in Kowel; he probably got on a train towards Sarny. The next morning in Kowel, I was captured by a Soviet patrol and escorted to a rallying point, from where I got deported to Shepetovka. After six days, I was sent from Shepetovka to Ostróg on foot – along with a group of around 1,500 people – and then to Hoszcza, Wołyń Voivodeship. In Hoszcza, I worked in a sand mine until March 1940. The sand was used for building a road connection between Korzec and Równe.

In March 1940, I was deported along with others to Olesko as impenitent *buntovshchik – lodzer* [rebel from Łódź], and then to Angielówka, Lwów Voivodeship. I was deported from Hoszcza with the following men: Cadet Sergeant Mieczysław Kostkowski (6th Infantry Regiment theater), Cadet Platoon-leader Chorbaczewski (the latter was taken away from Angielówka to Olesko in October and since that time I haven't heard of him), Sergeant Major Tadeusz Dziedzic (Command of the Commissariat Department), and many others, whose surnames I don't recall. In Angielówka, I worked at road construction until June 1940, but then I had a leg condition and the doctor declared me unfit for the job and the camp's foreman assigned me a job in cleaning the barrack we were living in. The road construction in Angielówka was finished in October 1940 and the whole camp was deported to Mościska, where I worked on stone crushing for the whole winter, with a one-month break caused by typhus. After being kept in quarantine, part of the camp – including Cadet Sergeant Kostkowski, Cadet Officer Polak, Bombardier Ryszard Muszyński (transport platoon), and myself, among others – were deported to Kamionka Las camp, outside Tarnopol. We lived in a shelter for Lwów's students, and we would go outside Tarnopol to work at the airport construction site.

I worked there until the outbreak of the Soviet-German war, then we marched to Zolotonosha (around 950 kilometers). We covered that distance in 25 days, being hustled 12 or 14 hours a day, almost without food. We would be given literally two biscuits and around half a liter of soup a day. It was even worse with drinking water, because the escorting guards wouldn't let us fetch it, and whenever somebody managed to draw water from a well and was noticed by the guards, they would spill the water and beat the offender with gunstocks. There were also cases of our colleagues falling ill or suddenly fainting. When a POW physician noticed it (Second Lieutenant Janczak, 18th Infantry Regiment, 6th Infantry Division), he would take care of them right away, seating them on the cart that was carrying food or guards' luggage, but if he hadn't noticed, it was hard to let him know – as it wasn't allowed to support others while marching – then one of the guards would stay behind and catch up after some time by car or other vehicle, but with no sign of the ill person.

Later, in Starobelsk, after announcing the Polish-Soviet agreement to us, the foremen and political commissars checking our [illegible word], would call the missing people “dead” or “killed” while reading out their surnames.

I joined the army in Starobelsk, right after the agreement was announced, and I began to organize an anti-aircraft battery along with Senior Artillery Sergeant Czapczyński, [illegible] Cadet Artillery Sergeant [illegible word]. Our job was to search for the people who had already served in such units, and we gathered approximately a hundred of them. Next, under command of Senior Artillery Sergeant Czapczyński, we arrived in Totskoye (USSR), where the 6th Anti-aircraft Artillery Regiment was finally formed.

I need to mention that the attitude of various foremen and political commissars towards us was initially hostile, but as time passed, some of them began to treat us a little better, to such an extent that they actually didn't forbid us from singing evening prayers, as long as we were doing this behind the closed doors of the barracks.

Almost all Jews, Belarusians, and Ukrainians, who were informing the camp superiors on various offenses (from Soviet perspective), like celebrating 3 May, 11 November, Marshal Piłsudski's death anniversary, etc., were living well. The rest, and especially those who stood firm in the role of soldiers and Poles, were constantly harassed by varied punishments.

When it came to medical assistance, as long as our doctor, a POW, was in the camp, it was relatively good, but it got worse when the doctor was a Polish Jew or a Soviet.

Food in our camps was dependent on the filled quotas, which were unattainable for an average POW, and so if somebody did 50% of the norm, they would get 500 to 600 grams of bread and the second cauldron, that is meat broth with an increased groats portion (the daily portion was 20 grams of raw groats a day). If one filled a quota of crushing stones for road construction (for example) – 1.3 cubic meters, or did the digging and carrying dirt in a wheelbarrow on a 50 meters distance – from 2 to 4 cubic meters, depending on the kind of soil, they would be given a kilogram of bread and the third cauldron. The third cauldron meant a dinner consisting of two meals, a soup, and potatoes or dry groats with meat or fish, the latter usually being unfit to eat.

There were only around 20% of people who were able to fill the quota, and around 70% who filled 80% of the quota. The rest had to deal with 400 grams of bread and thin soup.

It was even worse when it came to correspondence, as the right to send letters was unlimitedly given mostly to those who filled the quotas, while the people who filled up to 80% could send four letters a month. The ones who didn't fill the quotas could only dream of sending letters. Another thing is that some landowners from our area would make it easier to write families by sending the letters using their own address and surname, but if Soviets caught them, their whole families would be deported to Russia. Despite the repressions, they agreed to do it.

I received two letters from my friends from Stanisławów, who informed me about the death of my brother-in-law, attorney Jan Hypułkowski, who died in Dachau concentration camp. I didn't receive any news from home, neither from my parents nor wife, even though my colleagues who wrote their families always notified my family and provided my address. I would explain the lack of delivery of correspondences with the fact that I was a bad worker, as I mentioned above, and, as such, I wasn't allowed to correspond in the Soviet Union.

Collection of the Hoover Institution Library & Archives at the disposal of the Central Archives of Modern Records, Władysław Anders Collection. Reports, 800/1/0/-/47, account no. 747.

TOMASZ STRZELECKI

Tomasz Strzelecki, born in 1898, married.

I was captured on the night of 18/19 September 1939 in Tłumacz. Around 1,500 people were captured then. Immediately after capture, we were marched all day long, under escort, to Horodenka. We were given no food and no opportunity to rest. On the next day, we were subjected to a thorough body search. The things and all the money found on the captives were taken and we never got them back. We were also given no food on that second day and subsisted only on gifts from civilians.

Next, we were escorted to Volochysk and we spent two weeks there. We slept in the stables and in the open field, our daily food rations consisting of half a liter of watery soup and 100 grams of bread. Then, we were taken by train from Volochysk to Novograd-Volynskyi. We were housed in barracks but still had to sleep on bare ground. The rations were paltry; the prisoners would collect and eat raw cabbage leaves and beets. The barracks were indescribably filthy and we all had lice.

On 22 October 1939, we were transported to the quarry in Donbas and I remained there until May 1940. While I was there, we were subjected to interrogations.

During the vote, the prisoners were abused in an attempt to make them sign voting lists. If someone didn't want to sign, they'd be led out into the snow and kept there, in the freezing cold, for two to three hours at a time. People would also be sent to work in the quarry without proper rations.

In May 1940, we were subjected to a thorough search, during which our documents and objects of religious significance were seized and destroyed on the spot. We were packed into train cars, the cars were locked and sent away to Ukhta. While on our way, we were constantly searched and disturbed during rest. In transit we were given the following rations: 200 grams of bread and one salted fish.

We arrived in Ukhta on 16 June 1940 – we were transported to a spot next to the river and the train was unloaded there, in an open field. We lived in that open field until we built the barracks. We worked for 10 and sometimes even 14 hours a day, without any days off. If someone couldn't work, he'd get only 300 grams of bread and water as a ration. The labor quotas were so high that no one could actually meet them, on account of exhaustion.

The prisoners fell ill and died of various diseases. Among those who died was one Kraiński from the Poznań Voivodeship, a man named

Chrząszcz who was from somewhere near Warsaw, and many others whose names I don't remember.

Medical care was also shoddy; medicines were in short supply. There were also cases of sick prisoners being forced to work anyway.

I left Ukhta in August 1941, after my release. We were all searched after release. I joined the Polish Army in Jaźwiki [Vyazniki] and was later transported to Totskoye.

I did not participate in the vote for Russian legislative councils.

Collection of the Hoover Institution Library & Archives at the disposal of the Central Archives of Modern Records, Władysław Anders Collection. Reports, 800/1/0/-/48, account no. 256.

JÓZEF BABIARZ

Rifleman Józef Babiarz, a farmer by occupation, unmarried, born in 1909, village of Brzegi, Tarnobrzeg District, Kraków Voivodeship.

On 19 September 1939, I was disarmed by the Soviets in the settlement of Żarki. They took me to Kamenets-Podolskyi, where I was detained for five days. The food was very poor, only 150 grams of bread per day and some watery soup. Next, they transferred us to Równe. Throughout the entire journey, which lasted three days, we were given absolutely nothing to eat. They took us to the border post of the Border Protection Corps in Żytyń, where we were imprisoned from 3 October until 7 November. I worked at the station, loading and unloading stones from wagons, all the time receiving food as per the pathetic Soviet norm.

On 16 May 1940, they transported us beyond Lwów, to Zimna Woda, where we were forced to build a road, under appalling conditions. Many of us fell ill, while the food was barely edible; those who didn't fulfill the quota went starving. A friend of mine, Franciszek Marszałek from Jasło, was amongst those who succumbed to the hunger.

After three months of this ordeal they sent us – some 300 to 350 in all – to Gródek Jagielloński. The conditions there were somewhat improved, and we had medical care. But alas, after only a short while they drove us on foot, organized into two brigades, to Mościska. I remained there until 1 March 1941. In March, they transported us deep into Russia, to the township Dzelentsi (Ukraine). I lived there in an unheated barrack, suffering hunger and cold. We cleared roads of enormous snowdrifts; it was backbreaking toil. Using every last ounce of strength, you could earn 600 grams of bread. The working day lasted twelve hours.

Only in May 1941 did they send me to the township of Teofipol′, in the Kiev Oblast, where I worked as a carpenter. Toiling the sweat of my brow, I earned my bloodied slice of bread working on the renovation of an airfield. This took two months, and in July 1941 the NKVD drove us on foot for 19 days, right to the other bank of the Dnieper, with nearly no food or water. We were allowed to pause for no more than two to three hours a day, while the places that they chose for such rests were invariably muddy and waterlogged. When during this trek – in itself difficult to describe – any civilians attempted to give us a slice of bread, both their fate and ours would be unenviable. The first part of this odyssey finally came to an end in Zolotonosha. There they loaded us onto railcars and we set off for Starobelsk, where I remained for some time. I then fell ill and was taken to hospital. While there, I learned of the miraculous and wonderful Polish-Soviet agreement. From then on, the conditions started to improve right until our release. We were finally let go on 3 August 1941. I immediately enlisted in the Polish Army.

Encampment, 5 March 1943

Collection of the Hoover Institution Library & Archives at the disposal of the Central Archives of Modern Records, Władysław Anders Collection. Reports, 800/1/0/-/48, account no. 2483.

WYPOROWSKI

Name of the camp:

POW camp in Równe, Biała Street 12.

Social composition of POWs:

Privates (some cadets and a few officers in hiding).

Number of POWs:

In 1939 and 1940 – 700 on average; in 1941 – 200 on average.

Period of the camp's existence:

From October 1939 to June 1941.

Description of the camp:

Three-story building, formerly a mill.

Life in the camp:

The POWs were divided into four battalions, which were subdivided into brigades of 10–25 prisoners. They unloaded stone from the train, loaded it onto trucks, broke the stone – both by hand and with the help of machines – as well as boiled and loaded tar. Furthermore, a small group of around a hundred POWs worked directly on road construction. We had a small music band (that used mostly makeshift instruments), which would play only old Polish melodies. There were even some conflicts with the Soviet authorities over that repertoire. We hardly had time for cultural activities since the working day was 12 to 14 hours long and there were no days off except Soviet holidays.

Attitude of the NKVD towards Poles:

Równe housed one of the main NKVD offices so prisoners from other camps would be brought there for questioning. They'd bring people in for questioning, in a prison van, at any time of the day but most especially at night. Besides that the camp also had a Soviet tribunal that would try prisoners who were captured and suspected of wanting to cross the border. The punishments ranged from four to eight years in prison or in a stricter camp. Those found guilty would leave immediately.

POWs who distinguished themselves negatively:

Paweł Składanowski, Sergeant Drągowski (currently: 7th Infantry Division), Platoon-leader Jan Hupałowski (currently: Polish Army in Iran), Wapniarski (civil servant from Łódź).

Mortality in the camp:

Around six POWs died during my whole stay.

Collection of the Hoover Institution Library & Archives at the disposal of the Central Archives of Modern Records, Władysław Anders Collection. Reports, 800/1/0/-/48, account no. 39.

WŁADYSŁAW GŁUSZAK

Władysław Głuszak, senior rifleman, 44 years old, Roman Catholic, married, a carpenter by occupation, resident in Warsaw at Czerniakowska Street 206.

I was captured on 28 September 1939 near Lublin, from where on the same day we were driven on foot 65 kilometers to Chełm. Once we got there, we were loaded onto freight wagons (with a reduced capacity), 60 men to each, and received one loaf of Polish bread – all green with mildew – for 20 men. The journey lasted ten days, and during that time were given a loaf of bread (the same as before) once again, only this time per 18 men. In the main, we were fed by local civilians. After we arrived at our destination, that is Olesko in the district of Złoczów, we were detained in the castle, one hundred to a hall. For two weeks we slept on the ground. Later they made us plank beds, however they were so small that each of us had no more than 50 centimeters of room. Our daily ration comprised 400 grams of bread, a plate of fatless soup (given twice), and tea (poured out just once). The hygienic conditions were terrible, and our clothes were crawling with lice.

We were forced to work irrespective of the weather, even when it was minus 35–38 degrees [Celsius]. I had no shoes and no coat – only my uniform (which was torn); my companions were similarly dressed. I know of three murders committed by the NKVD, on 20 December 1939; the victims were colleagues who were trying to escape from our place of work. They were buried on 24 December 1939 in the Roman Catholic cemetery in Olesko. On 9 April 1940, I was transferred to the camp in Angielówka in the district of Złoczów, where we were also forced to labor. The quotas were impossible to fulfill. For example, the quota for crushed stone was initially 3.5 cubic meters, but they kept on increasing it daily, until finally it totaled 9.5 cubic meters. Our remuneration was 35–50 rubles per month. Next, I was moved to the camp in Mościska near Przemyśl, to Zelenche near Podwołoczyska, and then to Teofipol′ near Volochysk, where we toiled at the airfield. The daily quota was to cart away 12.5 cubic meters of sand to a distance of 50–100 meters on a wheelbarrow. We were forced to work from sunrise until late in the evening.

When the German-Russian war broke out, our plight got even worse. We were marched off on 2 July 1941. There were some 1,500 of us in total, the inmates of two camps, and the Soviets drove us on foot without mercy. The first four prisoners had revolvers put to their heads and were beaten with rifle butts in order to walk faster, while the rest had to keep pace, for those who lagged behind would also be beaten with rifle butts and have dogs set on them; many of my colleagues received bite wounds. During this march we received no more than half a liter of thin soup and 100–150 grams of bread per day. Some of my colleagues collapsed along the way, but whoever fell was done for – the guards would finish him off with rifle butts or bayonets. Between 8 and 15 men collapsed from exhaustion daily. On the twenty first day of this ordeal, after we had crossed the Dnieper River, I was unable to walk – my legs were swollen and bleeding, and I was completely spent. A guard hit me a few times with a rifle butt in order to force me on. I was resigned to my fate and ready to depart from this world and my colleagues, however the Soviets finally gathered us, the weakest – some 60 men in all – and loaded us onto trucks that drove us to a train station; once there, we were put on open wagons, 80 men to each. During this part of the voyage I fell seriously ill with dysentery; I didn't receive any medical care. I remember that after I regained consciousness, I found myself lying in a pool of water (it had been raining). Only after we arrived in Starobelsk was I examined by a doctor.

A dozen or so days later the Soviets read out Stalin's order granting us our freedom, and the NKVD gave each of us 500 rubles in damages. Thereafter I enlisted in the Polish Army and left for Totskoye; it was a very long time before I regained my health, ruined so terribly by the Soviets.

Collection of the Hoover Institution Library & Archives at the disposal of the Central Archives of Modern Records, Władysław Anders Collection. Reports, 800/1/0/-/48, account no. 1693.

ANTONI HRYNIUK

Personal data (name, surname, rank, age, occupation and marital status):
Antoni Hryniuk, corporal, 32 years old, farmer, unmarried.

Date and circumstances of arrest:

On 17 September 1939, I was captured along with my whole unit by the Germans near Sądowa Wisznia – specifically, in the Tuczapy village. Then, I was marched on foot towards Przemyśl for six days and managed to flee in Przemyśl; my friends and I fled on foot in the direction of Lwów. In Gródek Jagielloński near Lwów, we encountered the Soviet army and our own disarmed soldiers, who were returning to their homes in German occupied territory. We asked what had happened to them and what had befallen our units. They replied that the Bolsheviks had disbanded our army. From Lwów I took a train to Kowel. There, I was arrested by the Soviet authorities around 28 September. I was transported to Shepetovka (in Russia). The transit took four days and we were given no food – some of the men had a little extra with them and we subsisted on that. In each train car there [Illegible word] 80 to 100 men; the journey was hard.

Marched out of Shepetovka towards Polish territory on 4 October 1939. Camps: Radziwiłłów near Brody, Brody, Werba, Rudnia Poczajowska, Tarnopol, Czernielów Ruski. Then marched on foot into Russia – very hard journey, up to 50 kilometers a day, sometimes even without water.

Description of the camp or prison (grounds, buildings, housing conditions, hygiene):

The camps were mostly located away from the civilian population; we were kept in stables, barns or sheds. Our hair would often freeze to the blankets or cots – the temperature inside was below minus twenty degrees [Celsius]. We were packed very tightly and the conditions were highly unsanitary since the cold forced us to sleep in our clothes, in the dirt, with lice and without any chance to take a bath or change our underwear. Most of the men didn't even have shirts or long johns and those who did had no opportunity to wash them.

Social composition of POWs, prisoners, deportees (nationality, types of crimes, intellectual and moral standing, mutual relations, etc.):

Varied from 400–500 to even 3,000 men. They were almost all Poles – very few Jews, Ukrainians and Belarusians. Mutual relations were mostly very good but there would always be a couple of men who held the Soviet authorities in high regard and looked to cause trouble for the other prisoners. Such men sought to ingratiate themselves with the overseers and would unjustly accuse fellow prisoners, who would then have to spend time in the camp punishment cells or even get transferred to other camps. I know some of those men by name: 1) Stefan Sawczuk, 2) Kopciuch, 3) Jeremiej Owieczko, 4) Abramczuk. I haven't seen them anywhere now.

Life in the camp or prison (daily routine, working conditions, quotas, wages, food, clothes, social and cultural life, etc.):

Wake-up call at 4.00 a.m., then breakfast – half a liter of soup that was mostly water. March to work at 6.00 a.m. and work till 6.00 p.m. 12 hours of work every day, including on Sundays and holidays. As expected, they ordered us to do loads of work and gave us little food. The pay was miserly and even when we got a few rubles we couldn't buy anything with that. The bread and dinner rations were tied to labor quota fulfillment: it was either 400 or 600 grams of bread and dinner from the first or second cauldron. However, the work was so grueling that you'd almost be too exhausted to eat that 600 grams of bread when you got back to camp. In winter we had to go to work in torn shoes that had holes in them and without footwraps. Many people had no shirts or long johns. But if anyone refused to go to work, they'd be thrown into a punishment cell. That kind of cell was always made especially unpleasant. For example, in the Radziwiłłów camp it was located above a latrine pit.

Attitude of the NKVD towards Poles (interrogation methods, torture and other forms of punishment, communist propaganda, information about Poland, etc.):

They'd bring us for interrogation all throughout the day and night, questioning us in various ways. If a Pole was from the Eastern Borderlands, they'd pressure him to stop identifying as a Pole; they told him he was a Ukrainian or a Belarusian. If he persisted and said he was a Pole, they'd say: "You wait for Poland and desire Poland, but pigs will fly before Poland is a country again. And if it is ever reborn, then only as a Communist state." They'd also praise their own goodness but our men always had something to say about that. However, communists like that were always hard to convince; they would constantly insult our nationality and our religious convictions, blaspheme against God and disparage our faith. They'd make particular efforts to send us to work on Christmas, Easter and any other big holiday – any prisoner that tried to dodge work then would obviously be interrogated and land in a punishment cell.

Medical assistance, hospitals, mortality rate (provide the names of the deceased):

Shortages of medicines and other materials were common. I can't say anything definitive about the hospital situation since I was never in one, but fellow prisoners have told me that everything was also in short supply there.

Was it at all possible to get in contact with one's home country and family?

Keeping in contact with family was difficult – they wouldn't give us letters and when we finally did get one in a dozen, it was a few months or even a year late. I was from a Soviet-occupied territory, so my family had to live in difficult conditions anyway, but they still wanted to share their tiny bit of money or their last loaf of bread. When they came to see me, they'd often have to wait a couple of days before being given a visit permit by the camp overseer – if I didn't meet the labor quota, I was not be allowed to see them. If the visit permit was granted and the family was allowed into the camp, a political commissar would always be present at the visitation and I'd have just a couple of minutes or at most half an hour to talk to them.

When were you released and how did you manage to join the Polish Army?

I was released from captivity and joined the Polish Army on 25 August 1941 in Starobelsk.

Encampment, 24 February 1943

Collection of the Hoover Institution Library & Archives at the disposal of the Central Archives of Modern Records, Władysław Anders Collection. Reports, 800/1/0/-/47, account no. 576.

FRANCISZEK GOLIŃSKI

Personal data:

Franciszek Goliński, senior artillery sergeant, 43 years old, regular non-commissioned officer, married.

Date and circumstances of the arrest:

On 19 September 1939 I was imprisoned near Równe at the train station. From there, we were transported to Shepetovka, after an eight-day stay we went by foot to Zdołbunów, and from there we went by train to Dubno. Then we were marched on foot to Radziwiłłów, where I stayed until December 1940. From there we went by foot to Brody, and from there to work at an airfield in Stawki, near Tarnopol. After the Soviet-German war broke out we were transferred by foot to Zolotonosha, located over 600 kilometers from Tarnopol. The march was very tough: hunger, cold, poverty, exhaustion during the entire journey. Many people collapsed from exhaustion along the way – their fate remains unknown to this day. From Zolotonosha we went by train (on open platforms) to Starobelsk, where in August 1941 we were enlisted into the Polish army that was being organized there.

Generally, the conditions in the camps located on Polish territory were acceptable – we were housed in concrete buildings with bunk beds and straw mattresses inside. However, the conditions in the camps on Soviet territory were very bad. There we slept on the ground, which was often wet, without any cover or mattresses – we were absolutely freezing.

As for the nationalities there – the overwhelming majority of prisoners in all the camps were Polish soldiers. There were small numbers of Ukrainians and Belarusians. The level of intellectual standing was more or less the same, these were soldiers who had mostly graduated from elementary schools. If there were any illiterates or half-literates, they were usually Belarusians from the Polish Eastern Borderlands. There were also some people with secondary school or higher education – they were non-commissioned reserve officers mobilized into the army.

The moral standing was generally pretty good, except for some people, usually Ukrainians and Jews who had been converted to communism and had not been happy about their situation back in Poland, but now were glad to be working for Soviet Russia. They were indeed eager to work. As for the Poles, they held up well and stuck together. They were all positively disposed and were optimistic – their spirit was strong – they knew liberation would come and that was what kept them alive.

Camp life varied. It was slightly better on Polish territory because there was plenty of food (although of course you had to meet the rather exorbitant quota). However, those who met the required quota received good food, which was generally enough. There were many people who were not able to meet the quota – due to exhaustion or previous experiences – and they received 400 grams of bread and some soup of an inferior kind three times per day. Apart from that, the working conditions were not very satisfactory, although the demands of the camp authorities were high.

Cultural life was limited to readings of propaganda books that were of course boring for us, because we did not feel like listening to propaganda. It was clear for us that all of it was a treacherous lie.

Generally, the attitude of the NKVD was satisfactory, because they believed that if they wanted to find out anything during the investigations they could only do so by treating people well. However, if the authorities did obtain any information, it was useless because it was all based on lies – people testified anything just to be left alone and not summoned for interrogations anymore. The interrogations usually took place at night, which was of course very exhausting.

The hygienic conditions were horrific. Lice and fleas, caused by dirt and the lack of space in the rooms, constituted the greatest plague. However, the conditions gradually improved, because the authorities built bathhouses and disinfection chambers, so the number of lice decreased.

Medical help was quite all right. It was provided by Polish doctors who looked after people's health. They did everything they could so that sick people did not work by granting sick leave. The doctors were often reprimanded by the camp authorities because too many people had been granted sick leave, which was disadvantageous in terms of the required quota, according to the Soviets. In many cases, the doctors were dismissed and sent for forced labor, because they cared too much about the health of their colleagues.

In the camps where I was, the mortality was generally low. There were cases when prisoners were shot while trying to escape, but there were no epidemics.

I was released from the Starobelsk camp along with about 3,000 people and we were sent, by freight cars, to Totskoye, where an army was being organized. I was assigned to the 6th Light Artillery Regiment in September 1941.

Collection of the Hoover Institution Library & Archives at the disposal of the Central Archives of Modern Records, Władysław Anders Collection. Reports, 800/1/0/-/47, account no. 585.

JAN BARCZYKOWSKI

Personal data (name, surname, rank, age, occupation and marital status):
Jan Barczykowski, platoon-leader, born in 1914, regular non-commissioned officer, unmarried.

Date and circumstances of arrest:

On 16 September 1939, while withdrawing with the battle supply column of the "Wołożyn" Battalion of the Border Protection Corps, I reached Tarnopol. Leaving Tarnopol on 17 September, we made efforts to avoid the Russians and proceeded in the direction of the town of Podhajce, and from there to Halicz. In the evening of 18 September 1939 we were stopped by the Russians near the township of Dryszczów.

Name of the camp, prison or forced labor site:

Having laid down our arms, we were searched and marched off to Monasterzyska, and from there to Russia, to the township of Yarmolyntsi, while a week later we were transported by train back to Poland, to the station of Barszczowice near Lwów; from there we were taken to Jaryczów Stary, Niesłuchów and, after some time, to the following camps: Kupcze near Busk, Kozłów, Podliski Małe, Hermanów, Kurowice, Olszanica and, finally, Starobelsk.

Description of the camp or prison (grounds, buildings, housing conditions, hygiene):

In Jaryczów we lived in an abandoned stable; outside there were piles of manure. In short, the conditions were terrible. Niesłuchów: the living conditions were passable, we were housed in buildings and worked on road construction. Kupcze: we lived in a pigsty, surrounded by manure yet again. Kozłów: we had wooden barracks and tents, and slept on mean beds and straw mattresses; hygienic conditions were good, and we worked on building the Lwów–Równe road. Podliski Małe: we were quartered in pigsties next to a manor house (extreme stuffiness), and worked on the same road. Hermanów: we lived in pigsties, and worked on road construction. Kurowice: we were kept in pigsties and tents, again working on road construction. Olszanica: we were quartered in tents, and worked at the airfield; and – finally – Starobelsk: we lived in abandoned Orthodox churches and other buildings, all full of bugs.

Social composition of POWs, prisoners, exiles (nationality, type of crimes, intellectual and moral standing, mutual relations, etc.):

The number of prisoners – Poles, Ukrainians, Belarusians and Jews, from various social classes – varied between camps. A great sadness was palpable, and made all the worse by the Russians themselves, especially by their attitude towards us Poles. They frequently interrogated us at night, and never ceased to spread their propaganda, saying that Poland will be no more, that sooner hair would start growing on their palms.

Life in the camp or prison (daily routine, working conditions, quotas, wages, food, clothes, social and cultural life, etc.):

Depending on the camp, we would be woken up at three, four, five or six in the morning. We worked until 4.00, 5.00, or 6.00 p.m. We were forced to toil at road construction. If anyone refused, they would lock him up in the jail, which was in fact a dungeon, or in a cellar from which you had to bail out water. They demanded that we work to a quota, which was often so high that it was impossible to fulfill. What food we received was dependent on two factors: one, on the Soviets' unwillingness to give us anything at all, and second – on the degree to which the norm had been carried out. Meager as our rations were, they were further divided into categories. If someone carried out the norm, he would be rewarded with a bun or some other type of bread, with the aim being to encourage the others. Oftentimes people would collect various scraps just to keep alive, for they were so weak that they could not stand steadily. Frequently, we were unable to go out to work because our clothes were so worn out and tattered, while the Soviets were invariably unwilling to provide us with new apparel. Clothing was always hard to come by. In the camps, prisoners from different ethnic backgrounds would often be hostile to each other. Poles, for example, had to avoid nationalities that maintained closer relations with the Soviet authorities and sometimes helped them in their political agitation.

Attitude of the NKVD towards Poles (interrogation methods, torture and other forms of punishment, communist propaganda, information about Poland, etc.):

The NKVD would frequently take us for interrogations at night, which was extremely tiring; it was quite common for such examinations to end in detention in the punishment cell. Through their daily pep talks and lectures they wanted to convince us that Poland would be no more, that sooner hair would start growing on their palms, saying that Poland was badly governed, that its citizens went without food or clothes, and other such things.

Medical assistance, hospitals, mortality rate (provide the names of the deceased):

Infirmaries were set up at the camps, that is true, but they were frequently understaffed, while drugs were scarce.

Was it at all possible to get in contact with one's home country and family?

For a period of time some of us did receive letters from home, but if the Soviets determined that one of these lucky few worked with insufficient diligence – or not at all – they would confiscate his mail.

When were you released and how did you manage to join the Polish Army?

After the Soviet-German war broke out, we were transported, deliberately starved, to Starobelsk, from where following the conclusion of the Polish-Russian agreement and the arrival of Colonel Wiśniowski on 21 September 1941 we were sent to Totskoye, to the Polish Army that was being formed there.

Collection of the Hoover Institution Library & Archives at the disposal of the Central Archives of Modern Records, Władysław Anders Collection. Reports, 800/1/0/-/48, account no. 2008.

ADOLF HOŁDAKOWSKI

Personal data:

Adolf Hołdakowski, platoon-leader, 33 years old, farmer, married.

Date and place of arrest:

I was disarmed in Lwów on 22 September 1939 but later managed to flee Russian captivity. I was eventually stopped by the NKVD while on the run in Zdołbunów and sent to Shepetovka.

Name of the camp, prison or forced labor site:

Initially, I was detained in the POW camp in Shepetovka, then in the Równe labor camp – until 15 May 1940, next from 15 May 1940 to 28 January 1941 in the Omeliany labor camp near Równe, and then from 28 January to 2 July 1941 in the Yarmolyntsi labor camp in the Ukrainian SSR.

Description of the camp or prison (grounds, buildings, housing conditions, hygiene):

The Równe camp was a building, specifically a large mill; the living conditions were bearable (there were around 600 people in total). The Omeliany camp consisted of tents, from 100 to 200 men per tent. The Yarmolyntsi camp was a bunch of tents in an open field – that one had a population of around 1,000.

Social composition of POWs, prisoners, exiles (nationality, type of crimes, intellectual and moral standing, mutual relations, etc.):

Prisoners were mostly of Polish nationality. There was a small percentage of Ukrainians, Jews and Belarusians.

Life in the camp or prison (daily routine, working conditions, quotas, wages, food, clothes, social and cultural life, etc.):

The average day in the camp went as follows: wake-up call at 5.00 a.m., airfield construction work from 6.00 a.m. till noon, dinner break from noon till 1.00 p.m., further work from 1.00 p.m. till 7.00 p.m., dinnertime from 7.00 p.m. till 9.00 p.m. and sleep time from 9.00 p.m. onwards.

The working conditions were very harsh. Labor quota: mine 1.2 cubic centimeters of small-particle crushed stone aggregate a day. Rations very poor – 400 to 600 grams of bread, watery soup twice a day plus tea and 20 grams of sugar. The issued clothes and shoes were torn and old. Wages were only promised, never actually paid. No entertainment and no books or newspapers either.

Attitude of the NKVD towards Poles (interrogation methods, torture and other forms of punishment, communist propaganda, information about Poland, etc.):

The NKVD's attitude towards Poles was very negative. Prisoners were detained in punishment cells for the slightest infractions. Political commissars held communist propaganda lectures twice a week and all prisoners were forced to attend them. We had no information about Poland.

Medical assistance, hospitals, mortality rate (provide the names of the deceased):

Medical assistance was available but it was of very poor quality. The medics among us were the ones who provided all the actual medical care.

Was it at all possible to get in contact with one's home country and family?

In camps located within Polish territory we could contact our families by letter. In Soviet camps we had no contact with our families or with the home country.

When were you released and how did you manage to join the Polish Army?

Once the German-Soviet conflict began, the whole camp in Yarmolyntsi was combined with the camp in Proskurov and all the prisoners (1,500 people) were marched under escort deeper into USSR territory. The prisoners had to walk 30, 40 and sometimes even 50 kilometers a day. The daily allotment of food during the march was 200 grams of bread and half a liter of soup, and sometimes we wouldn't get anything at all. Rest stops were very short. We rested mostly in the bushes, in fields, in muddy places or in various kolkhoz stables. The worst thing was the complete lack of water. Many people collapsed along the way out of weakness and exhaustion. The whole march route was around 900 kilometers. When we got to our destination, we were loaded onto flatcars and taken to Starobelsk. The conditions during transit were awful – there was no free space, no protection from the rain and the food allotment was a measly 100 grams of bread per person. I remained in Starobelsk until 25 August [1941].

After the signing of the Polish-Soviet agreement, I was released from captivity and joined the army.

Collection of the Hoover Institution Library & Archives at the disposal of the Central Archives of Modern Records, Władysław Anders Collection. Reports, 800/1/0/-/47, account no. 586.

IGNACY WASIAK

[Ignacy Wasiak, cadet platoon-leader]

Name of the camp:

a) Hoszcza, 30 kilometers from Równe in the direction of [illegible word]
b) Angielówka near Olesko – Złoczów District
c) Mościska near Przemyśl
d) Teofipol′ – opposite Krzemieniec on the Soviet side, 14 kilometers from the border.

Social composition of POWs:

a), b), c) and d) – mostly privates, a few officers.

Number of POWs:

a) 923
b) 350, later 450
c) over 1,000
d) 411.

Description of the camp:

a) Border Protection Corps barracks – electric light, running water, toilets in the building, bath available, sleeping arrangement: some slept in beds (two beds per three men) and others in cots. Overall very good conditions;
b) a one-story barrack – a well and a bath at the location, overall conditions acceptable;
c) a number of one-story barracks – no access to water, bathing opportunity provided at the location, highly unsanitary conditions (cramped, infested with lice and dirty), lack of heating fuel, cold, overall conditions very bad;
d) a brick building (kolkhoz stable or barn) – no access to water, opportunity to bathe once every two or three weeks, acceptable sanitary conditions, overall conditions bearable.

Period of the camp's existence:

a) arrived on 8 October 1939, left on 26 April 1940,
b) arrived on 26 April and left on 15 October 1940,
c) 18 October 1940 to 1 March 1941,
d) 1 May to 2 July 1941.

Life in the camp:

a) Prisoners divided into battalions – 100 men per battalion – subdivided into brigades of 25. Performed forced construction labor, building the Lwów–Kiev highway. We hosted two theater revues in the beginning of 1940, with the approval of camp authorities. However, because the shows had an obvious propaganda slant (especially the second one), they were abandoned.
b) Prisoners divided into brigades; performed 12 hours of forced construction labor a day, building the Lwów–Kiev highway. We would sing Polish patriotic military songs at night (*Warszawianka* [La Varsovienne], *Boże, coś Polskę* [God Save Poland]).
c) Prisoners divided into brigades; performed forced construction labor, building the Przemyśl–Lwów highway. From January to March 1941, we organized shows that included satirical pieces about camp life and recitations of artistic works, such as *koncert Jankiela* [Jankiel's concert, part of the Polish epic *Pan Tadeusz*], *Reduta Ordona* [*Redout of Ordon* by Adam Mickiewicz], *Piramidy, czy wy macie…* [*Conversation with the Pyramids* by Juliusz Słowacki] and very good pieces written by our fellow prisoner Czesław Rosiński. Furthermore, the shows featured performances by a four-part male choir directed by Henryk Kufirski and an orchestra conducted by Malinowski. There were around eight shows in total; camp command was relatively supportive.
d) Prisoners divided into brigades; performed forced labor for 14 hours a day, building a military airfield. No rest or cultural events.

Attitude of the NKVD towards Poles:

a) Initially, frequent questioning at night intended to identify the officers. Constant communist propaganda. Failure to meet the labor quota, refusal to leave for work, and all disciplinary infractions punished severely – with detention in a punishment cell.
b) Suspect POWs were questioned by a persecutor in August and September 1940; prisoners who refused to sign a personal data questionnaire were punished: threatened, put in detention or sent to another camp.

c) Work avoidance was punished with detention in the freezing cold, specifically in a shed made out of wooden planks and lacking a floor or beds. No propagandizing, as it was considered completely ineffective.
d) Like in camp c with the exception that after the outbreak of the German-Soviet war we were read an edict about the USSR entering the state of martial law.

POWs who stood out either positively or negatively:

a) Zygmunt Królikowski – a tireless propagator of communism among the POWs and a traitor. Zarzycki – a vile man who acted as a spy and provocateur in return for permission to skip work. Skalski from Grodno – a crass thief who stole shoes, coats and uniforms from the other prisoners and, afraid of being punished, offered his services to the camp command, therefore becoming a snitch and provocateur. Rida [?] – he lifted our spirits with his words and actions, giving us hope of a better future.
b) –
c) Cadet Platoon-leader Mieczysław Rostkowski – his unshakably positive attitude and great faith in the righteousness of our cause encouraged us to endure and not break under pressure. He had a mysterious way of knowing and spreading news among the prisoners, whether about the radio addresses of the Commander-in-Chief to the nation, the distinguished service of our troops in Norway, or the assembling of the Polish Army in Syria.
Corporal Czesław Rosiński gave us news that strengthened our love for Poland, increased our longing for it and gave us hope of its resurrection.
Henryk Kufirski, through his dedication to Polish music, and [illegible surname], through dedication to the spoken mother tongue, strengthened our belief that Poland is a mighty nation that cannot just pass away, that this present storm will eventually end and we will once again bask in the warm glow of freedom.

Collection of the Hoover Institution Library & Archives at the disposal of the Central Archives of Modern Records, Władysław Anders Collection. Reports, 800/1/0/-/48, account no. 14.

PIOTR AFFEK

Personal data (name, surname, rank, age, occupation and marital status):
Piotr Affek, senior sergeant, 38 years old, regular non-commissioned officer, married.

Date and circumstances of arrest:

On 22 September 1939 I was taken into Soviet captivity in a town near Włodzimierz. Then I was escorted to the train station in Włodzimierz, where we were loaded into railway cars, 60–70 people per car, and taken to Shepetovka.

Name of the camp, prison or forced labor site:

I was in the following camps: Shepetovka, Zahorce Wielkie, Rudnia Poczajowska, Łuka Wielka, Zastawie, Starobelsk.

Description of the camp or prison (grounds, buildings, housing conditions, hygiene):

Living conditions: Shepetovka – military barracks, concrete floor. There were so many of us that we had to sleep in rotation, as there wasn't enough room to fit all of us. Hygienic conditions were awful. Zahorce Wielkie – cowsheds filled with manure. There was a large heap of liquid manure in front of them. It was impossible to walk across it. Rudnia Poczajowska – a barn, half of it roofless. We slept on bare planks. There was no straw. Łuka Wielka – farm stables. There was a lot of manure around. It wasn't removed until the very end of my stay there. Zastawie – sheds that had once stored concrete. We built bunks inside. Everyone was allotted 40 centimeters of a bunk to sleep on. We were marched off from Zastawie under heavy escort, driven day and night without rest. The marching conditions were awful. We weren't allowed to take water with us. Food was out of the question. We lived on nothing but grain, which was obtained when one of us managed to detach himself from the column. On the way we were subjected to rigid discipline. We weren't allowed to take one step off to the side. I saw people who were so famished and exhausted that they were no longer able to walk. In such cases Soviet guards stabbed them with their bayonets, leaving their bodies unburied. They drove us in this way for 21 days, from Zastawie to Zolotonosha.

Social composition of POWs, prisoners, exiles (nationality, type of crimes, intellectual and moral standing, mutual relations, etc.):

Except for a few Jews, all the prisoners were of Polish nationality. Intellectual level – average. Mutual relations were very good.

Life in the camp or prison (daily routine, working conditions, quotas, wages, food rations, clothes, social and cultural life, etc.):

Daily routine: we woke up at 5.00 a.m. After breakfast, at 6.00 a.m., we set out to work. Working conditions were very harsh and the work quotas were set much too high for anyone to meet them, for instance to remove 1.2 cubic meters of stone during one day, which was simply impossible. Pay depended on the meeting of work quotas, as did food rations. And none of us was able to meet them. Food rations were divided according to the so-called caldrons: the first, second and third ones. The third caldron was for those who filled 100% of their work quota. They received 800 grams of bread and three hot meals. Those who met 80% of their quota were given 600 grams of bread and two hot meals.

The first caldron was for those who failed to meet 80% of their work quota. The latter received 400 grams of bread and two hot meals. The first caldron was called a punitive one, and the camp head, in referring to it, used to say: "if you fail to meet your quotas, you are going to have rations that only smell of groats." And we all received rations from the first caldron, because none of us ever managed to meet the work quotas. In terms of clothes, our situation was also very difficult. We walked ragged, almost naked. In order not to go around naked, everyone had to patch their pants together.

We were all on good terms with each other. The Soviets, fierce in the pursuit of their propaganda, tried to convince us of the advantages of communism and we were lectured on the ideas of Marx and Lenin during obligatory meetings (*beseda*). They also told us that Poland would never be restored.

Was it at all possible to get in contact with one's home country and family?

Except for a small number of those who were in the camp head's good graces, nobody received letters.

When were you released and how did you manage to join the Polish Army?

I was released from captivity on 26 August 1941 in Starobelsk, and this is where I joined the Polish army.

Collection of the Hoover Institution Library & Archives at the disposal of the Central Archives of Modern Records, Władysław Anders Collection. Reports, 800/1/0/-/48, account no. 2004

KALINOWSKI

Personal data:
Kalinowski, second lieutenant.

Name of the camp:

Hołownica estate near Korzec, Równe District.

Social composition of POWs:

In principle the camp was intended only for reserve privates, but there were some officers and regular non-commissioned officers among us – they hadn't provided their actual data to the authorities.

Number of POWs:

At inception the camp held 300 people and later expanded to 600.

Period of the camp's existence:

The camp was established on 13 October 1939. I left it in the end of December 1940 (it continued to operate until the outbreak of the Russian-German war).

Description of the camp:

The camp was located in one of the Hołownica estate buildings. It was a small place, so it was extremely cramped and we all suffered from a long-lasting lice infestation (almost until spring). In the spring, a few additional tents were erected in the camp since the number of prisoners had doubled. The whole camp area – a quadrilateral field of 200 square meters – was surrounded by two rows of barbed wire and guarded by three men in the daytime and from six to nine at night. The nightshift also had two dogs. It was cramped and stuffy in the summer; an unpleasant odor coming from the latrine situated next to the building only made things worse.

Life in the camp:

All POWs were basically divided just into brigades. There were on average 25–30 men per brigade, although at first the groups numbered anywhere from 20 to 100 men. Notable labor assignments in the camp included kitchen duty, construction and furnishing work for the camp, fuel harvesting, work for the NKVD. Forced labor outside of the camp involved work on the Novograd-Volynskyi–Równe highway, particularly road widening, earthworks, stone mining at the quarry, road tarring, paving, work at the asphalt and concrete factory, etc. This was hard work and the Soviet authorities wanted to finish the construction project quickly, so during periods of maximum work intensity they did everything they could to make prisoners reach their labor quotas. We were threatened with court trials, the weaker workers were publicly labeled enemies of Communism and so-called Stakhanovites would get better food, etc. All prisoners were sent out to work for 12 hours a day. In the 1939–1940 winter season, some of the men would be taken by car to work in Novograd-Volynskyi, which was 48 kilometers away, and in transit they would be prohibited from moving an inch in the car even though the temperature went as low as minus 40 degrees [Celsius]. Unsurprisingly, after that kind of commute the men were not just unable to work but almost unwilling to live. We would all return from work around 8.00 or 9.00 p.m. Insufficiently productive workers were put in punishment cells. Despite the mistreatment of Polish prisoners in comparison to the Ukrainians and Belarusians, and despite the initial snitching by the latter, the Polish POWs successfully closed ranks and formed a separate faction in the camp. They would show disdain for the others, always stressing their Polish identity and unshakable resolve. If the political commissar visited, he would often leave quickly, unable to defend himself from the ensuing verbal attacks.

Attitude of the NKVD towards Poles:

The NKVD authorities were hostile to the prisoners and sought to eradicate all signs of our Polish identity. We were told at every opportunity that we should forget about Poland and that we need to go through a long quarantine to rid ourselves of our "bourgeois" inclinations. Merely speaking, laughing or slowing down during march to work was cause enough to be reviled, beaten and put in the punishment cell after return to camp. In winter, if a prisoner was seen idling at his work assignment, he would be forced to sit in the snow until it was time to go back. Then, after we got back, he would be put in the punishment cell as an enemy of Communism.

Every once in a while an NKVD commission would come to the camp, seeking to weed out officers, regular non-commissioned officers, *pomeshchiki*, participants of the 1918–1920 war, police officers, some state administration employees, etc. Many of the prisoners, who had been preselected for questioning, would be summoned before this commission and the NKVD would try to make some of them admit to things they hadn't actually done.

They were asked many questions that were tricky to dodge properly without preparation, such as: "What is your opinion of a Soviet Poland?", "What do you like about Russia?", "Would it have been good if the Polish government had completely allied with Russia before the war of 1939?" The initial phase of the questioning was usually very polite – we would even be offered cigarettes – but they would turn to shouting and threats when the politeness didn't have the desired effect. Periodically, some of the prisoners would be rounded up and transferred elsewhere – this usually happened to the ones who were reluctant workers. Some of them were later found at other nearby camps. In the winter season of 1940–1941 in the Proskurov camp, the punishment for small infractions – such as refusing to go to work because one lacked shoes – was detainment in underwear only in an unheated shack made out of wooden planks; it was meted out regardless of the freezing cold weather.

Deaths in the camp:

Kazimierz Szymiec, a worker from Wilno, and one Błażewicz also from Wilno (whose name I can't recall) both died in the Hołownica camp. Błażewicz was, specifically, shot while attempting escape on 28 April 1940.

POWs who stood out either positively or negatively:

Those known for negative behavior at the Hołownica camp were: Michał Zdanowicz – paver, employee of the District Directorate of State Railways in Wilno, brigadier and *desyatnyk* [leader of ten] in the service of the NKVD, who would accuse others of hostility to Soviet authorities, refusing to work, harboring a "Polish spirit," etc; Włodzimierz Żuk – a Ukrainian and a Soviet-aligned snitch who lived near Hołownica and was indirectly responsible for the death of POW Błażewicz from Wilno because Błażewicz was planning to escape from the asphalt and concrete factory, Żuk found out about it by unknown means and informed the NKVD, who set an ambush for Błażewicz.

Addendums:

One of my most horrible memories, which I cannot describe vividly enough, is the forced march to the other side of the Dnieper River that some of us POWs had to suffer through. My last camp was Yarmolyntsi (30 kilometers away from Proskurov). We marched for over three weeks from 3.00 a.m. to midnight or 1.00 a.m. the next day, with almost no food: they'd give us 50–100 grams of bread for three of four days and sometimes a bit of groats. Some walked barefoot. Those who didn't have the strength to keep going and fell behind were lost forever – shot dead. The NKVD showed no humanity whatsoever. We had to use dirt side roads; a destination 20 kilometers away could actually require up to 50 kilometers of marching. We were marched this way to Zolotonosha. There, completely exhausted and with almost no will to live, we were finally put on a train and sent to Starobelsk.

Collection of the Hoover Institution Library & Archives at the disposal of the Central Archives of Modern Records, Władysław Anders Collection. Reports, 800/1/0/-/46, account no. 8.

HENRYK GANSINIEC

Henryk Gansiniec, platoon-leader, 31 years old, regular non-commissioned officer, unmarried.

On 19 September 1939 I was disarmed and taken prisoner by the Soviets in Łuck. I was kept there in the barracks until 25 September, when about 2,000 people were loaded onto a train and transferred to Shepetovka. Fifty people were loaded into each railcar. For the journey, we received 500 grams of bread and about 100 grams of lard. We traveled like that for five days. On the third day of travel, everyone received 300 grams of rusks, but we had to get water by ourselves, putting canteens outside the windows during stops and asking passers-by for some water to drink.

The day after we arrived in Shepetovka we received 300 grams of bread and a quarter liter of soup. On 5 October 1939, about 5,000 people were taken outside and led as far as Ostróg. Many of us collapsed along the way because of hunger and exhaustion. People were also beaten and kicked, and were then left to fate's mercy on the road. Five people died, but I do not know their names.

After arriving in Ostróg, at the barracks of the 19th Cavalry Regiment, we spent the night in a stable that was wet from horse manure. We slept on one another's legs. After one night in Ostróg we were each given 400 grams of bread and were marched further, to as far as Zdołbunów. There, we were loaded onto a train, 60 to 70 people in a single dirty railcar that still had manure in it, and taken to Dubno. After we'd been unloaded we were taken to a hop house, where civilians brought us something to eat – we hauled it upstairs using a rope, as they were not allowed to get close to us. On 13 October, about one thousand people (after we had received 500 grams of bread each, because we did not want to go) were escorted to Werba. Having spent a night in a sawmill, we were escorted to Radziwiłłów.

From 15 October I was in Radziwiłłów (a railroad building), from 25 May 1940 – in Sitno (tents), from 9 August – in Brody (castle), on 16 August I went by train to Rohatyn, and from 21 August I was in Rohatyn (pigpens). February 1941 – Janów Lwowski (a wooden barrack), from 7 May to the outbreak of the Soviet-German war – Lwów-Skniłów (a wooden barrack).

The location selected was usually away from settlements, fenced off with 2.5-meter high barbed wire. We lived in tents or wooden barracks, so when it rained water poured onto our heads and we were unable to sleep (we were marched to work in the morning). From 300 to 400 people lived in such a barrack. We had no soap and no change of underwear, and we rarely bathed or were sent for disinfection.

There were Poles, Ukrainians, Belarusians and Jews in the camps. The level of intellectual standing was average, moral standing was satisfactory, and the camaraderie between us was all right.

Life in the camps was very hard. Its quality depended on the quotas, which were difficult to meet. We were woken at 4.00 a.m. and at 5.30 a.m. we set off for work, where we then spent 10–12 hours. We had to walk 15 kilometers to get to work. On our way to work we were forced by the escorts to march faster. They set their dogs on us. When we reached the destination we were unable to work, having walked for several kilometers. The guards mocked us, saying, for example, "Let God work instead of you." There often were no tools to work with, and if one failed to meet the work quota (unloading stones – that had been looted – from 18 to 20 three-ton trucks in the space of 10 to 12 hours, and taking 8 cubic meters of dirt to a spot 200 meters away in wheelbarrows, etc.), he would get 400 grams of bread and watery soup. For propaganda, those who met the quota were given groats at work – so-called *prembludo*. Remuneration was for those who met the quota – at 20 to 30 rubles per month; those who did not meet the quota were forced to pay for the food they received. Sundays and Saturdays were not work-free. After arriving from work in the evening and eating combined lunch and dinner, which invariably failed to satisfy our hunger, there was no opportunity to rest, because political instructors would call on us to attend communist talks and convince us how good life was in their country.

News concerning Poland was that Poland would no longer exist; we were told that laborers in Poland had been badly treated, beaten, etc., which caused our indignation, and we argued about that.

The medical assistance was very poor, there were no medications, and the hospitals were overcrowded. As for mortality – in the camp in Radziwiłłów, Szczepański from Silesia was shot dead. He was buried at the cemetery in Radziwiłłów. During the evacuation from the Polish territory to Russia there were cases of execution by shooting and deaths from exhaustion, about 20 people – I do not know their names.

On the way to a camp near Zborów six people who had been murdered in a horrible way were found. They had knife wounds, their eyes had been gouged out, etc. The corpses were found in a basement, in water.

The evacuation was very difficult. We went on foot from Lwów to Zolotonosha, covering up to 40 kilometers a day. The food – up to 200 grams of bread, sometimes a little soup, quarter a liter. If the local people tried to give us some water to drink we were not allowed to take it, and we were forced to drink water found on the road, or we dug holes in the ground during stops and waited until they filled with water. We marched from 23 June to 17 July 1941. On 17 July we were loaded onto a freight train in Zolotonosha, with 70 or more people per railcar.

We were unloaded in the forest beyond Poltava station, and we stood there for four days in the mud and rain. Sleeping was out of the question, we weren't even allowed to break off some branches and sit on them under the trees. People were swelling from exhaustion.

We did not have much contact with the home country. I received three letters, although I sent many more.

On 28 July 1941 we were unloaded at Starobelsk, where on 25 August 1941 I joined the Polish Army.

Encampment, 24 February 1943

Collection of the Hoover Institution Library & Archives at the disposal of the Central Archives of Modern Records, Władysław Anders Collection. Reports, 800/1/0/-/47, account no. 570.

MICHAŁ KASZA

Michał Kasza, corporal, 28 years old, farmer.

I was taken into Russian captivity on 19 September 1939 in Sarnki Dolne. We were searched, disarmed, and divested of ammunition and many other things, such as watches and razors. Then we were marched under escort to Kamenets-Podolskyi. This journey took seven days, including two nights of rest which we spent in the open air, in the rain. The journey was very hard, because we didn't get anything to eat. We were taken to Husiatyn, where we were given a short break, and the Polish civilian populace went to the commander of the escorting unit to ask permission to give us some bread. After this modest meal we were marched on. Whenever we entered some bigger town, [illegible word] threw pieces of bread at us, just to see how we would fall upon the crumbs of black bread to alleviate our hunger. We passed by those crumbs and didn't pick them up in order not to show them that we were hungry, and upon seeing this they gave vent to their anger.

Then we crossed the border. In the first town we heard them shouting that they would finish us off and we wouldn't see Poland ever again. In Kamenets-Podolskyi we were taken to the barracks, where we spent seven days. On the eighth day they took us to the train station. They said that they were taking us to Siberia, where we would all croak. In the wagons we received one fish per day for twelve people and one 2-kilogram loaf of bread for forty people. This was repeated over ten days. We were brought to Równe, from where we walked to the barracks in Żytyń, where there were 3,000 soldiers. Eight rows of barbed wire hung over our lives there. They began to cook soup from rotten fish for us and gave us 400 grams of bread per person. Although it was freezing cold, we didn't receive any coal to make ourselves warm. We were driven out for hard labor. Later on we were divided into small camps. We moved to mud huts. There wasn't even any water for washing there, let alone food, and we had to melt snow to obtain some. There was so much lice that I'm grateful they spared our lives. It was impossible to get rid of them, because during the day we had to work on the road, and at night there wasn't any light or water. When the doctor visited us, he said that he couldn't do anything, as he was always being escorted.

On 2 March we were taken to a gulag camp in Niesłuchów, where we were again marched for forced labor. We were taken to the camp in Słowita, and after a month to Olszanica, where we were tormented with work on the airfield.

We were severely punished for mentioning the restoration of Poland. The briefest mention of Poland entailed incarceration in prison, and I shall now describe what the prison looked like: it was a basement dug into the earth, which after spring rains was filled with water to such a degree that it was impossible to pour it out, and it kept leaking from the surface and the sides, and as a result one had to stand knee-deep in water both during the day and at night. Any food was out of the question, there was only some sour cabbage soup to drink once a day. When we walked to work, we were forced to quick march. When we couldn't obey due to exhaustion, they told us to lie down in the mud, then kicked us and beat us with rifle butts. On Sundays, when we were driven out for work but refused to go in order to celebrate the holiday, they told us to stand to attention facing the sun and then to lie down in the mud. We had nothing to smoke; if they gave us some tobacco, they didn't give us newspapers to roll it in, and when they gave us some newspaper, they didn't give us tobacco. We were divested of books; we were forbidden to read Polish books. We were searched and robbed of any clean change of underwear from Poland, knives, etc. When there were no more shoes or underwear, we were told that we would be issued some if we kept working.

THE GERMAN-RUSSIAN WAR

When the war between Germany and Russia broke out, we were marched to Russia. We were in a pickle: we were so hungry and it was so hot that we could barely walk. But there was no other way, because we were beaten; that was not the end, we simply had to go. Many kilometers later night fell on us, and as many suffered from night blindness, they had to be led. Those who couldn't walk on their own couldn't count on any help. The escort walked in the back, and those who fell to the ground were finished off with a bayonet. In Złoczów, following a break in a gulag camp, four of our soldiers were killed in this way. We were loaded into wagons at some Russian station, and then the wagons were sealed; we didn't receive food or water, and air raids continued over our heads, not leading to victory this time.

We came to Starobelsk, where there were several thousand prisoners. One day they announced to us the signing of the Polish-Russian agreement. Then Lieutenant Colonel Wiśniowski came and began to organize a Polish army. Thanks to our beloved Commander, our days of captivity were over and a new life began for us.

Collection of the Hoover Institution Library & Archives at the disposal of the Central Archives of Modern Records, Władysław Anders Collection. Reports, 800/1/0/-/48, account no. 2429.

TEODOR MICHALAK

Teodor Michalak, senior rifleman, 38 years old, married, factory worker.

I was called up on 30 August 1939 into the 44th Infantry Regiment in Równe; after 20 days, together with the whole reserve battalion under the command of Major Gołąb, I found myself in Łuck, where we were taken into Soviet captivity.

Of course, that memorable day of 19 September marked a radical change in my life. This is because that date was the beginning of wandering from place to place between various labor camps, a time of intense communist propaganda as well as moral and physical suffering.

After a brief stay in the Russian territory (Shepetovka), where we were brought for a very short time, we returned on foot to the Polish territory, to Zdołbunów, and then went on to Dubno. We were quartered in the building of a hop-processing plant, and the whole burden of supplying us with provisions rested with the local population, who organized a campaign on their own initiative in order to save the POWs from starvation. After spending nearly two weeks in Dubno, we found ourselves in Werba, where they started using us for roadworks, digging ditches, logging, etc. Our living quarters were the buildings of the local lumber mill, strongly guarded by Soviet soldiers. Two "rooms" could accommodate 1,200 people on four-decker bunks. We were fed twice a day with soup, and the rations of bread varied depending on the stocks. The sanitary conditions were horrible, there was no doctor at all. We were rushed to work at gunpoint.

The previous group of captives had been taken to Radziwiłłów, where they were still put to work at building the freeway from Novograd-Volynskyi to Przemyśl.

From that moment, normal work began according to Soviet regulations: with quotas for all kinds of work, raised to the highest limits. Food in that period was very poor and grossly inadequate to the work we performed. I would like to stress here that there were those among us who – having taken the posts of foremen – became outright mercenary renegades and exploited their companions in misery more than the Soviet despots did. Add to this the shortage of water in the Radziwiłłów camp, and you can imagine the hygienic and sanitary conditions.

Regarding the campaign of "raising communist political awareness," it was systematically carried out by political officers; it must be said that the campaign did influence some group of the prisoners, though only a small one. This obviously caused a number of quarrels between true citizens of our country and these degenerate scoundrels. Good relations with them were out of the question. But in the group of people who retained their Polish spirit despite intense agitation and physical persecution, the mutual relations were warm and friendly.

We remained in Radziwiłłów camp until 16 May 1940. From there, we were transported to the village of Rodatycze, where we were quartered in the outbuildings of a Franciscan convent. We stayed there for three weeks, and then we were transferred to the camp in Gródek Jagielloński. Objectively, it should be said that the living conditions in this camp – food, accommodation, and hygiene – were adequate. This was particularly thanks to the camp's commandant, Surkov, who was fair and honest with people.

We returned from that camp to Rodatycze in July and remained there until February 1941. In Rodatycze we celebrated Christmas, in a cheerful and merry mood, with an orchestra that consisted of prisoners of war, and with the invited Soviet authorities, who looked approvingly at the fact of celebration being held this time, despite its purely religious character.

It should be stressed here that the first Christmas in captivity, in Radziwiłłów, had been celebrated in sorrow and tears, and the Soviet authorities reacted by destroying and trampling the Christmas trees we prepared.

The next stage of our journey was Janów near Lwów. This camp meant a deterioration of living conditions, both in terms of sanitation and in terms of accommodation, as well as supplies. As a result, numerous protests took place here, involving refusal to take any food. Then we were transferred to Sknilów near Lwów, where we were put to work for the construction of a concrete airfield. The living conditions were horrible; the buildings were unheated and wooden, and we walked nearly waist-deep in mud. In this camp, I spent two days in solitary confinement, without food, for tearing a newspaper with a photograph of the Soviet cabinet and using it to roll cigarettes. The sanitary conditions were appalling.

The German-Soviet war broke out. The following day we were gathered and set out towards the Soviet border. We marched 800 kilometers on foot in 24 days to the town of Zolotonosha. This period was the worst in the whole painful ordeal we had been through. People fell down due to fatigue and exhaustion caused by hunger. Those who lagged behind were killed, had dogs set on them, etc. We marched 22 hours a day and rested wherever we found ourselves when night came – we slept under the open sky. A two-kilogram loaf of bread was the food for 16 people, and we were not allowed to drink water at all. After spending one day in Zolotonosha, we were transported as far as Poltava, where we stayed a week in conditions so dreadful that a lot of people fell seriously ill and were sent to local kolkhozes.

From Poltava, we departed for Starobelsk. Already on the way there we heard rumors about a Polish-Soviet pact and the Polish Army being organized, but no one wanted to believe these rumors. On 1 August 1941 in

Starobelsk, all the prisoners of war were assembled and a Soviet dignitary read out the Russian text of the Polish-Soviet pact, which was then translated into Polish. That was a very touching moment, when the assembled people sang the Polish anthem and *Boże, coś Polskę…* [God Save Poland]. We felt that our link with the motherland was strong and indissoluble; we understood that the moment of our liberation from captivity was near, and that we would be part of the Polish Army that was in the making.

From that time, we were not taken to do any work, except when we volunteered to do it, and the food and sanitary conditions improved considerably. Still, we had to wait until 24 August, when Lieutenant Colonel Wiśniowski arrived and set about organizing us into an army. On 3 September 1941, we left for Totskoye, and this is when we started regular work in the ranks of the Polish Army.

Collection of the Hoover Institution Library & Archives at the disposal of the Central Archives of Modern Records, Władysław Anders Collection. Reports, 800/1/0/-/48, account no. 2129.

WŁADYSŁAW PALICZEWSKI

Personal data (name, surname, rank, age, occupation and marital status):
Władysław Paliczewski, ensign, born 22 January 1900, regular non-commissioned officer, married.

Date and circumstances of arrest:

On 19 September 1939, as I was traveling to the Division Reserve Center, I was taken captive by the Bolsheviks near Złoczów. I was taken to Shepetovka and later, on 4 October 1939, transferred with around 2,000 other POWs to Podliski Małe near Lwów, to work on widening and asphalting the Lwów–Równe–Kiev highway.

Name of the camp, prison or forced labor site:

Podliski Małe – from 10 October 1939 to 8 September 1940
Jaryczów Stary – from 8 to 30 September 1940
Podliski Małe – from 30 September 1940 to 28 February 1941
Słowita near Lwów – from 28 February to 31 May 1941
Olszanica – from 31 May to 23 June 1941
Starobelsk in Russia – from 8 July to 2 September 1941.

Description of the camp or prison (grounds, buildings, housing conditions, hygiene):

In camps located in Polish territory the POWs were housed in estate barns or tents. The quarters were cramped, dirty due to overcrowding, foul smelling and awfully humid. We made floors, cots, benches and tables by ourselves. In winter we used bricks from dismantled chicken coops to build makeshift heaters, but they weren't powerful enough to heat the large area of the barns we lived in; we were freezing cold at night. We built a bath, a laundry and a disinfection room, with some minor help from the guards, to fight the dirt and the lice – we eventually did get rid of the pests.

Social composition of POWs, prisoners, exiles (nationality, type of crimes, intellectual and moral standing, mutual relations, etc.):

Among the POWs were men of varying social class – from a reader of the Wilno University to an unskilled worker – but 80% of them were farmers and workers. Most were Poles; there were 30 Belarusians, 10 Jews, 5 Ukrainians, 5 Lithuanians and 12 Poles who identified as Germans. The Poles, Jews and Lithuanians were agreeable to one another – only the "Germans," Ukrainians and Belarusians isolated themselves. The groups mostly displayed a lot of solidarity with one another and an unwavering belief in their future ultimate victory.

Life in the camp or prison (daily routine, working conditions, quotas, wages, food, clothes, social and cultural life, etc.):

On average we worked 12 hours a day in two shifts (day and night). The assigned food rations differed according to whether one had met one's labor quota and these quotas would rise as they were being fulfilled, eventually exceeding the relevant regulations. Those who met their quotas got some money, a kilogram of bread and a larger overall food ration. Quota fulfillment was accomplished – or, quite often, successfully faked – mainly by the physically stronger POWs, who would then share their food with the weaker ones; the weaker ones would have found it very hard to live on their allotted 400 grams of bread and some thin soup. We saved our military uniforms from wearing out by staging a strike and getting camp command to issue us denims and rubber boots for work.

Attitude of the NKVD towards Poles (interrogation methods, torture and other forms of punishment, communist propaganda, information about Poland, etc.):

The NKVD questioned only a small group of POWs who were suspected of being officers or anti-Bolshevik agitators. The interrogations took place in the evening, after our return from work. The tone was initially pleasant but would change later and the men would be threatened with court trials or executions, but since the guilty party never admitted to what they were accused of and all witnesses supported their testimony, the cases were eventually dropped for lack of evidence. Besides, the solidarity among the prisoners and our hostility to the Bolsheviks, which we manifested at every opportunity both in words and deeds, eventually convinced them the we were all anti-Bolshevik agitators, at which point the interrogations were discontinued. Communist propaganda, while extensively planned, mostly didn't actually reach the prisoners – no one went to the lectures, excusing themselves with tiredness due to overwork. Negative information about Poland was immediately repudiated, forcing the enemy into silence.

Medical assistance, hospitals, mortality rate (provide the names of the deceased):

Medical aid was available through our fellow prisoners who were physicians. Unfortunately, we severely lacked medications. Initially, every sick prisoner would be sent to the hospital in Lwów, which provided an opportunity for him to escape. Later, infirmaries were organized within the camp and only the very sick were sent away to the hospital. Deaths from tuberculosis: Senior Sergeant Ignacy Czubek from the 63rd Infantry Regiment and Private Perła. When the Bolshevik-German war broke out, POWs were marched into Russia; during that march, in Zborów (still on Polish soil), the following men were killed with revolver shots: Stachowicz, Ptaszyński, Józef Kamiński, Kieliszek, Skarżyński. They and one more man – whose name I can't recall – were all killed because they were too famished and exhausted to keep walking. Furthermore, Jan Dymek and a man named Hyniec were wounded during an escape attempt near Złoczów. Four men went insane.

Was it at all possible to get in contact with one's home country and family?

Maintaining contact with families was not easy. A letter from Warsaw would take six weeks to arrive in Podliski Małe by official means. Since only prisoners who met their labor quotas were allowed to send letters, we devised a way to send them indirectly: going through a *desyatnyk* [leader of ten], with return addresses that belonged to Lwów residents. These residents were Polish Military Organization members who were in close contact with us and readily helped us despite the significant risk of being arrested and deported. This indirect mailing route allowed us to halve the time of letter delivery.

When were you released and how did you manage to join the Polish Army?

After arrival in Starobelsk, 12,000 POWs were put together in one place, in complete isolation from the outside world. We waited like that until the second half of August, when the amnesty was announced. A few days after the announcement, we were visited by a delegate of the newly forming Polish Army in Russian territory – Certified Lieutenant Colonel Kazimierz Wiśniowski. He arranged transport for the POWs to Totskoye, where the Polish Army divisions were forming up.

Collection of the Hoover Institution Library & Archives at the disposal of the Central Archives of Modern Records, Władysław Anders Collection. Reports, 800/1/0/-/48, account no. 1285.

KONSTANTY WOLSKI

[Konstanty Wolski, lieutenant]

I was an inmate of the POW camp in Dubno that housed 1,112 prisoners in total. The POW population consisted of soldiers (40%), officers (30%), police force members (20%) and members of the Border Guard (10%). The camp in Dubno was in operation from 7 October 1939 to 23 February 1941. We were quartered in a hop house – the conditions were bearable. We were divided into units called *sotnya* and brigades. We did construction-related work on the highway leading from Równe to Lwów. We read Polish books provided to us by Poles. The NKVD authorities organized propaganda lectures and provided us with books and newspapers, both in Russian and Polish. The interrogations were performed by a political commissar that was permanently stationed in the camp and observed the prisoners closely. Punishments were dealt out for refusal to work.

From among the notable prisoners who assisted other POWs, and who were Polish Military Organization members, I knew the following: Lieutenant Jan Szafer from the 16th Infantry Regiment, Platoon-leader Jan Roszczyk from the 16th Infantry Regiment, Cadet Hieronim Miernicki from the 16th Infantry Regiment, Corporal Opacki from OZM [?]. There were also many others. These men took care of the material needs of the sick, lifted the spirits of their fellow prisoners, and provided them with access to books in Polish.

Additionally, from 27 September to 4 October 1939 I was detained in the POW camp in Shepetovka. There were around 18,000 of us in total in that camp – officers (commissioned and non-commissioned), privates and Border Guard members. Between 4 and 5 October 1939 the whole camp was disbanded; some of the men were taken deeper into Russia (officers and police force members), while others were transferred to camps in Polish territory (officers and police force members who had not been discovered).

I cannot give any more details about POW life because I was eventually arrested by the NKVD for promoting Polish independence, strengthening patriotic feelings among fellow prisoners and caring for their material needs via the Polish Military Organization. As a result, I was put in the Dubno prison, where I remained for 11 months. On 24 February 1941, I was transferred deeper into Russian territory – to Ukhta, in the north – where I stayed until 16 December 1941. On 17 January 1942, I joined the Polish Army, where I still serve. I've been continuously employed at the supply management department.

Encampment, 22 December 1942

Collection of the Hoover Institution Library & Archives at the disposal of the Central Archives of Modern Records, Władysław Anders Collection. Reports, 800/1/0/-/48, account no. 7.

WŁODZIMIERZ PILEC

[Włodzimierz Pilec, rifleman]

On 26 September 1939, I was taken captive by the Soviets as a Polish soldier – this occurred near Łęczna. From there, I was force-marched, along with other prisoners, to Sarny; the march took a few days and we weren't given any food on the way. In Sarny we were put on a cargo train and taken to Olesko. The train journey to Olesko took around three weeks. We were issued no rations and we lived solely on food given clandestinely by civilians.

In Olesko we were put in an old castle; there were a couple thousand of us POWs there and the place was so cramped that we had to sleep basically on one another. We stayed there until March 1940.

Throughout the whole of winter we were forced to work building a highway – even when the temperatures went down to minus 48 degrees [Celsius] – and few of us had warm clothing. Many suffered frostbite on legs, hands and ears. In the end of December 1939, I personally witnessed the following incident: while we were working in the bitter cold, four of the POWs ran some distance away from the group – possibly with the intention of escaping. When the guards saw this, they started shooting at the men. The prisoners stopped but two of them had been hit: one in the lungs and another in the leg. The Soviet soldiers ran up to the two remaining ones, immediately shot one dead and started beating the other with the butts of their rifles. The POW who had been shot in the lungs was left lying in the snow for approximately three hours and then forced to start walking back to the camp. When he could no longer walk, he was just left behind in the snow. On the next day, we saw only bloodstains in that place – the wounded man had probably died.

In March 1940, we were transferred to Lack [Lackie Wielkie?] near Brody, where we remained until May 1940; while there, we were forced to mine stones.

In May 1940, we were transported to Brody, where we worked until the outbreak to the Soviet-German war. On the second day after the outbreak of that conflict, we were told that we would be going into hiding in the woods. We weren't permitted to take anything with us and instead of being led into the woods we were marched off to Złoczów.

While near Złoczów, we were passing some Soviet soldiers and tanks when German planes showed up and started bombing the Soviets. We were ordered to fall on the ground as we stood – in marching formation – and when some of the prisoners attempted to hide in nearby ditches, the Soviet guards who were escorting us opened fire on the POWs. Several people died that way. Our group numbered around 2,000 prisoners but was only allowed to actually seek shelter after an explicit command: we were led into some wheat that grew further afield and lay there for several hours. Eventually, roll-call was called, but many men had fallen asleep in the wheat and those ones were shot on the spot. Thus, several more POWs lost their lives that day.

We were then force-marched to Tarnopol. The journey took around four days and any prisoner who lagged behind was shot. Among those killed during the march were: 1) Jankowski from Warsaw, 2) Rafał from Kraków, 3) Dynich [?], and many others. From Tarnopol we were driven on foot to Zolotonosha and then sent by train to Starobelsk. There, I remained until my release in August 1941.

Collection of the Hoover Institution Library & Archives at the disposal of the Central Archives of Modern Records, Władysław Anders Collection. Reports, 800/1/0/-/48, account no. 366.

STANISŁAW GŁOWIAK

Stanisław Głowiak, corporal, 40 years old, border guard, unmarried.

On 18 September 1939 around 5.00 p.m. I arrived in the town of Złoczów, Lwów Voivodeship, with several hundred companions. The whole unit was commanded by Major Ruciński, while my company was led by Captain Socha. In Złoczów I noticed several hundred civilians, mostly men, standing next to the town hall. They were immediately dispersed. Major Ruciński then assigned us to posts throughout the town, because the local residents had been robbing the barracks, stealing uniforms, blankets, and other military items.

On 19 September 1939 around 8.00 a.m., I was arrested and disarmed near the town hall in Złoczów, together with the above-mentioned companions. Major Ruciński, Captain Socha, and Lieutenant Daprzalski, former Border Guard Deputy Commissioner, were also arrested. About 15 minutes after being arrested we were escorted to the Złoczów–Tarnopol road, about three kilometers from Złoczów, and we stayed in the field by that road for a day without any food. On 20 September about 9.00 a.m., we were escorted back to Złoczów, where we were released.

As soon as we were released, individual soldiers scattered in groups in different directions. I marched off with a certain group of soldiers towards Kowel. When we arrived in Kowel, my companions and I were arrested again by the Soviet authorities, the NKVD. During the march to Kowel, defenseless Polish soldiers were attacked by Ukrainians, who confiscated the last of their money and their uniforms.

I spent a day in Kowel and then we were taken by freight train (in covered cars) to Shepetovka (Russia), where on 30 September 1939 we were placed in old military barracks. There were several thousand Polish POWs in the camp. The personal details of individual soldiers were written down and we were searched; they took away razors and other sharp objects. Food: once a day some very watery soup and 400 grams of bread.

On 5 October 1939 we left Shepetovka and marched off in the direction of Ostróg (Poland). During that journey, many soldiers collapsed from exhaustion in the middle of the road, some of them were run over by vehicles because of the dark.

On 6 October we arrived in Ostrów, from where we departed two days later and marched to an estate in the town of Podliski, Lwów Voivodeship. We arrived in the Podliski estate on 10 October, and on 12 October we were escorted again, to the Żydatycze estate, Lwów Voivodeship. On 14 October 1939 we began work on widening the Lwów–Żydatycze road. Initially, the soldiers were reluctant to work, but the Soviets forced us, threatening us with arrest and a reduction in our food rations.

At work, we were supposed to meet a certain percent of the quota, from 25 to 200. The kind of life each soldier had depended on the percentage of the quota he met. Based on these quotas, the Soviets organized three cauldrons and bread rations.

The soldiers who met 110–200% of the quota received the best food – 1,200 grams of bread and the third cauldron. Those who met 100% of the quota received 800 grams of bread and food from the third cauldron. If you met less than the full quota, that is, 75% – you were given 700 grams of bread and food from the second cauldron. For 50% – 600 grams of bread and food from the second cauldron, for 25% – 400 grams and the first cauldron, which was the worst. We were given food from the cauldrons three times a day.

The camp in Żydatycze was about [illegible number] square meters in area, was encircled with barbed wire, and a watchtower was built at each corner. In the middle of the camp there was a long building that had previously held cattle. We slept in that building, initially on straw, but later on bunk beds were assembled. In addition two sheds were built from boards. One of them served as an infirmary, and the other one as a kitchen. A pit was dug next to the latter, about 4 meters deep, which was covered with a couple of poles and served as a toilet.

There were about 800 of us in the camp – about 70% were Poles, 20% were Belarusians, and 10% were Ukrainians.

The Soviet government considered the following actions crimes:

1) criticizing the Soviet regime,
2) escaping from a camp,
3) encouraging prisoners in the camp to refuse to work.

The Ukrainians and some Belarusians were hostile towards Poles, and reported everything about us to the Soviet authorities – whether someone had once worked as a government official, had been a member of the Riflemen's Association or the Military Preparation.

Work was organized as follows: we were woken up at 6.00 a.m., at 6.30 we had breakfast, at 7.30 we marched off to work, from 12.00 to 1.00 p.m. we had dinner, which was delivered to work. We finished work at 5.00 p.m., had supper at 6.00 p.m., and curfew started at 9.00 p.m.

For meeting 100% of the quota at work, we were paid three rubles per day.

The Soviet authorities, that is, the NKVD, were very hostile towards Poles. We were interrogated based on information provided by the Ukrainians, some Belarusians, and other POWs.

Medical help was provided as follows: people suffering from non-infectious diseases were treated in the camp, in a zone for the sick, while those with infectious diseases were transferred to a hospital.

Apart from the Żydatycze camp, I was also in the following camps: Stary Jaryczów, Kurowice, and the last one – Olszanica, Lwów Voivodeship.

In Olszanica, where we stayed until the outbreak of the German-Russian war, our task was to build a huge airfield. On 23 June 1941, as a result of a German air raid on the camp, we abandoned it and were escorted towards Złoczów.

In Złoczów, while we were resting in the morning, there was a German air-raid, during which soldiers immediately started escaping and hiding in rye. The Soviet escorts opened fire and killed a dozen or so Polish soldiers. The Soviets shot at the soldiers even from a distance of about two meters and stabbed a few of them with their bayonets. Then we marched through Tarnopol to Volochysk (Russia). While we rested in the Zdołbunów camp, a dozen or so soldiers hid in one of the buildings under boards in the attic and in the basement. With the help of a few dogs, the NKVD found all the soldiers who had hidden. The soldiers were beaten with whips and kicked, and then escorted along our column already standing on the road and ready for marching off, after which they were taken back to the camp. After three minutes, they were all executed by shooting.

While marching from Olszanica to Volochysk we received from 150 to 200 grams of bread and some watery soup per day. The convoys did not even let us drink water. After about two days, others from a different column told us that in the Zdołbunów camp they had seen a dozen or so Polish soldiers lying in a basement filled with water – their tongues had been cut out and their faces had been cut. One of them was a pilot whose name I knew, Stachowicz from Warsaw.

We travelled from Volochysk to Starobelsk (Russia) by freight train (covered cars).

The march column and the train were commanded by a major going by the name of Szerszyl. People claimed he was Ukrainian. During the march, some of our companions asked Major Szerszyl to let us have some water and to increase the bread rations. He answered: "It's your payment for the year 1920."

We were given barely about 50% of the food that was intended for us during the journey. Therefore, when we got off the train at Starobelsk station, about 40% of the soldiers were unable to walk because their legs had swollen (including mine). The distance from Starobelsk station [to the camp] was about 4 kilometers.

In the camp in Starobelsk until the non-aggression agreement was signed by Poland, England, and Russia, we received 400 grams of bread, some very watery soup twice a day, and several dozen grams of very small and salty fish.

It was difficult to communicate with families who lived under the German occupation, because many of the letters never arrived in the camp.

The Soviet authorities provided the following address for sending letters to the Żydatycze camp, Lwów Voivodeship:

Eastern Ukraine, Równe, postbox no. 37, group IV.

On 26 August 1941, in the Starobelsk camp, I was released from Russian captivity along with several hundred Polish soldiers, with whom I immediately joined the Polish army in Starobelsk.

Collection of the Hoover Institution Library & Archives at the disposal of the Central Archives of Modern Records, Władysław Anders Collection. Reports, 800/1/0/-/47, account no. 1306.

HENRYK RÓŻYCKI

Henryk Różycki, platoon-leader, 18th Infantry Regiment, 3rd Company.

DUBNO CAMP, POLAND

I was interned in this camp from 2 October to 7 December 1939. In the initial period right after capture, there were around 2,700 POWs there. For the first few days we weren't called to work, with the exception of a few men who worked at the concrete plant and most of the Jews, who were tasked with bringing us our meager rations. Afterwards, the forced labor began in earnest – we did construction work on the highway. The NKVD strongly pushed the narrative that Poland was gone forever; if we complained about anything, they told us: "You'll get used to everything." Among the POWs were some noble Polish officers I knew personally and there was a large percentage of loyal Polish men in general, but there were also some horrible ones that tried to cause us more grief that the Soviets themselves. This group included Ukrainians, Belarusians and a fraction of the Poles. The most notable troublemaker of Polish extraction was Corporal Gauden – when I got to know him better, I concluded he was a truly vile individual; he attempted to mold the younger POWs among us to his liking.

WARKOWICZE CAMP, POLAND

I stayed there from 7 December 1939 to 7 May 1940. The camp housed around 900 POWs. While at this camp, I witnessed the Soviets destroying our historic heritage; they built a latrine at the local cemetery, dismantled buildings, destroyed various paintings, etc. One of my fellow prisoners, a man named Świderski, who was a father of five, was killed at this camp for climbing a fence. They shot him from such close quarters that he had a gunshot burn. His body was taken somewhere – I don't know where.

During this internment, I met many soldiers that deserved commendation. Among them were: Second Lieutenant Walczak, Cadet Osakiewicz, Cadet Cyran, Master Sergeant Idzikowski and Rifleman Walenty Prokop from the Lublin Voivodeship – he in particular was a hundred percent loyal to Poland (and was probably killed by the Bolsheviks during our journey to Starobelsk).

ROMANÓWKA CAMP, POLAND

Internment period: 7 May to 22 November 1940. The camp initially housed 600 POWs, but the prisoners would be transferred elsewhere in punishment for even the smallest of infractions. This is where I really learned what [illegible] meant. The rations were very poor and we were assigned hard forced labor. They would send us out in bitterly cold weather nearly barefoot to clear snow from the local roads or dig the hardened ground. The NKVD really wanted to mold us to their liking but we were a stubborn lot – some did stumble and break, but [illegible word] only small fraction. The biggest [illegible word] that I met during my captivity was war veteran Petrov (Belarusian) – he was in charge of that whole camp.

BUILDING AN AIRFIELD NEAR TARNOPOL, POLAND

Internment period: from approximately 22 November 1940 to 27 June 1941. The camp housed around 2,000 POWs. Initially, they worked us to the bone because along with the airfield they were also building some apartment blocks and really wanted to finish the airfield on time (which they failed to do). We were also mistreated here. Overall, at all of those camps we lived in abysmal conditions, crammed almost one atop another and suffering constantly from lice infestations. Finally, there was the journey to Starobelsk: we were given some [illegible] once a day, no [illegible] in the barred windows, overall horrible conditions.

Collection of the Hoover Institution Library & Archives at the disposal of the Central Archives of Modern Records, Władysław Anders Collection. Reports, 800/1/0/-/48, account no. 65.

JAN MAROSZEK

Jan Maroszek, lance corporal engineer, born in 1906, factory worker, married.

On 24 September 1939, near Kowel, I was captured along with various units. After spending three days there, I was transported to Brody and placed in the local military barracks. The conditions of my stay were very terrible and unhygienic; all I was fed was buckwheat groats with no salt. This continued until 27 October, when we were taken by car to Sasów. There, our group of 300 men began their camp life and enslavement.

The first day of forced labor was 1 November, All Saints' Day. I was rushed to work, escorted by the NKVD, bitter at heart and filled with memories of our fallen brothers-in-arms. We had to walk over 6 kilometers to work, to the mine or quarries. And this kind of work continued all winter, with very poor food and no sleeping blankets. The hard, triple-decker bunks were swarming with lice and full of dirt. This continued for some time, but later disinfections gradually started.

In April, escorted by a convoy armed with machine guns, we were marched in close-order column to Podhorce, to the stables of one of the landed estates, in order to do road construction. The work was subject to so-called quotas, which were impossible to meet, and this meant that we couldn't get sufficient food and pay. It was like that in various workplaces. I worked in Sądowa Wisznia and in Czerlany – doing airfield construction this time – 12 hours a day, very hard and arduous work mixing concrete, listening to the sounds of concertina music during lunch break and with various propaganda speeches to listen to. Because the German-Soviet War broke out, I was taken away from the camp in Czerlany, marched for seven days to Volochysk, and put on a freight train. With the doors and windows closed tightly, with no air, water, or food, I was transported to Starobelsk. Completely worn out, I was enlisted in the army in Starobelsk in September 1941.

14 March 1943

Collection of the Hoover Institution Library & Archives at the disposal of the Central Archives of Modern Records, Władysław Anders Collection. Reports, 800/1/0/-/48, account no. 1754.

EDWARD PIEKUT

Edward Piekut, bombardier, 28 years old, cobbler, unmarried.

On the night of 18 September 1939, the [illegible] Division that I was in was stopped and disarmed by Soviet "liberators." That was in Sasów. We spent the rest of that night at the local school and in the morning we were driven on foot towards the border. We asked when we would get food and were told that good people would give it to us – since there are, apparently, no good people in the Ukraine, we marched hungry. They promised us that we would be fed in Shepetovka. I did get food there: a piece of bread and half a liter of soup (supposedly made from groats) for three days. Hungry and under a strong NKVD escort, we were put on a transport. We were supposedly going to Kiev, to get our release papers and be able to go back home, but we ended up in Novograd-Volynskyi, where we got a close-up view of the Soviet paradise and its propaganda lies.

There were around 12,000 of us POWs there. We were divided into smaller groups, sent out to the smaller camps in the area and transformed into workhorses: going only from the barn to work and back again. The living conditions were unbearable and the sanitary situation isn't even worth describing – even knowledgeable people like physicians couldn't avoid getting lice.

I was put in Żerebiłówka; throughout the whole of winter we were given only two opportunities to bathe and wash our underwear. To get water to wash we had to boil snow, which was difficult because 75 men had to use one heater. The sleeping space was 41 centimeters per person. I was part of the POW group that "did not submit to Soviet law," so we frequently changed camps. I was interned in Żytyń, Jaryczów Stary, Kozłów, Podliski, Kurowice, Hermanów and Olszanica (which was my last normal camp).

Among the noteworthy camp arrangements were the thick barbed wire fences – there were three rows of barbed wire, of sufficient height to deter escapes. The camps were located in places with partial isolation from the civilian population and the POWs were quartered in buildings intended for farm animals or in tents.

There was a physician but medications were in short supply – the sick would be released from medical care based on a percentage quota.

Cultural life as organized by the Soviets consisted mostly of the political commissar's talks, wherein he pontificated extensively about the Soviet paradise and its worthy people, such as Marx, Lenin, etc. They gave us their reading material but, frankly, the ink on the pages should've turned red from embarrassment, considering what lies they printed. There were articles by Boy-Żeleński and Wanda Wasilewska, and slogans plastered all over the walls. We were threatened that Poland would never be restored, told that it had been sold out and that only communism could bring happiness to the working-class people. Then, one day they finally found out that their crazy graft was rejected by the Polish soil and said: "There will be Poland."

The labor was hard, the food rations were normally paltry and went down to completely horrible if one didn't meet one's quota. The labor quotas were huge – I'm not a weak man and even today I wouldn't be able to handle them.

The pay was calculated to be precisely such that after camp-related deductions we were left with only a couple of rubles. I can't even tell what we were supposed to buy for that, possibly [illegible word].

Then, finally, 22 June 1941 arrived and with it the outbreak of the [German-Soviet] war. The comrades were fleeing and took us with them. On this journey we suffered great mistreatment and losses in men because our red oppressors would sometimes give us just one loaf of bread and a bucket of water for 49 men for the whole day and then say: "That's all – there will be more tomorrow." Those too weak to march while starving fell to the ground and were "treated" with bullets and bayonet stabs. This was also how I lost a friend, Reserve Corporal Jan Kieliszek from the 1st Anti-aircraft Artillery Regiment in Warsaw (address: Staszica Street 5). He and five other prisoners (whose names I don't know) were all murdered in the Zborów camp. Their bodies were found, full of grisly wounds, in a basement with water and cabbage. This is how we discovered the horrible crime committed against the defenseless – a crime that the Soviets hid from us. They know full well that many of our brothers died during that journey to Starobelsk; the Soviets burned paperwork that documented their fate.

Starobelsk is a known hellhole of its own – the scribbles on the walls testify to the years-long misery of those who had been there; the prison there has the world's largest bedbug population. The hunger I suffered there made me nearly lose my mind.

Eventually, the sun did shine on us prisoners, as our government's wise actions opened the door to our freedom. The political commissars started singing a different tune; the Polish Army was forming up. I joined in the end of August 1941.

Encampment, 25 February 1943

Collection of the Hoover Institution Library & Archives at the disposal of the Central Archives of Modern Records, Władysław Anders Collection. Reports, 800/1/0/-/48, account no. 617.

JAN JĘDRZEJEWSKI

Jan Jędrzejewski, senior artillery sergeant, 40 years old, married.

Having clashed with the Germans southeast of Chełm Lubelski, the 1st Reserve Regiment unit newly formed from scattered soldiers of various divisions was defeated. The Regiment withdrew in chaos roughly in the direction of Hrubieszów. Me and many others, got through to a settlement, whose name I don't recall now, near Hrubieszów, where we stayed overnight hosted by Polish civilians. The battle ceased almost completely. We found out from the locals that Soviets crossed the Bug River and were advancing to the West. The situation was hopeless. We discussed our next steps as the sun rose, and the officers (several of them were with us) couldn't make a decision. Around 2.00 p.m., on 25 September, the Soviets took over the town and advanced further, while others gathered us Poles together in one place, where we stayed guarded until the next day. The next day, after separating several officers and more than a dozen of non-commissioned officers, they loaded 25 of us onto cars and took us to a prison in Włodzimierz, where after a thorough search and seizure of our valuables (such as watches, etc.) and an investigation, they shipped us out by rail, in closed wagons, to Kowel.

The next day, having organized a huge rail shipping of POWs, they took us locked, under escort, across the border, to Shepetovka. The journey inside overcrowded wagons was horrible, mainly due to the lack of air. After two days of this kind of journey, with several hours of break in Zdołbunów, we arrived at the destination, where we were led to the barracks. The conditions were terrible due to the space being overcrowded by the huge grouping of POWs and civilians, whom we had already encountered. Normally, there could be a maximum of 2,000 people fitted into those barracks – but there were around 12,000 squeezed in there. Hygienic conditions were indescribable; food was insufficient, consisting of a piece of dark bread and a little soup once a day – not every day, as they didn't prepare enough.

Attitude of the gendarmes towards the POWs was cruel. We were mentally harassed at every corner; those who fought in 1920 were sought out. I stayed there for around five days. Another search was made and thorough descriptions of each of us were prepared; we were organized into bigger groups. I was in one of such groups. 1,500 of us, under careful watch by the NKVD, set off on foot, and after two days of marching with no food, we arrived in Hoszcza, Równe District. They informed us we would live and work there. Living and hygienic conditions in the barracks taken over after

Border Protection Corps Battalion were good. Food was insufficient. At that point, we were working indoors – on camp construction.

After a 14-day stay in Hoszcza, a group of 150 people were divided and moved to Babin, 7 kilometers from Hoszcza, towards Równe. Living and hygienic conditions – in a stable – were indescribable. Lodging quarters were not adapted to at all; food was insufficient. Work, which consisted of preparing materials for road construction, was extremely hard. As work efficiency seemed little to them, they introduced quotas, which were impossible to attain – for example, digging 18 cubic meters and moving it 5 meters further within 10 hours. The amount of bread and food quality was assigned based on the filled norms, as the food was divided into the so-called first, second, and third cauldron.

Intellectual standing was average, moral standing was high, except for a small number of Ruthenians, Belarusians, and several Hitler supporters.

Attitude of the NKVD towards the Poles was cruel. Whenever they could, they harassed the POWs mentally and physically. News about Poland and the army would get to us through civilians.

Communist propaganda spread on a wide scale. In each camp, there was a political commissar dedicated to that purpose. But the Bolsheviks were very lousy at the art of propaganda, and despite their trickery, it came with a great difficulty for them. During the talks about the Communist Party, the welfare in Russia and praising its political system, the POWs laughed at the liars, disrupting the talks with hissing and booing.

Medical assistance depended on the access to medicines, some of which were constantly lacking.

Communication with the family: one postcard during seven months.

As work was almost finished there, a group of 80 POWs was selected, also from other camps, and in June 1940 we were moved in a rail transport from Równe to Żabno, Mościska District, to work on road construction as well. Living and hygienic conditions, as well as food, were the same as in the first camp. Attitude of the NKVD towards the POWs was much worse here. The camp chief and his associates were bandits. The camp doctor was limited from issuing sick leaves for the ill. Ill people were just sent to work, and those who refused to go were locked in punishment cells and given one meal a day. On the first day of Christmas, they wittingly sent us to the road construction site, and when we refused to work, they had us stand to attention for half an hour in the freezing temperature of 28 degrees [Celsius] below zero. Many POWs suffered from leg frostbite then.

At the beginning of March 1941, the whole camp was taken to Czerlany, Gródek Jagielloński District. Conditions were similar to previous camps. Work on airfield construction was extremely hard, and in addition to that, the workdays were prolonged from 10 to 12 hours, and included Sundays. No breaks for rest were given at all.

After the war with Germany broke out, we were led to the east under heavy guard of the NKVD. The march went on day and night and was accompanied by the retreating army in order to shield them from bombardment. We were exhausted to the limits because of the short breaks and poor nourishment. Dry, salty fish was the only food on the way. We didn't receive bread at all. In order to terrorize the prisoners and make them obedient, a POW, whose surname I don't remember, was shot dead for no reason, and another prisoner named Sutkowski, whom I later met in Starobelsk, was wounded by the same bullet.

When the Polish army was being formed in Starobelsk, I joined its ranks.

Collection of the Hoover Institution Library & Archives at the disposal of the Central Archives of Modern Records, Władysław Anders Collection. Reports, 800/1/0/-/47, account no. 746.

WŁODZIMIERZ POŁUJASZ

Personal data (name, surname, rank, age, occupation and marital status):
Włodzimierz Połujasz, bombardier, 28 years old, farmer, unmarried.

Date and circumstances of arrest:

We were taken captive by the Soviets near the Romanian border on 27 September 1939. There was no way to avoid this: they ambushed us from both the front and the rear. Initially, they wanted to execute us all. They told us to drop all our gear, including coats, haversacks and masks, then marched us off to a nearby barn (full of manure) and ordered us to sleep there. The barn was small and cramped: 117 soldiers had to fit inside. They gave us no food then – in the morning some civilians brought us bread and tea. After dinnertime on 29 September, they led us off to the prison in Sambor. On 30 September, they gave us one eighth of a liter of supposedly groats soup that tasted mostly like water. There were around 6,000 of us there. Later, they issued us release documents and let us head home; in Lwów we boarded a train to Kiwerce. Upon arrival, we were attacked, loaded onto trains and sent hither and yon – this lasted from 4 to 11 October. Food was given out every third day: 900 grams of bread and half a liter of canned fish per six men.

Name of the camp, prison or forced labor site:

I was detained in the camps in Olesko, Złoczów and Brody. We arrived in Olesko on 11 October and for the first three days were given no food at all, such that we were too famished to even walk. When they did start cooking food for us, they used very wormy peas for the soup. Per day they gave us only a quarter of a liter of that soup and 600 grams of bread that tasted like it was just raw, unprocessed dough. The soup was basically all water. The food was distributed at 5.00 p.m.

We weren't allowed to go to a latrine. We had to relieve ourselves basically right where we stood. The place was so filthy that you couldn't even walk through safely.

There were 1,264 of us there. We were given almost no water and the one we did get stank of manure. They made us go to work even when we were sick. If someone didn't go, he'd land in the punishment cell. The labor quota was 7 cubic meters per man. They tried to entice us to meet the quota by telling us we'd get more food – *prembludo* or a small piece of rotten herring.

Description of the camp or prison (grounds, buildings, housing conditions, hygiene):

My first camp was located in the castle in Olesko (the one that had belonged to king Jan III Sobieski). For around two months we slept on barren ground, basically one atop another. Then they made us some cots and we slept on the wooden planks in our clothes – there were no mattresses or coverings; each man slept in what he wore. Lice lived on us the way ants live in anthills.

Social composition of POWs, prisoners, exiles (nationality, type of crimes, intellectual and moral standing, mutual relations, etc.):

There were 1,264 POWs of varied nationality in Olesko camp. The majority were Poles, with a small number of Jews, Belarusians and Ukrainians.

Life in the camp or prison (daily routine, working conditions, quotas, wages, food, clothes, social and cultural life, etc.):

Living conditions in the camp were miserable, both in 1939 and in 1940; I needed outside assistance from my family, specifically extra food, to be able to function. I don't know what would've happened to me if they hadn't sent and brought stuff from home. Mostly prisoners couldn't really work, and therefore couldn't earn anything, because they were too exhausted. If the civilians wanted to bring us something, soldiers and the camp overseer wouldn't let them.

Attitude of the NKVD towards Poles (interrogation methods, torture and other forms of punishment, communist propaganda, information about Poland, etc.):

The NKVD treated Poles very badly – they told us that Poland would never be restored. The reemergence of Poland was just as possible as hair growing on the inside of a palm. During the 27-day forced march from Brody all the way to Zolotonosha, the Soviet lieutenants punched and hit the prisoners on the face with the butts of their rifles if the POWs lagged behind – and the prisoners were too weak to walk because they weren't being given any food. We were also in danger of being bombarded. 48 of our men died and 200 were gravely wounded, but I don't know the names of the victims.

Medical assistance, hospitals, mortality rate (provide the names of the deceased):

No medical care was provided in the camp because there were no medications. Even if someone did go to the physician on account of being sick, the physician pronounced him healthy. Two men were killed and another two were wounded during an escape attempt on 22 December, but I don't know their surnames.

Was it at all possible to get in contact with one's home country and family?

I wrote letters home and received letters back. My father visited me – when he came, we were allowed to speak for two and a half hours under supervision. The supervision was there to prevent me from talking about the Soviet Union, for example from saying that things are bad in the camp.

When were you released and how did you manage to join the Polish Army?

I was released in Starobelsk and joined the Polish Army while in Starobelsk, within USSR territory.

Encampment, 25 February 1943

Collection of the Hoover Institution Library & Archives at the disposal of the Central Archives of Modern Records, Władysław Anders Collection. Reports, 800/1/0/-/48, account no. 623.

JAN GOLONKA

Personal data (name, surname, rank, age, occupation and marital status):
Jan Golonka, corporal, 45 years old, clerk at the Polish Spirits Monopoly in Tomaszów Mazowiecki, Łódź Voivodeship, unmarried.

Date and circumstances of the arrest:

I was arrested by the Soviets on 29 September 1939, a few kilometers from the Minkowice railroad station (between Rejowiec and Lublin) with the rest of the 6th Light Artillery Regiment. We were escorted on foot 60 kilometers to Chełm Lubelski, where the entire transport of prisoners of war was loaded onto a train and taken via Zamość, Włodzimierz Wołyński, Kowel and Równe to Shepetovka, and then on to Sarny. There, officers, officer cadets, regular non-commissioned officers and policemen were separated from the rest. The rest were told they would be sent back home. We were asked if we had received enough food and pay, because our officers had escaped to Romania. The Soviets distributed communist leaflets and newspapers. Then after two days, we were again loaded onto a train and transferred to Brody.

Name of the camp, prison or forced labor site:

After we had bathed and shaved, we were taken to Olesko, Złoczów District, where we (about 1,500 people) were accommodated in the old castle of Count Sobieski. Initially, the conditions there were horrible – only part of the castle was habitable (the rest was being renovated), but a few days later work began on building bunk beds and distributing straw, and then they provided straw mattresses, opened an infirmary and built a kitchen, etc. Registration began, and we were told that we would be working on the construction of the Kiev–Lwów highway. We were split into units and occupations, and prisoners who spoke Russian were appointed commanders. The Germans were separated from the rest, and around the middle of December 1939 they were sent back to Germany. [Illegible word] were also promised a return home then, and following negotiations with the Germans, we were solemnly assured of it, but it depended on the progress of the works. The promises were of course not kept.

The work was hard, temperatures fell well below zero (winter 1939/1940), we had no warm clothes. That caused some people to attempt to escape while at work or on the way to the work site. In the course of an escape attempt during our return to the camp on 21 December 1939, two prisoners were shot dead, one was injured, and one managed to escape. After the second escape attempt by several prisoners at night, all of them were caught, they were all stripped of their clothes and placed in a punishment cell in only their underwear; then they were taken away – we never found out where to.

Rudnev, the head of the camp, was quite humane. He granted the sick and poorly-dressed people leave from work, but when he was absent (he usually arrived after we had left for work), the NKVD officers mercilessly chased everyone out. In spring 1940, a dozen or so prisoners of war (mostly Belarusians and Ukrainians) were selected and sent to Równe for training – later on they became guards at another camp. At that time, the conditions inside the camp improved markedly, because several hundred of our companions were transferred to a new camp situated 10 kilometers away, in Angielówka, where barracks had been built. In the new camp, those most in need received boots, clothes and underwear, and a good bathhouse was built there, etc. This was all thanks to Rudnev, who was soon succeeded by another man [Gorbachev]. He did not implement anything new in the camp, and was usually drunk.

In October 1940, a hundred other prisoners and I were transferred to a different camp, to Babin, 22 kilometers west from Równe. We worked there for only two weeks, and on 21 December I was sent along with a party of 160 other people to the Susk forestry management near Klewań, to fell trees. The working conditions were tough, we worked in knee-deep snow, and most of us were inexperienced in such work – so accidents happened. In my group, Fidelus, a worker in a slaughterhouse in Łódź, suffered an accident when he got entangled in bushes and didn't manage to jump away in time from a falling oak. No medical help was provided – he remained lying in the frost for a few hours following the accident before he was taken to hospital. In mid-February 1941 I suffered frostbite to the toes on both feet (we were working every day, even when it was more than 30 degrees below zero outside), and seven other prisoners and I were sent back to the camp in Równe.

Medical assistance was provided in the Równe camp – compared to the camp in [illegible] (where a paramedic was brought in only after there had been several accidents) it was much better, but during my stay [illegible] about 10 prisoners died of tuberculosis in March 1941. They were mostly sick people brought to Równe from other camps. At the end of April 1941 we were sent with a transport of about 400 people to Skniłów near Lwów, where we were to build a military airfield. I was there when the German-Soviet war broke out. On 22 June 1941, I was working the night shift when the Germans dropped bombs on the airport under construction, at 4.00 a.m. Two men were injured, one man called [illegible] from Wieluń died during the retreat (on his way to [illegible]). On 23 June, the entire camp was wrapped up and we went by foot, in a group of about two thousand people, via Złoczów, Tarnopol, Podwołoczyska, Vinnytsia, Skvyra and Belaya Tserkov to Kaniv on the Dnieper River, where we crossed the Dnieper in groups of 50 people by a railroad bridge, and we reached Zolotonosha on 17 July. This march from 23 June to 17 July 1941 represented a single terrible streak of torture. We made 40–50 kilometers a day; there were days when we did not receive any food and were not allowed to collect water, we were lucky if someone managed to collect a tiny bit of foul-smelling water from a puddle. When people sometimes wanted to give us something along the way, the NKVD soldiers escorting us did not allow them, saying: "They shot at our people, and you are giving them water!", explaining to the bystanders that we were German. Along the way, we were joined by others, so the column kept getting bigger. Those unable to walk were beaten with rifle butts, and whoever collapsed and fainted, was gone. That was how over 200 people from our transport disappeared without a trace. During the march we were bombed several times by German bombers – for the first time as soon as we passed Vynnyki near Lwów, and then near Proskurov, Vinnytsia, and near Skvyra, where 18 people died as a result of the bombing and over a hundred were injured, mostly from the camp in Brody. On 17 July 1941 we were loaded onto a train in Zolotonosha, and taken to a place a few stations beyond Poltava, where we were unloaded at a small station and taken to a young forest. We spent five days there, out in the open air the whole time. On 26 July we were again loaded onto a train and taken to the prisoner-of-war camp in Starobelsk in the Donetsk Region, where we arrived on 28 July and where I was when the Soviet-Polish agreement was signed, on 30 July 1941.

Description of the camp or prison (grounds, buildings, housing conditions, hygiene):

We lived in buildings of various kinds in the camps. In the camp in Olesko, we lived in an old brick castle, in Susk and Babin – in tents, in Równe – in an old brick mill, in Skniłów – in barracks. All the buildings were cramped, hygiene was bad, there was no [illegible]. There were bathhouses and a *dezokamera* in all the camps.

Social composition of POWs, prisoners, exiles (nationality, type of crimes, intellectual and moral standing, mutual relations, etc.):

My companions were mostly prisoners of war imprisoned in September 1939, from the areas occupied by the Germans. Only in the Równe camp was there also a small number of former Polish soldiers who had been arrested in their homes in 1940 and 1941 by the Soviet authorities. Most people were of Polish nationality, there were small numbers of Belarusians, Ukrainians, and Jews. Most of the Belarusians and Ukrainians worked as "unescorted," and were allowed to leave the camp with special passes. But the Soviet authorities also divided the Belarusians into two categories: those who were trustworthy, and those who were not. Almost everyone was told that they should already be home and that they shouldn't have listened to the Polish military authorities, but rather should have left their troops as soon as the fighting started. The morale was generally good, but it was noticeable that some people were disheartened, especially shortly after they had been imprisoned and in summer 1940, following the fall of France. There were also cases when prisoners informed the Soviet authorities of what other camp-mates did or said, etc. There were also numerous cases, especially at the end of 1940, of Poles trying to pass as Germans, hoping that they would thereby return home sooner.

Life in the camp or prison:

Life in the camp was difficult – no contact with families, hard work, poor food, miserable clothes, low pay for the job, high quotas that were difficult to meet – that all had an impact on the prisoners' morale. We left for work early and returned late, and often worked for months without a day's rest. In many camps there were common rooms with newspapers and books – obviously the content was communist, and apart from that [illegible].

Attitude of the NKVD towards Poles:

All prisoners in every camp were carefully registered and photographed – additionally in October 1940, the NKVD thoroughly investigated prisoners' entire lives (from birth to the current day), their family, property, etc. People were not tortured during interrogations in the camps I was in. In every camp there was a so-called political commissioner who held frequent talks in the communist spirit.

Medical assistance, hospitals, mortality rate:

In almost every camp there was an infirmary managed by a doctor who was also a prisoner of war – except for the camp in Susk.

Was it at all possible to get in contact with one's home country and family?

From January to September 1940, prisoners of war received letters from their families, later [illegible] contact with the home country.

When were you released and how did you manage to join the Polish Army?

I was released from the prisoner-of-war camp in Starobelsk on 4 September 1941, I joined the Polish Army on that day and left with a transport to Totskoye.

Collection of the Hoover Institution Library & Archives at the disposal of the Central Archives of Modern Records, Władysław Anders Collection. Reports, 800/1/0/-/47, account no. 517.

ADAM WĄSOWSKI

I will not go into all the details of my nearly two-year-long captivity and stay in various camps, in which I had to work from dawn to late at night with miserable food and such "camp comforts" as sleeping mostly under my own coat (often soaked through with water and reeking of nondescript foul odors). It was impossible to maintain even basic bodily hygiene, considering the frequent lack of water and scarcity of opportunities to change one's underwear. The situation made one so miserable that, even being as exhausted as one was from the hard labor, one would get up at night to hunt lice or burn them off at some campfire. Underwear was mostly worn without washing until it just tore completely. This was also true of shoes and other things used by us "slaves." And despite all this we were supposedly the lucky ones because we worked within our own territory, as those who were sent to Russia in 1940 and later came back told us. The following year, I lived through the things they'd described.

Camp life was hard and led to prisoners developing various illnesses, including even mental breakdowns. It featured constant searches, interrogations and frequent detention in punishment cells, wherein people sat literally naked in temperatures more than twenty degrees below zero, with only a little bit of warm water being provided to stave off the cold. I'd like to note here that this punishment was meted out to one of my acquaintances from the Sądowa Wisznia labor camp, but the man was young and had a good constitution so he survived this torture. Some men were detained like this for wearing the Polish military eagle insignia, others for failing to meet their labor quota, etc. There were hundreds of reasons. They also bored us senseless with Bolshevik propaganda. This hell continued until the outbreak of the German-Soviet war, when we saw a sliver of hope that things might change somehow. That hope, however, merely glimmered a little and soon died, replaced by an even greater torment – we were now being force-marched, constantly starving and exhausted. On the way, we weren't even allowed to go to any of the nearby streams to wet our parched lips.

While we were marching, there'd regularly be some sort of shootout that resulted in a number of our men going missing. I specifically remember that, according to my friends who took a headcount, somewhere between 1,600 and 1,800 of us marched out of the camp in Czerlany and around 300 were probably lost on the way. We would also frequently hear shooting when we were leaving a camp: we would be marched out of the camp and stopped, then they would go back looking for men who stayed behind and hid somewhere (for example in an attic or under the floor). I also remember that while we were resting in one such camp, someone went down to the basement and found five bodies of our men killed with bayonet stabs – one of those was an officer from Lwów and the others were from other parts of Poland. Furthermore, there were supposedly many dead bodies in the wheat outside the camp perimeters.

We had one more noteworthy unnerving experience – somewhere outside of Złoczów we were led off the road, into a meadow with some alder shrubs, the Soviets arranged us in a sort of quadrangle formation and told us to rest. What was actually happening was this: they were worried about being intercepted by German troops and had been told that if they were intercepted, they should dispose of all the POWs, using grenades (which each of them was issued in Złoczów). One of the POWs overheard the relevant conversation. Luckily, no Germans were sighted and we went on our way. Eventually, sick, exhausted, with legs swollen from exertion, we arrived someplace where we were loaded into train cars – 80 men per car – shut inside and sent onwards. As food they gave us a tiny amount of bread, a few small salted fish and some water. We arrived in Starobelsk half dead. Life there was miserable: the exhaustion led to various illnesses, such as typhus, our beds were just bare wooden planks and we suffered a bedbug infestation. It was truly hell! And it would have certainly been the last journey of our lives, but the agreement was signed. That agreement ended our time in hell.

Collection of the Hoover Institution Library & Archives at the disposal of the Central Archives of Modern Records, Władysław Anders Collection. Reports, 800/1/0/-/48, account no. 386.

TADEUSZ CYRAN

I

Name of the camp:

Shepetovka.

Composition of POWs:

Concentration camp comprising soldiers of all ranks.

Number of POWs:

Several thousand.

Period of the camp's existence:

My stay lasted from 28 September to 5 October 1939.

Description of the camp:

Barracks, brick buildings. Concrete floor. Living conditions: minimum sustenance, soup once a day, 300 grams of bread. Huge overcrowding of people made it impossible to maintain personal hygiene. No medical assistance for the sick.

Life in the camp:

Divided into blocks and hundreds. No work. Initial organizational work carried out. First registry of internees recorded.

II

Name of the camp:

Dubno.

Social composition of POWs:

Primary purpose: for POWs who were to work in the Eastern part of the Lesser Poland region. The camp included soldiers of all ranks. Officers hid their true rank.

Number of POWs:

2,000 at first. 700 remained on a permanent basis.

Period of the camp's existence:

My stay lasted from 8 October to 19 November 1939.

Description of the camp:

A hop field on the Ikva River. Very cramped in the first days. Bedding on the floor made of hop sacks. The Polish population was very supportive; entry to the camp was not prohibited in the first days. After the vast majority was sent to other rooms, living conditions improved slightly. Bunks were built. Medical assistance was organized, meals regulated.

Life in the camp:

We were divided into hundreds. Work on the roads in western Ukraine began at the end of October. We worked under the watch of a convoy. Work was supposed to be voluntary but punishments were used for those who abstained from the very first days.

III

Name of the camp:

Warkowicze (19 kilometers from Dubno in the direction of Równe).

Social composition of POWs:

Camp for privates. Two officers hiding incognito. Several cadets.

Number of POWs:

Around 600.

Period of the camp's existence:

Until 2 June 1940.

Description of the camp:

Camp established beside a cemetery. Large tents with double canvas, 125 people in each, heating from two iron furnaces. Scant fuel. Cold, cramped, and dark. Food meagre. No concern taken for hygiene. No water on the campgrounds. Infested with lice.

Life in the camp:

Division into work brigades. Rivalry propaganda began. Three cauldrons were introduced. Lack of warm clothing and footwear, forced to work out of hunger. Resistance got the punishment cell. The "demoralizing" elements were taken to other camps. Propaganda talks were organized about the USSR and its benefits. Two propaganda films were shown. Prisoners from the territories occupied by the USSR were taken away.

Deceased:

One POW was shot during a mass escape, several were wounded. The deceased was called Świderski (from Kamionna village near Łochów).

IV

Name of the camp:

Mołodawa (11 kilometers from Dubno in the direction of Równe).

Social composition of POWs:

Privates.

Number of POWs:

Around 400.

Period of the camp's existence:

From 2 June to 3 November 1940.

Description of the camp:

The camp was established in a field. Tents, one wooden barrack. Administrative buildings: barracks. The tents were damaged, the roofs of the buildings leaky, as a result of which we felt the heavy rain. The best food from my entire period in captivity. It was possible to buy dairy products at relatively low prices. Lice were eradicated. The living conditions of the sick were improved.

Life in the camp:

We were divided into brigades. Forced labor building roads. 12-hour workdays. Sundays and holidays banned. Several cases of escape. Fates of the escapees unknown.

Deceased:

One POW fell beneath a tractor wheel when returning from work and died. I do not remember his name.

V

Name of the camp:

Turyczewo [?] near Smyga (Krzemieniec region).

Social composition of POWs:

Privates.

Number of POWs:

110.

Period of the camp's existence:

From 15 December 1940 to 22 April 1941.

Description of the camp:

Forester's buildings. Housing conditions fairly good. Cramped. Fuel in abundance. Poor food. High labor quotas made earning opportunities impossible.

Life in the camp:

We were divided into brigades. Work chopping wood. Health of POWs good thanks to the healthy environment in spite of hard labor and poor food. No cultural entertainment.

VI

Name of the camp:

Świętosław near Skole.

Social composition of POWs:

Privates.

Number of POWs:

I don't know.

Period of camp's existence:

Liquidated on 27 June 1941.

Description of camp:

Wooden barracks, fairly solid. Food dependent on the quotas fulfilled. Generally poor.

Life in the camp:

Work in quarries, hard and dangerous. High quotas. Intense propaganda. Forced lectures. Increased discipline.

Radical change after the outbreak of the war between the USSR and Germany. Food rations made smaller, but forced labor was abandoned. The camp was hurriedly liquidated on 27 June 1941 and the evacuation to Starobelsk began, lasting until 23 July 1941.

Collection of the Hoover Institution Library & Archives at the disposal of the Central Archives of Modern Records, Władysław Anders Collection. Reports, 800/1/0/-/46, account no. 44.

BOLESŁAW ZIELIŃSKI

Bolesław Zieliński, corporal, 33 years old, hairdresser, married.

The Soviets disarmed me and part of my unit on 22 September 1939 in Werba near Włodzimierz Wołyński and sent us by train to Shepetovka.

On 5 October 1939, I and around 2,000 other men began a march on foot to Ostróg. The march was very hard on us, since we had been basically starved while in Shepetovka and food was also lacking during the march itself. As a result, many of my fellow prisoners were left behind. After walking approximately 60 kilometers in one day, we arrived – late after nightfall – at a stable belonging to the 19th Uhlan Regiment. There, we rested for two days.

On 8 October 1939, we marched out on foot to Hoszcza (Równe District). There, we were quartered in the Border Protection Corps barracks. A week later, some of the POWs – including me – were sent to the camp at the Tudorów estate. I remained there until 2 January 1941. We were housed in one of the granaries and in a barn; the barn was damp with and stank of manure. The sanitary conditions were very bad – for two months we slept on bare wooden planks without pallets. Because we lacked a bath, a laundry room, etc., there was a massive lice infestation: each night a group of prisoners would be waiting under a lamp to kill a couple dozen lice so we could get a few hours of decent sleep. On average the camp housed around 400 POWs. Most of them were Poles, then some Belarusians, Ukrainians and Jews. Relations with the minorities were strained because they were favored by the Soviet authorities and were given posts of higher authority in the camp hierarchy, e.g. of overseers, shop clerks, warehouse managers and such.

On 2 January 1941, with the weather being 30 degrees [Celsius] below zero and very windy, we were taken in cars to Równe. There, we were loaded into small cargo train cars (40 men in each car) and sent on an eight-day train journey to Volochysk (near the Zbruch River). The train cars let in air from outside, so we suffered greatly on account of the biting cold and strong wind. While in transit, we weren't allowed to leave the train cars, so we had to relieve ourselves inside them. We didn't have sufficient water, coal and wood. We were fed mainly bread and herrings; besides that we got a small amount of sugar and fatback.

After arrival, we were led to an old, ruined stable – there were around 500 of us. We would be let out one by one to relieve ourselves since the camp wasn't yet surrounded with barbed wire. The first month was particularly difficult as the lack of a proper kitchen, lack of space, lack of warm underwear and clothing in general, combined with the freezing cold weather, resulted in many prisoners falling ill with cold. The conditions improved once we personally built the second living barrack, a kitchen, a bath and a *dezokamera* (which is indispensable in Russia), and were set to work; we performed hard forced labor mining stone.

For work we would be divided into brigades of 25 to 50 POWs and sent out under a strong escort. A headcount was taken multiple times before we left the camp and also a couple of times after our return. To maintain decent health, we wrapped ourselves in blankets if we had them. We also commonly took one or two straw pillows and stuffed them under the blanket, in the chest or back area. For all this hard labor we were given rations as follows: for fulfilling 100% of one's quota – 800 grams of bread, soup and some fish or meat (which often stank badly); below 100% – 400 to 600 grams of bread and some soup but no fish or meat. Working days were 8 to 10 hours long and would extend even to 12 hours when the demand for labor was high. The attitude of the escorting guards was very often vulgar; they would frequently insult our national and religious convictions. Maintaining any sort of social and cultural life was difficult, since the prisoners were often segregated and transferred to other camps if the authorities noticed that they were getting along well.

The attitude of the Soviet authorities towards Poles was hostile. After our return from work, the political commissars would organize meetings in which they publicly derided those who either couldn't or wouldn't work. Such person would be called an enemy of the people, *otkaznik*, *sabotazhnik*, etc. They threatened us with "polar bears," i.e. with deporting the difficult prisoners to Siberia. In these meetings they also pushed the narrative that the Soviet system was the best and that Poland had been a country of "lords, capitalists and officers that had oppressed working people." We were prohibited from practicing our religion, personal things of cultural significance were destroyed, Polish books were disposed of and only communist brochures and writings were permitted as reading material. Interrogation sessions took place at night – the interrogators would demand that we identify the officers, police force members and military police among us, and also indicate which prisoners were reluctant to work or hostile to the Soviet system.

Cadet Franciszek Mrówka, a teacher from Oborniki in the Poznań District, died in captivity.

Contact with the home country and with family was extremely limited. I sent a couple dozen letters and received only a few postcards back from my family. The best way to send letters was through trusted people that had access to the camp.

After the outbreak of the war between Germany and the USSR, our whole camp – of which around 80% were POWs who identified as German, plus some Belarusians and a few Poles – was loaded onto a train at the Volochysk train station. The train cars and the windows were shut tight. We weren't allowed to open a window on pain of death, even though there were 40 men in the 16-ton train car, water was scarce and the temperature went as high as 30 degrees [Celsius]. After the train had already been filled with POWs and a strong escort had been provided to guard it, German planes showed up and attacked it. They shot at the train from their machine guns. We were also attacked a couple of times by German planes while underway to Starobelsk; many bullets and bombs were sent in the direction of that train.

On 6 July, we arrived in Starobelsk – we were led to a large camp that had previously housed Polish officers and cadets.

Every day new prisoners would arrive at the camp, driven on foot by the NKVD. They had been forced to march for hundreds of kilometers and told horrible stories about their ordeal. For instance, that a weak, exhausted POW who could no longer walk would simply be executed by the escorting soldiers. Furthermore, POWs from the Brody camp had grenades thrown at them by German airmen during the march – several men died and many were wounded.

The living conditions were horrible: we lived in lice and bedbug infested wooden shacks that had their windows blocked off with barbed wire, which would have been extremely dangerous if a fire ever occurred at the camp. The rations were miserable – we got an allotment of very thin millet soup and 400 grams of raw wholemeal bread that we would dry in the sun to avoid stomach trouble; I know of a case where a prisoner died at the local Orthodox church after eating that raw bread. The bedbugs were such a nuisance that most of the prisoners initially slept outdoors (until that was prohibited).

On 25 August 1941, after the amnesty proclamation, Certified Lieutenant Colonel Wiśniowski arrived at the camp – which was then a few thousand POWs strong – and started organizing infantry, artillery and other companies and battalions with the help of the officers who were among the POWs.

On 1 September, the gates of the camp opened and we marched out – in torn clothing, barefoot and hungry but in formation. We marched to the station and then traveled by train to Totskoye. This time the train cars were open.

Encampment, 22 February 1943

Collection of the Hoover Institution Library & Archives at the disposal of the Central Archives of Modern Records, Władysław Anders Collection. Reports, 800/1/0/-/48, account no. 643.

CAMPS IN KRIVOY ROG AND THE DONETS BASIN

Contrary to the provisions of international law, the Polish POWs were used on a mass scale as unpaid workforce. They shared the fate of thousands of Polish civilians deported deep into the Soviet Union for forced labor. In the photograph: a group of women felling trees, Sverdlovsk area, 22 November 1940.

Photo. NN / KARTA Center

MAKSYMILIAN BARANOWSKI

Maksymilian Baranowski, cadet platoon-leader, "Children of Lwów" 6th Tank Battalion.

I was taken prisoner by the Russians on 19 September 1939 near Tłumacz. In Horodenka we were subjected to a thorough search, during which literally everything was taken from us: our army overcoats, belts, blankets, canteens, spoons, private monies, rings, watches, silver and gold chains and crosses, and suchlike.

Between 19 and 23 September 1939 we didn't receive food even once. Thereafter we were transported to Volochysk in freight wagons; the conditions were terrible, with a few dozen men crammed into each car and no food or water. We remained in Volochysk for around two weeks. The conditions there were just as scandalous. The food – once daily we would be given a few spoons of soup (or rather water) and a morsel of bread. Next, we were all deported deeper into Russia. I ended up in Marhanets (in Ukraine), where I was imprisoned until April 1940. During winter we were not given any heating fuel, and we had to sleep on planks or on the concrete floor, with nothing to cover ourselves. The food was poor. We were forced to work in decrepit and unsafe manganese mines – without the necessary safety clothing. As a result – and despite the repressions – 90% of us ceased working in January 1940. From this time on, the authorities became more oppressive, and on a few occasions we were denied our daily meals. We would be driven out into the extreme frost (minus a few dozen degrees centigrade) without warm clothing, having to wait five or six hours just to be let back inside the barracks. In addition, nightly interrogations, inspections and body searches became more frequent. Agitators started to appear en masse, encouraging us to go to work – obviously unsuccessfully.

In the beginning of May, we were punished for our "rebellion" by being sent to the Komi Republic (between Kotlas and Arkhangelsk), to work on the Kotlas–Ukhta railway line. The conditions were appalling: penal food and filthy, dilapidated barracks infested with rats, bugs, vermin. In addition, we were set quotas that 90% of the prisoners simply could not fulfill. We would be driven out to work in the heaviest frost (minus 50–60 degrees centigrade) wearing inadequate clothes, with rubber shoes on our feet. The majority of us fell seriously ill with scurvy and rheumatism. The nocturnal interrogations intensified (with one person being summoned three or even four times during a single night), as did transferrals of men from one labor camp to another. The guards treated us brutally, frequently shoving and pushing us, or even using their rifle butts. Those who resisted were locked up in dark, damp cells, where they would be given soup once daily and 300 grams of bread.

We suffered these conditions for over a year, until July 1941.

We were freed under the amnesty in August 1941 and left for the newly established army camp near Moscow, and from there to the Polish Army that was forming in Totskoye.

26 March 1943

Collection of the Hoover Institution Library & Archives at the disposal of the Central Archives of Modern Records, Władysław Anders Collection. Reports, 800/1/0/-/48, account no. 2413.

ANONYMOUS

[Sergeant]

Name of the camp:

The POW camp in Marhanets (Dniepropetrovsk Oblast).

Composition of POWs:

The camp included soldiers of all ranks, but the Soviet authorities didn't know that there were also officers in the camp.

Number of POWs:

Throughout the entire existence of the camp, there were about 500 POWs.

Duration of the camp's existence:

The camp existed for nearly seven months, that is, from the moment our soldiers had arrived from Novograd-Volynskyi up until they were taken away to the northern camps (from 28 October 1941 to 22 May 1942).

Description of the camp:

The camp was situated outside of town, near the manganese mines. It was located in four buildings, formerly occupied by laborers. The building was divided into ten rooms and could accommodate about 150 people. Right next to the rooms there was a kitchen and a dining room for a hundred people. Everything was surrounded by a tall slate fence.

Life in the camp:

About 75% of the people there worked in the manganese mines, the rest – in various wood storehouses. People were placed in the buildings (the so-called barracks) according to their occupation. Each barrack had its commandant (prefect) chosen from the POWs. Those working in the mines were divided into brigades. The work in a mine or outside of the mine was forced. We got paid, however, not directly, but [illegible word] to the canteen. It must be noted that the maintenance cost of one prisoner was calculated as seven rubles per day. The remuneration for working in the mines ranged between four and ten rubles. As a result, about 50% [of the prisoners] were unable to pay their living expenses, 25–35% could pay for the food, and about 15% would receive several rubles of compensation, and the so-called Stakhanovites would receive several dozen rubles per month.

Working at the mines was hard, dangerous and life-threatening due to the very primitive equipment and incompetent organization of work. That's why, in the second part of December, people stopped going to work, excusing themselves due to exhaustion. This resulted in repressions, which included being escorted to work by guards, getting arrested or isolated in a barrack built especially for this purpose, etc. When none of that helped, and the attendance of laborers kept decreasing, the administration of the mine, or more precisely – the administration of the mine trust, announced that on 1 January workers would get paid directly and they could use the money to buy food at the canteen. On 1 January 1942, everybody was to receive an advance payment for five days, naturally, once they had signed the receipt and committed themselves to work. After this order, 90% of people stopped working and the mine canteen stopped feeding them. There were various committees and, after negotiations with our soldiers and various deliberations, it was eventually decided that everyone who didn't work would get 300 grams of bread and some soup once a day. We received such rations of food until the end of our stay in the camp.

Apart from the harsh working conditions, there was also another reason why people jointly decided to live on 300 grams of bread and soup that contained no more than 20 grams of cereal. Word got around, spread by the civilians, that all POWs who didn't want to work would be sent back to their country and only those who worked willingly and efficiently would be kept. That's why people would rather starve, sleep on bare planks with no mattresses nor blankets, and use their uniforms to cover themselves with throughout the entire winter (all sets of bed linen were taken away with the beginning of January, and our coats were taken away when we were taken into captivity) than work, as they were convinced that they would be sent home.

Attitude of the NKVD towards Poles:

During the first month of our stay there was a lot of propaganda work. Various campaigners were sent to us to inform us about their system, their program, the organization of work, and culture that was catching up with American culture, etc. At the same time, they would test our opinions about all aspects of their life, our views, moods. That came very easily to them, as we couldn't – for quite understandable reasons – sit still and listen to the things we were told, which often insulted our ambitions regarding the nation, culture, etc. And so various inspectors from the NKVD started to interrogate us, looking for officers and priests. They would frequently perform searches, especially at night. They would isolate about 150 people, whom they thought to be non-commissioned officers, rebels and dangerous individuals. They interrogated us in this way and wrote protocols until the end, until our departure.

POWs who distinguished themselves:

There actually were no prisoners who were outstanding in any way. One can only add that while almost all of the Poles did not work out of solidarity, the Belarusians and Ukrainians continued to work, justifying it by saying that since they came from territory that was occupied by the Soviets at the time, they had to comply with their orders.

Collection of the Hoover Institution Library & Archives at the disposal of the Central Archives of Modern Records, Władysław Anders Collection. Reports, 800/1/0/-/46, account no. 22.

WACŁAW EJSMONT

Wacław Ejsmont, born on 10 August 1914 in Sheibaki; education: three classes of elementary school; farmer; unmarried, Polish national, Roman Catholic, resident at Nowogródek Voivodeship, Lida Commune and District. Performed active military service in 1937 with the local 77th Infantry Regiment unit in Lida.

I was taken captive on 26 September at the Zdołbunów railway station, where we were put into Soviet train cars under the guard of an armed escort. At night the train set off, and everyone who attempted escape was shot at. The cars were sealed. On the morning of 27 September we arrived at the station in Shepetovka. We stayed there for seven days. We received food once in 48 hours: 200 grams of bread and a quarter of a liter of soup – nothing but water. On 1 October we were loaded onto freight wagons and transported to Kiev, where we got breakfast. We spent the entire day at the station and left in the evening. On the following day we arrived at the camp in Novograd-Volynskyi, where we received food twice [a day]: soup and 500 grams of bread. We stayed for three weeks in that camp, until 27 [October. Next] we were deported to Ukraine, Dnipropetrovsk Oblast, Chortomlyk station. 500 men were brought there for work in an iron mine. For two weeks, our life was quite bearable: we were herded to work under escort, but at that time there was no prescribed amount of work to do. Two weeks later the quotas were introduced, and from that time on we had to live off the money we earned ourselves. The quotas were very high, so we didn't agree to them. In retaliation we didn't receive any food for three whole days. Accordingly, we refused to go to work from 24 December on. Then they forced us to go to work and used all methods of harassment: arrests, death threats, various forms of punishment, and Soviet propaganda saying that we would never again set eyes on Poland and our families, as they would torment us to death. In that camp we received 400 grams of bread and water twice a day. We spent six months in such conditions, from 1939 to 21 May 1940. Then we were deported northwards, to the Republic of Komi, where we were forced to perform earth works only, that is, building a railway line. We worked under very harsh conditions: we had to transport the excavated earth at a distance of 200–300 meters, and the prescribed amounts were 7 cubic meters of earth in summer and 5 cubic meters in winter. For meeting 25% of the quota we received 50 grams of bread and soup twice a day, but it was made of water only. On holidays I used to evade work; as punishment we would be put under arrest for five days, receive 300 grams of bread and water once a day, or be forced to go to work by having dogs set on us and being hit with rifle butts. Temperatures fell to 47 degrees below zero, and we had to work without clothes and shoes. To be exempted from work one had to run a temperature of 40 degrees or have a broken leg or a broken arm. Five people died suddenly at night, but I don't know their surnames. It was so until the very end, that is, until our release.

On 15 July 1941 we were transported to Polish camps. My camp was called Vyazniki. On 25 August 1941 I enlisted in the Polish Army. On 1 September we left Vyazniki for the camp in Tatishchevo; 5th Infantry Division, 14th Infantry Regiment, 9th Rifle Company.

Collection of the Hoover Institution Library & Archives at the disposal of the Central Archives of Modern Records, Władysław Anders Collection. Reports, 800/1/0/-/48, account no. 2298.

EDWARD ZNAJDA

Edward Znajda, corporal, residing in the Augustów District, Sztabin Commune, Kopiec village.

I was mustered to the Polish Army in Kobryń on 29 August 1939. On 18 September 1939, I was disarmed by the Red Army in the city of Równe and was taken into Russia as a prisoner of war. They brought us to Shepetovka, where we stayed for two weeks in terrible conditions. We did not get any food at all during the first three days, until they began giving us half a liter of meatless soup and 200 grams of black bread, and nothing more. After two weeks, they loaded us into train carriages and transported us to Novograd-Volynskyi, where we stayed throughout October in door-less and window-less barracks while the temperatures dropped to 10 degrees below zero. They gave us food once a day – if they gave it at all – and our soldiers died one by one as a result.

As many as 1,600 soldiers were transported from Novograd-Volynskyi to Zaporozhye on the Dnieper, where we went to work in a factory (heavy industry). The work was very hard and done in poor conditions; some went to work barefoot or in tattered sandals in temperatures of 20 below zero. Those who did not make it to work were put in an isolation cell (a small, dark, window-less cell that was dirty and stinking and so low that it was only possible to hold one position with your back bent). I spent 14 days there on two separate occasions. I was given 200 grams of bread and a liter of water, and every third day I received a liter of warm, thin, and meatless soup.

We organized a Christmas tree in the barracks in time for the holidays and celebrated Midnight Mass, as a result of which 31 soldiers were arrested and brought before the war tribunal. Except for myself, these included: Cadet Henryk Cap, Cadet Bronisław Łęgowski, Platoon-leader Jakubowski and the riflemen Koleryński, Zeliński and Konstanty Żukowski. I do not remember the names of the rest. This is what happened: they called me to their office which was located outside the camp. When I arrived, I noticed an NKVD officer sitting at the table. I did not recognize him because he had never been in the camp. He got up, pointed to a chair and told me to sit down. When I sat down, he gave me cigarettes, and said: "Comrade Znajda, you will be our man, you must help us. Here, I will read to you," and began to read that my duty as a child of a metallurgist, i.e. member of the working class, was to help them catch anyone working against Soviet Russia and to point them out; they would know what to do then. He presented me with a paper to sign, which stated that I, Edward Znajda, voluntarily agreed to cooperate with the NKVD and will obey all orders.

He suggested that I sign, but I refused. Following this, that same NKVD officer suggested very politely that I take a taxi to the city with him. I did not know what he meant. He took my arm and told me: "Let's go for a walk," and led me out to where the taxi was waiting. We got in. When we left, he reprimanded me and said, "Sit still, don't move." I had a feeling it would be like that. As it turned out, he drove me to prison, where the real torture began.

They began to interrogate me. Day and night, they would not let me rest; they tortured me in various ways for a month and a half. They kept me, naked, in an isolation cell on bare cement – the clothes I had were taken away from me I was only allowed to dress when I was taken for interrogation. They really wanted me to hand over the officers and the bourgeoisie – as they called them – constantly hammering it into my head that I was the son of a worker and should help them because of that, but I categorically refused. They sentenced me to six years of work in the labor camps. The same happened to my colleagues, and they even got as many as eight or ten years. They sent all of us to the labor camps in the taiga in the North, where we worked in very, very difficult conditions: hungry, naked and forced to work in temperatures up to minus 50. It got to the point that I was not able to climb onto the bunk without help. In a word, it is impossible to describe or talk about that ordeal in such a short outline.

There were 103 Poles in the camp where I was being kept, the rest were of various nationalities. A total of seven people out of our group of 103 died over the course of a single month in the north, and that number gradually dwindled until there were only 70 left two years later. Were it not for the amnesty, each of us would have met that same fate: only destruction.

My name was similarly read out in the amnesty and I was cleared for release, but my colleagues received documents, and, when I asked why there were no documents for me, I was told: "You will stay here, you will never know freedom again." In addition to me, there were 24 who did not receive any documents and who heard the same as me. On the second day, they sent us back to the camp, and the real torture began. We were desperate: the amnesty had passed over us and we were being treated as the worst element of all; we were kicked and beaten in a beastly way with clubs.

Of the 24 of us, five died of hunger and misery, and I was released on 7 April 1942 as a result of the intervention of my colleagues-in-exile who were at the Polish outpost in Kirov. They gave me documents for the right to remain in the North, from which I did not have the right to leave, but I took a risk and walked 345 kilometers on foot, eventually arriving at the Polish military outpost in Kotlas. I do not know where I found the strength to go so far. I suppose hope for the future gave me strength. In this way, I broke out of Hell, which is in the land of the Soviets, and not in any afterlife. It was only when I was in Russia that I understood how to value our Polish life and how to respect everything that is in our beloved Poland.

10 March 1943

Collection of the Hoover Institution Library & Archives at the disposal of the Central Archives of Modern Records, Władysław Anders Collection. Reports, 800/1/0/-/46, account no. 387.

STEFAN DANILECKI

Personal data (name, surname, rank, age, occupation and marital status):
Stefan Danilecki, corporal, born on 8 June 1908, farmer by profession, married.

Date and circumstances of arrest:

I was arrested as a Polish soldier on 22 September 1939 in Lwów, in a group of about a thousand people. We were searched and for the rest of the day we were marched in the direction of Tarnopol. We spent the night under escort. In the morning the escort was gone. We went homeward, but on the way we were caught by the Red Army men, led to the station and transported to Shepetovka.

Name of the camp, prison or forced labor site:

I spent three weeks in Shepetovka, three weeks in Novograd-Volynskyi (POW camp), and then from 1 November 1939 to 15 May 1940 I was in the 9th hamlet (labor camp) in Zaporozhye. On 15 May I was deported northwards, to Kotlas (labor camp).

Description of the camp or prison (grounds, buildings, housing conditions, hygiene):

In Shepetovka there were wooden barracks. They were so cramped that some of us had to stay out in the open air. The hygienic conditions were terrible. In Novograd-Volynskyi there were summer barracks, and both the housing and hygienic conditions were the same as in Shepetovka. In Zaporozhye there were buildings made of clay, but furnished with pallets and mattresses. The hygienic conditions were bearable, as we could finally take baths. In Kotlas we had to build the huts ourselves, for which we used boards and wood. While the huts were under construction, we lived on the road, in the open air. We also made pallets to sleep on ourselves. We had found Kotlas a wilderness and left it a fully developed camp.

Social composition of POWs, prisoners, exiles (nationality, type of crimes, intellectual and moral standing, mutual relations, etc.):

Only Polish soldiers. There were about 15 Jews, but I don't know whether there were any other national minorities. Mutual relations were good and friendly.

Life in the camp or prison (daily routine, working conditions, quotas, wages, food, clothes, social and cultural life, etc.):

An average day in Zaporozhye: wake-up at 5.00 a.m., breakfast, work from 7.00 a.m. (slave labor), dinner at 3.00 p.m., free time, supper at 10–11.00 p.m. In Kotlas: wake-up at 4.00 a.m., work from 5.00 a.m. to 4.00 p.m., then free time. We worked at railroad construction.

In Zaporozhye we used to play tricks on the Bolsheviks who marched us off to work. They tried to force us to go and we were running away. Our labor didn't yield any results. Remuneration depended on meeting the work quota. The work quota was: unloading 35 tons a day; remuneration: 5–6 rubles. When someone didn't fill the quota he didn't receive any payment and on top of that had to pay a fine. We received food three times a day, there was soup for dinner and some thick groats. We received 800 grams of bread per day. It was enough for someone who didn't work, but it was insufficient for a laborer. Those who didn't work received only half of the ration. We were issued clothes (padded jackets). There wasn't any cultural life as we lacked means to organize it. Only propaganda literature was available. We had friendly relations and lived in harmony.

Quotas were established at railroad construction in Kotlas. Meeting 100% of the work quota entitled one to full board, consisting of: soup – without any nutritional value (without even salt) – twice a day and 900 grams of bread. For filling 35% of the quota one could get 450 grams of bread and soup once a day. We had the same clothes that we had been issued in Zaporozhye. There wasn't any cultural life.

Attitude of the NKVD towards Poles (interrogation methods, torture and other forms of punishment, communist propaganda, information about Poland, etc.):

I was interrogated about five times in Zaporozhye and once in Kotlas. None of us signed his testimony, as the Soviets were trying to force us to take Soviet citizenship. For skipping work or failing to meet the work quota we were punished with confinement in a dark cell with nothing but 300 grams of bread and water. Kabanov, the NKVD major, punished us frequently and severely. Communist propaganda was spread in the form of lectures delivered by political commissars. It was less intense in the north, and was limited there to propagating the Stakhanovite labor. The NKVD spoke of Poland only in foul and derogatory terms, claiming that Poland – if ever – would be reborn red, as one of the Soviet republics.

Medical assistance, hospitals, mortality rate (provide the names of the deceased):

The medical assistance was virtually non-existent, limited to issuing rare medical leaves for those who ran a very high fever. The rest of the sick were driven out to work. The mortality rate was low.

Was it at all possible to get in contact with one's home country and family?

It was virtually impossible to get in contact with one's country and family. The majority of us received but one letter, and there were some who didn't manage to establish any contact with their families.

When were you released and how did you manage to join the Polish Army?

I was released on 20 July 1941 and transferred in a Soviet transport to Vyazniki, and then I left in a Polish military transport for Tatishchevo, where I joined the 5th Infantry Division.

Collection of the Hoover Institution Library & Archives at the disposal of the Central Archives of Modern Records, Władysław Anders Collection. Reports, 800/1/0/-/46, account no. 2106.

KAZIMIERZ ŻMIJOWSKI

Kazimierz Żmijowski, platoon-leader, born 15 February 1910, bachelor, farmer.

I was taken into captivity by the Soviet army on 18 September 1939.

The camps I was interned in were as follows: Kamenets-Podolskyi, Kozelshchyna, Shyrokoye (near Krivoy Rog), Sapożyn (near Równe), Volochysk, Podwołoczyska, Starobelsk.

The camp in Kamenets-Podolskyi was a transit camp. The camp in Kozelshchyna was set up in a former monastery where there were lots of church buildings that have since been turned into a club. There were also lots of large, well-maintained buildings there. Some of us slept on the wooden floor in those buildings, some on the stone floor of the church, on any mattress that anyone could get their hands on. The rest lived in the stables and tents which were put up separately and which housed the officers, non-commissioned officers and police.

The camp in Shyrokoye (near Krivoy Rog) was in a large single-story building with a sink with cold water, central heating, electric light, sleeping partly in bunks, partly in beds with bedsheets. The washroom was by a shaft; washing every day after work in the shaft.

The camp in Sapożyn (near Równe) was in a building that had previously been used by the border guard prior to the invasion of the Soviet army. We slept in bunks.

The camp in Volochysk was in two stables of which one was shared with cattle. We slept in bunks.

The camp in Podwołoczyska was in a large Russian [?] building where films had been screened before the war. We slept on multi-level bunks and so it was dark, stuffy and cramped.

The camp I was put in in Starobelsk was comprised of tents. We slept on the rags we had gone to great trouble to bring with us. The composition of the prisoners with regard to nationality and military rank was different in each camp. There were more than 6,000 prisoners in Kozelshchy na, the majority of them Poles; regarding their military rank, around 40% of them were officers and non-commissioned officers. There were 300 prisoners from regions occupied by the Soviet forces in the camp in Shyrokoye (near Krivoy Rog). Poles accounted for 60% of the prisoners there, the rest were Belarusians, Ukrainians, and Jews. There were no officers. The rest of the camps were very similar in terms of nationality and number of prisoners.

Life in the camps varied. We did not work in Kozelshchyna, we only fought off starvation and, later, lice. We worked 24 hours a day in three shifts in the shaft at the camp in Shyrokoye (near Krivoy Rog).

The work was very hard because the mines lacked the proper ventilation and the quotas, which were raised from time to time, were extremely high. At the beginning, in one type of work where I was put, we had to shovel 16 tons of iron ore and transport it on a trolley, pushing it for 300 meters with our bare hands. This was the quota for two men, which was rewarded with one ruble and 12 kopeks per trolley. Later, the quota increased to two carts per two men, and the salary dropped to 90 kopeks per cart.

At the same time, we had to pay about 6 rubles for decent food that was so sorely needed after such hard work, at least 3 rubles for breakfast, the same for supper. Altogether, food cost around 12 rubles, while the average earnings were about 8 rubles a day. In the first months, we had to pay for the lodgings as well. Later, this was given to us for free because everyone had such a large debt and there was no way to pay.

It reached the point that we had to start a hunger strike because most of us had no way to buy bread. They did not want to pay in advance because everyone had so much debt. As a result of the hunger strike, four of us were taken away somewhere unknown, the price of food was slightly reduced – but not for long – they gave us advances on our salaries and we had to struggle [illegible]. As for clothes, we usually had our military uniforms that still served. Later on, we supplemented these with our own jackets. The worst was with footwear. When ours was ruined, we received either canvas shoes, or old rubber ones which did little to protect from the cold and nothing to protect from the water.

Social life was generally good, except for people who – out of fear or for other reasons – tried to serve the Soviets by reporting all the conversations they overheard. Fortunately, there were few such people and after a short time, we were able to recognize them and avoid them. Cultural life was deplorable, resulting from a lack of freedom of movement, a lack of freedom of speech, good books or any good entertainment. What's more, unfortunate news came from abroad and often unpleasant news came from home. The implanting of communist propaganda by the political commissars took place during talks that were held on an almost daily basis and which we were physically forced to attend after work. They tried to turn us into communists. We were often told that there was no more school in Poland, no more bread, clothing, etc., which seemed very odd. We were constantly told that Poland would cease to exist, and that it would only return when pigs learned to fly.

Medical aid left much to be desired due to a lack of medicine and the previously established numbers of sick people who could be released from work at one time.

Majewski from Wilno, less than 30 years of age, died at the camp in Podwołoczyska following an accident at work that was caused by the lack of a foreman to manage the labor. Three others died in other camps, but I do not remember their names.

We maintained contact with home via letters from family and friends which came several times a month and which used metaphors to describe the most important events and the orders of the occupying authorities. You could also learn a lot from those who had visited their loved ones in Poland.

Following the amnesty, I was released from captivity at the camp in Starobelsk at the beginning of September 1941. I joined the Polish army in Totskoye in the same month.

Encampment, 25 February 1943

Collection of the Hoover Institution Library & Archives at the disposal of the Central Archives of Modern Records, Władysław Anders Collection. Reports, 800/1/0/-/47, account no. 644.

JAN DARASZ

Personal data:

Jan Darasz, platoon-leader, 42 years old, senior guard with the Border Guard, married.

Date and circumstances of arrest:

I was taken prisoner by the Soviets on 18 September 1939 in the town of Biała, near Tarnopol, together with the employees of the administrative office of the "Bogumin" Polish Border Guard. The Soviets seized a two-horse carriage with arms: light machine guns, anti-tank rifles, grenades, and uniforms. They behaved ruthlessly towards us, guarding and treating us as if we were bandits.

Name of the camp:

1) Volochysk at the Polish-Soviet border; 2) Novograd, Ukraine; 3) Marhanets, Ukraine; 4) Marhanets "3 barracks"; 5) Svizhok [?] beyond Kotlas.

Description of the camp:

In Volochysk several thousand people were placed in the stables. Marhanets – as long as we didn't refuse work, the conditions were bearable: we lived in barracks, there were both beds and blankets, and tolerable food three times a day. However, we were required to work very hard. Marhanets "3 barracks" – deplorable conditions: pallets made of wood shavings, a bowl of watery oat soup once a day, tea was out of the question; we were also forbidden to cook anything on our own. We received 500 grams of bread per day. People suffered a great deal. They fell ill and swelled from hunger; 20% had their legs swollen so much that they walked like utter cripples.

We left for the North on 21 January 1940. Accommodation was in barracks. Lots of bugs. Food and clothes depended on meeting work quotas. Poles were assigned to the first caldron, the rest – mostly Ukrainians – had the third caldron. The work was very hard, we worked at railroad construction.

Life in the camp:

In Marhanets, the Soviet authorities offered to change our status so we would become mercenaries. Since we refused – as this might have resulted in imposing USSR citizenship on us – the Poles were imprisoned in Marhanets "3 barracks." The Poles acted decisively and in solidarity. In order to press our demands – we were especially concerned with the maintenance of prisoner-of-war rights – we staged strikes.

Social composition of POWs:

Poles, Belarusians, Ukrainians from Poland, a few Jews, Russians, USSR citizens. The latter treated us rather kindly and with a sort of respect. The Ukrainians always kept apart, waiting for the German victory; they were hostile towards the Poles to the point where they were informing against us. At first, the Belarusians were also prejudiced against us, but with time – as they came to know the Soviet realities – they abandoned their pro-Russian stance and grew closer to us.

Attitude of the NKVD towards Poles:

The NKVD tried to win us over to the USSR. On the one hand, they repeated ad infinitum and ad nauseam that Poland was lost, while on the other they tempted us with the prospect of improving our living conditions, offering jobs, remuneration, and even freedom and marriage on Russian territory. This propaganda produced the opposite results. The actions taken by the Poles didn't suit the NKVD, and they tended to cover these up even at the expense of concessions.

Medical assistance, hospitals, mortality rate:

The medical assistance was inadequate. There weren't enough hospitals, especially in Ukraine. Someone was considered ill only when he ran a temperature of at least 38.1 degrees. The doctors worked on the assumption that people in the camp were healthy, and all they needed was better nourishment. Therefore the more emaciated ones were assigned to the so-called tenth caldron. The mortality rate for the whole period was calculated at 2%. As regards deaths among my personal acquaintances, guard Kasprzak from Turek, near Łódź, died in the camp. The most widespread diseases were scurvy, pneumonia, and tuberculosis.

Was it at all possible to get in contact with one's home country and family?

We received letters from our country, both from the German and the Soviet-controlled territories. Despite the fact that everybody wrote letters, no more than of us 25% received answers.

When were you released and how did you manage to join the Polish Army?

On 15 July 1941 the prisoners were transported to a Polish camp near Vyazniki, where on 24 August 1941 the released men were sworn in as soldiers of the Polish army.

Encampment, 13 January 1943

Collection of the Hoover Institution Library & Archives at the disposal of the Central Archives of Modern Records, Władysław Anders Collection. Reports, 800/1/0/-/48, account no. 1682.

MAKSYMILIAN UŁASIUK

Maksymilian Ułasiuk, bombardier, 2nd staff platoon/5PA [5th Light Artillery Regiment?]

Name of the camp:

Camp point Zaporozhye by the Dnieper River near Dnipropetrovsk.

Social composition of POWs:

Privates, police, railway workers.

Number of POWs:

1,500.

Period of the camp's existence:

From 27 October 1939 to 23 May 1940, when everyone was transported to the Komi ASSR.

Description of the camp:

Single-story, low-rise buildings on a small square surrounded by barbed wire. The area was near an iron foundry which was very unpleasant for prisoners. Smoke and iron dust were constantly pouring into the area and penetrating into the living quarters.

Life in the camp:

The attempt to organize the prisoners into brigades failed. We were forced to work in the factory and unload wagons. We cleaned the camp ourselves. We went to the bathhouse very rarely. There was dirt. Bed bugs were rife. Food: 400 grams of bread and meatless soup twice a day, half a liter each time. The employed (Belarusians, Ukrainians, Jews) received a kilo of bread.

Attitude of the NKVD towards Poles:

Forcing labor with threats, harsh punishment cells. Interrogations were very unpleasant, frequently at night, searches – weekly. Polish documents were taken away. Prisoners were harassed and assured that they would never see Poland again, that the name of Poland would cease to exist forever. Solidarity among Polish POWs was high. Ukrainians and Belarusians were separated and given better conditions. Letters were not delivered to prisoners. There were cases of arrests of prisoners who tried to organize themselves to fight for better conditions or who urged others to avoid work. The prisoners were robbed of little things: tooth powder, brushes, spoons, forks, etc.

POWs who stood out either positively or negatively:

Two Ukrainians stood out negatively (I don't remember their names).

Medical assistance, hospitals, mortality rate:

One prisoner lost a leg at work in the foundry, a second lost a finger.

Collection of the Hoover Institution Library & Archives at the disposal of the Central Archives of Modern Records, Władysław Anders Collection. Reports, 800/1/0/-/46, account no. 57.

IGNACY JAŁOWACZ

Ignacy Jałowacz, uhlan, born in 1899, a farmer, married, with two children; auxiliary armored squadron, Auxiliary [Armored] Weapon Division.

Date of arrest: 18 September 1939 as a POW.

Name of the camp: Kozelsk. We were interned behind barbed wire for a whole month, we did not work. The food was very bad, there was only water and cabbage, we received 400 grams of bread – we were hungry. We lived in an Orthodox church. They kept us guarded and locked up. There were around 3,000 of us in the building. They made a record of our places of residence and kept lying that we would return to our families. That was how they got us to the station. 60 people were loaded into 16-ton wagons, so that half were sitting and half had to stand. We were fed stale bread and water. We were directed to the foundry in Krivoy Rog. I worked on unloading iron ore and I received meagre payment: 30 rubles a month (when a plate of soup cost [number missing] rubles) and 400 grams of bread. I worked for seven months. They continued to aggravate us and told us not to expect to return to Poland, because it would be no more.

We were hardly given any medical aid. When a man was sick and did not go to work, he was not given food.

The quota was not feasible – we were pouring with sweat, but simply couldn't unload 10 tons of iron ore. After a while, we were transported to the Tuligłowy camp. I worked on the road there. There was a quota of 12 meters [illegible]. I worked for three months. From there they took us to the airbase in Sknilów near Lwów and I worked there for a month.

I received a payment of 30 rubles a month for work. In addition, we were given the following food: soup – to this day I know not what it was made from, it was plain water – and we received 500 grams of bread. I worked there until the outbreak of the Soviet-German war. Then an evacuation took place – we were fed once a day, rushed day and night, we did not receive any water and were beaten with rifle butts and pushed around. We marched for 28 days. We were chased to the Zolotonosha station and loaded onto a train – 65 people per wagon. They didn't let us rest. We were transported to Starobelsk. We arrived there on 28 July 1941. We lived in tents and were overseen by guards. We received 800 grams of bread.

We were released on 28 August 1941 when our army was being formed and I was assigned to the artillery of the 6th Infantry Division. I served in Totskoye.

12 February 1943

Collection of the Hoover Institution Library & Archives at the disposal of the Central Archives of Modern Records, Władysław Anders Collection. Reports, 800/1/0/-/47, account no. 1306.

JAN SOFRONIUK

Personal data (name and surname, rank, age, occupation and marital status):
Jan Sofroniuk, senior sergeant, 44 years old, regular non-commissioned officer, widower.

Date and circumstances of arrest:

I was taken into Soviet captivity in Strusów near Tarnopol on 17 September 1939 as I was travelling to Romania with my daughter, who did not want to remain alone at home following the death of her mother on 25 June 1939.

My daughter and I arrived in Kamenets-Podolskyi on 20 September 1939. My daughter was immediately taken from me and I gave her into the care of Mrs Poniatowska, the wife of a major from the 1st Heavy Artillery Regiment. After a thorough inspection, a recording of our personal data and a dinner of bread, millet and coffee, we were put onto a train later that same night.

Name of the camp, prison or forced labor site; Description of the camp or prison (grounds, buildings, housing conditions, hygiene):

From 24 September until 13 October 1939 – Tiotkino in the Sumy Oblast. Summer barracks, cold and cramped. Poor food, thin soup twice a day, [illegible], 400–500 grams of bread, sometimes a few sugar cubes. They hounded us to work exclusively within the area of the camp, digging toilets, carrying water, cleaning up waste, etc., and took mostly officers and policemen to do it.

After separating the officers and policemen from the privates, and after segregating the prisoners who came from the German and Soviet partitions, they took the prisoners from the Soviet partitions to Krivoy Rog and the German partition probably went home. I do not know where they took the officers and policemen. The fact is, however, that Major Aleksy Poniatowski and Captain Stanisław Kraiński, with whom I stayed very briefly in Tiotkino, have so far not returned to the army.

From 18 October 1939 until 22 May 1940 – Krivoy Rog, Kolachevskaya station, Lenin ore mine.

Housing conditions sufficient; quantities of food sufficient, quality insufficient: borscht, soup, groats, tea and 800 grams of bread three times a day. I worked on the railways, most worked in the shaft. From 1 January

1940, they paid 50 rubles every ten days, that is 5 rubles a day, with which we could buy in a canteen: borscht, soup, groats, tea and 800 grams of bread three times a day, all of it in oil. Whoever earned more than that was paid the difference. The work on the railway lasted seven hours, i.e. from 8.00 a.m. to 3.00 p.m.

In April, this failed too, and they began to pay irregularly, especially to those who earned less than 5 rubles a day. For example, I was paid only 50 rubles in April.

After arriving at the Kolachevskaya station, I wrote two letters to the Red Cross in Moscow and in Kamenets-Podolskyi, concerning my daughter who stayed in Kamenets-Podolskyi, but I did not receive any replies. After writing a letter to Brześć on the Bug River, I received a letter from my daughter stating that she and Mrs Poniatowska had arrived in Brześć on 10 October 1939.

From 27 May until 7 June 1940 – Busk (Lesser Poland region). Poor quarters: cowsheds, sleeping on bunks, dirt, sloppy. 11 hours of work on road construction, [illegible] depending on the achieved quotas, earnings from zero to 250 rubles.

From 7 June until 15 October 1940 – Jaryczów Stary (Lesser Poland region). Work and living conditions as in Busk. Leave was regulated to be given every two weeks, but in fact it only came every few months; they counted rainy days which prevented us from working as leave.

From 15 October 1940 until 15 March 1941 – Podliski near Lwów. Work and conditions [illegible] in Busk, except the fact that, with the exception of a few days, we did not work from 1 November 1940 and 15 March 1941. Rzęsna Ruska near Lwów; I worked tidying the base in hall no. 1 in Lwów. They did not pay us for two weeks of work. The barracks were new and damp, food insufficient, [illegible] fish every day.

From 15 April until 3 May 1941 – Zimna Woda near Lwów. During this time, I worked building our barracks in Skniłów. The shifts were 11 hours long regardless of the weather; they took us in carts, transported us like livestock. Terrible barracks, the water leaked onto our heads when it rained; the mud was up to our knees and we had to wade 300–400 meters through it to reach the road.

From 3 May until 23 June 1941 – Skniłów near Lwów. We built the barracks ourselves; food sufficient but of poor quality, fish every day, meals cooked on oil; soup cooked on meat was brought in the afternoons (half a liter), but this was a propaganda scheme as there were many civilians working at the airfield.

There were many grocery stores with bread, sugar, sweets, gingerbread, lemonade, beer, bacon, butter, milk, ice cream and even newspapers at the airfield where we had to work. In addition to those was a shop selling shoes, underwear, soap, cutlery, clothing, even alarm clocks. It was all to entice both us and the civilians to work harder because there was nowhere to get these items in normal civilian life.

The work was very urgent and difficult in shifts from 7.00 a.m. until 7.00 p.m. with not a single break in the day. Payment was meagre and I did not receive a salary for several days in May or for 21 days in June.

I was working the night shift using machines to break rocks on the night of 21 June. At around 3.15 a.m., four planes flew overhead and dropped bombs on the railway lines a few kilometers from our location. A few minutes later, nine planes flew past and started to bomb the area 200 meters from us. Everyone in our two brigades – that is around 50 people – managed to come out unscathed, however four of the imported workers pouring concrete were killed and 18 of them were wounded.

In the afternoon of 23 June 1941, they took us through Lwów, Tarnopol, Volochysk, Proskurov, Kaniv, and after that whole ordeal they hounded us to Zolotonosha where they loaded us into wagons 70 at a time and took us to Starobelsk. Rifleman Gaj – I do not remember his first name – was mentally ill and was killed by the NKVD convoy during a stopover in Podwołoczyska on the night of 28 July 1941.

Everyone was physically exhausted when we reached Starobelsk. Our legs were swollen. Life was miserable until the contract was signed, it got a little better after that. We slept in tents, stretched out on the bare earth.

On 24 August 1941, Lieutenant Colonel Wiśniowski arrived at the camp surrounded by the NKVD authorities and read out a memo ordering the formation of a Polish army in the USSR.

Medical examinations on 28 August.

Departure from Starobelsk on 3 September.

Arrival in Totskoye on 8 September 1941.

Life in the camp or prison (daily routine, working conditions, quotas, wages, food, clothes, social and cultural life, etc.):

Cultural-educational life grew very poor. Firstly, because everyone was tired after working all day; secondly, because there was only communist reading.

Was it at all possible to get in contact with one's home country and family?

I only wrote letters to my daughter in Brześć on the Bug River.

Collection of the Hoover Institution Library & Archives at the disposal of the Central Archives of Modern Records, Władysław Anders Collection. Reports, 800/1/0/-/48, account no. 2073.

ALBERT JANCEWICZ

Albert Jancewicz, corporal, 30 years old, farmer.

I laid down my arms on 22 September 1939. I was captured in Zdołbunów and deported to the USSR to a place called Shepetovka.

The camp was situated within military barracks. The food rations were scarce – we starved. Hygiene was non-existent. Health care was poor; there was high mortality. As for cultural and social life, as well as the national composition, it's hard for me to say as I only stayed there shortly.

I was moved to Novograd-Volynskyi, where I stayed from 4 to 23 October 1939. It was better there in terms of food (easier to barter). The camp was full of chaos; everybody was struggling to survive. I deluded myself with thoughts of freedom, and that lifted my spirits. The labor consisted of going away to work at road construction, or sometimes to a kolkhoz. It wasn't any better than Shepetovka.

On 27 October 1939, I came to Zaporozhye. Living conditions were good. Medical care was sufficient. Working conditions varied depending on where you landed. Remuneration was reasonable. Work ethics high at the beginning. Communist propaganda was huge, the lectures were initially well-attended, but then gradually boycotted. There was a strong tendency of the Bolshevik authorities to hold POWs as contract workers. Strikes were a response to this, with strong solidarity (80%). There were two strikes: first during Christmas (with a religious background), and another in February, which was supposed to make our release happen sooner. As a result of the strikes, the camp divided into three groups: the first one consisted of those who refused to work, usually coming from German-occupied territory, Poles exclusively; the second group was neutral; the third group included those loyal to work (mostly Jews, Ukrainians, Poles, and Belarusians) and the peasant and working-class people. Cultural life was limited to the organization of a few performances of an orchestra and a choir. When we encountered local civilians at work, the interest in Poland was high.

I left on 18 May and arrived on 4 June 1940 in an NKVD labor camp – the 5th unit delegated to build a main iron railway.

I spent the first days of work in the Urdoma settlement. Urdoma is located about 150 kilometers northeast of Kotlas. Taiga all around, the only path which connected it to the world was a road made of logs laid across. The camp was surrounded by a fence, with "storks" – watchtowers – in the corners. The work started at 8.00 a.m. and finished at 6.00 p.m. It consisted of logging, digging, and earthwork. The quotas were always impossible to attain. Food rations were scarce. Living conditions were terrible (a hundred people in each primitively built barrack), bunk beds were often made of logs, there were no bed sheets. People fell ill with dysentery, and around autumn, masses were ill with scurvy. 30% suffered from night blindness due to a lack of vitamins.

Daily routine: a watchman did the wake-up call by ringing the gong; we then received rations of bread according to the norms we had filled; breakfast was then given, which consisted of one meal (usually wheatmeal or a codfish). Brigadiers led us to work near the gate. Here the counting and checking started, until finally a guard would give the order: "Step to the right, step to the left" and so on – the march started. Of course, we would try our best to walk as slowly as possible. After arriving, everyone was given some work to do. The hard and unrewarding struggle began. Around noon, *prembludo* – a meal – was brought to the worksite. Whoever had the first cauldron would receive soup; those who had the second cauldron would get a 150-gram pie made of barley flour. Before 6.00 p.m., work results of each worker were inspected. Then, the result was compared to the norm in the camp's offices, and the amount of bread and the type of cauldron were designated. After returning from work, the work supervisors would put poor workers in front of the foreman, who would threaten them with court or prison, and forced improvement at work, often locking them up in a punishment cell. Every day, there was a check-in for brigadiers and *desyatniki* [leaders of groups of ten], and if any of them defended the workers (their colleagues), they were considered supporters of sabotage and replaced.

Intellectual standing varied; social relations were better than ever before. There was no cultural entertainment of any sort. We were forced to listen to propaganda.

During work in the forest, Chlemtacz from Borysław was killed. Except for that, in the neighboring colony – during a railway accident – 18 POWs were killed; I don't know their surnames.

Throughout my whole stay in the North, I received two letters.

On 10 July 1941, I was taken to a camp in Talitsy, where all the interned POWs were gathered. On 31 July, the NKVD authorities read out an amnesty that liberated us, and from that point we were treated as free citizens. On 5 August 1941, a representative of the Polish army in the USSR, Lieutenant Colonel Sulik-Sarnowski, took command from the NKVD.

I was accepted into the Polish Army by a Polish-Soviet commission.

Encampment, 7 March 1943

Collection of the Hoover Institution Library & Archives at the disposal of the Central Archives of Modern Records, Władysław Anders Collection. Reports, 800/1/0/-/47, account no. 471.

FRANCISZEK POPKO

Franciszek Popko, uhlan, born in 1909, farmer, Polish national.

I was taken captive on 18 September 1939 in the town of Nowojelnia, where they disarmed us and took our horses and marched us to Stołpce. In Stołpce we were kept for three days. They said that they would give us passes and release us back home. They didn't give us anything to eat, but the civilian population brought us baskets of bread and threw it to us. So if you caught a piece of bread, you could survive on it. On 21 September 1939 they loaded us into wagons and transported us to Kozelsk. The journey took five days; we arrived in Kozelsk on 25 September 1939. They didn't give us anything to eat on the way; when we arrived in Minsk, the civilians bought some bread and gave it to us. In Kozelsk we received 400 grams of soggy black bread and half a liter of soup, made of I don't know what – some scarce cabbage leaves were floating in it – and if we got our ration at 10.00 a.m., we received the next at 8.00 p.m. on the following day. We stayed in Kozelsk until 19 October 1939.

There were 12,000 of us in Kozelsk, including the officers. Our quarters were very cold and cramped, there was no place to sleep. Later on they deported us to Krivoy Rog, and the journey there took six days. They told us that we would work for a while and then they would release us home. We toiled until 15 December, and then we rebelled and refused to work because they had lied to us. We didn't work for seven days and didn't want to eat throughout that time, but it was all to no avail. We had to go to work, because the NKVD men forced us. It was a wretched existence; we got five rubles per day and had to buy food at the canteen, but we could get nothing more than 800 grams of bread and soup with oil, and meat was out of the question as 100 grams of sausage cost three rubles. Our quarters were lousy, the place was so cramped that we had to turn on our other side on command; there were 300 soldiers in the barrack, and the room was 30 meters long and 6 meters wide; we slept on pallets. I worked in an iron ore mine [illegible] 20 to 30.

Medical assistance was poor. When I fell ill on 13 January 1940, they refused to recognize my illness as a legitimate one and to give me treatment, but all the same I couldn't work. I didn't have anything to eat because I couldn't receive any money since I didn't work; my friends gave me some bits and pieces of food for three weeks. Then my illness was finally acknowledged and I was issued a sick leave and received five rubles per day.

We were very badly treated. On 19 May 1940 we were deported from Krivoy Rog to the Polish territories, to the township of Ostra Góra near Przemyśl. I didn't work because I was sick and the commission assigned me to the hospital. I left for the hospital on 26 July and stayed there until 19 September. In the hospital I was guarded, they watched me so that I wouldn't escape. The doctors were Poles and very good specialists; this was in Lwów. On 19 September 1940 they took me from the hospital to a camp in the township of Tuligłowy; I had a leave from work for a month that had been issued to me at the hospital, but they didn't accept it and on the second day they drove me to work. I couldn't work because I was still very weak, so I wasn't able to earn more than 400 grams of bread.

On 23 January 1941 they deported me to Zborów, where I worked at roadworks until 13 May. Then they deported me to the stone quarries in Stanisławów. The work was hard and we had to toil 12 hours a day in two shifts: one at night and the other during the day. I couldn't earn more than 400 grams of bread. Medical assistance was poor.

After the outbreak of the war, that is on 27 June 1941, they marched us away. They drove us like cattle; those who stumbled and fell were immediately finished off. At the station in Dolina near Stanisławów they loaded us into wagons, 80 people to each 18-ton wagon, and transported us for 24 days to Starobelsk. They gave us one bucket of soup per 80 people a day, so we all looked like corpses. In Starobelsk we received 400 grams of bread and soup twice a day. After the signing of the Polish-Soviet agreement we received 700 grams of bread.

On 26 August Colonel Wiśniowski came and announced to us that we were no longer prisoners, but soldiers of the Polish Army. And that's what I am to this present day.

Collection of the Hoover Institution Library & Archives at the disposal of the Central Archives of Modern Records, Władysław Anders Collection. Reports, 800/1/0/-/48, account no. 2339.

ALEKSANDER JANCEWICZ

Personal data (name, surname, rank, age, occupation and marital status):
Aleksander Jancewicz, corporal, 39 years old, concrete worker, married.

Date and circumstances of arrest:

Taken into Soviet custody on 19 September 1939 in Równe.

Name of the camp, prison or forced labor site:

Deported to Moscow and then to Pavlishchev Bor.

Description of the camp or prison (grounds, buildings, housing conditions, hygiene):

Bricked barracks, 120 people living in a room meant for 30 people (sleeping one on top of another). Pine forests surrounded the area. The barracks were dirty, full of lice and bugs. There wasn't a single bath for three months.

Social composition of POWs, prisoners, exiles (nationality, type of crimes, intellectual and moral standing, mutual relations, etc.):

There were solely POWs in the camp, including one barrack for officers. Mutual relations were very good. Moral standing was rather high.

Life in the camp or prison (daily routine, working conditions, quotas, wages, food, clothes, social and cultural life, etc.):

A roll-call took place at the square at 6.00 a.m., then breakfast (only those who forced their way actually received it – there weren't enough cauldrons). After breakfast, we'd just swat lice. Dinner was either at 11.00 p.m., or not at all. Not only was there a shortage of food, but also a shortage of water. We were wearing our military clothes. There was no cultural entertainment.

Attitude of the NKVD towards Poles (interrogation methods, torture and other forms of punishment, communist propaganda, information about Poland, etc.):

Mortality rate was high; a few people were actually shot.

Medical assistance, hospitals, mortality rate (provide the names of the deceased):

Health care was done by our own means; we used Soviet medicines.

Was it at all possible to get in contact with one's home country and family?

I didn't have any contact with my family in that camp.

In November 1939, I was deported to Krivoy Rog to work in the "Gigant" mine. We lived in clean barracks, there were medical inspections, and we had our underwear laundered. Food rations were reasonable. The Soviets offered us to work as free men, but we turned that proposal down. A strike broke out – subsequently, we had a break from work. The NKVD forced us to use the canteen to force us to work, but only some left to do so. Those who didn't want to work were taken to the North (including me), and the working ones were sent to camps near Wołyń.

I became ill on the way and stayed in a hospital in Knyazhpogost for a month. Wieczorek died in that hospital. I was taken from the hospital to the 12th settlement, 2nd unit, where I stayed for a month. Then I was sent to the 19th settlement (but was unable to work). I didn't work. On 1 October 1940, I escaped the camp along with Captain Mendel. Platoon-leader Czerwiński and Corporal Odyniec were with us. We walked through taiga for 19 days. Corporal Odyniec, who went off to get food, turned us in to the gendarmes' hands. Unwilling to be placed in a work camp again, we ran away. I was wounded in the left leg (knee) while escaping. Platoon-leader Czerwiński – who was ill – could not run, and Captain Mendel didn't want to leave me wounded, despite an opportunity to escape. I was put in the hospital, and the others were placed in a punishment cell. I was placed in a camp in Koryazhma. Another attempt to escape failed and I was moved to a camp in Aykino. Our yet another escape attempt also failed, because a Ukrainian from our area exposed us. I was assigned to work in a carpentry workshop, and then to the 9th settlement, but I wasn't admitted there because the entry in my file mentioned three escape attempts.

Then I was taken to a trial in court, but my case wasn't looked into. I was deported to the 41st settlement, 2nd unit, and worked in the forests there until May 1941.

Before the amnesty, I was taken to the prison in Knyazhpogost and received my sentence there: three years. I was sent to the 4th penal colony of Pechora. Before I was released, I had spent the whole time in a punishment cell.

When were you released and how did you manage to join the Polish Army?

I was released from the camp on 3 September 1941. I then left for Totskoye to join the Polish Army. I was assigned to the 6th Light Artillery Regiment.

Collection of the Hoover Institution Library & Archives at the disposal of the Central Archives of Modern Records, Władysław Anders Collection. Reports, 800/1/0/-/47, account no. 577.

WACŁAW JANKOWSKI

I laid down my arms at 1.30 p.m. on 25 September 1939 at Unii Lubelskiej Street in Brześć on the Bug River. The rest of my unit did the same, surrendering all kinds of weapons. After disarming us, the Bolshevik authorities told all the privates (except for the officers) who lived near Brześć to return home and ordered the others – who lived further afield – to march towards the train station. We were detained upon arrival. We were surrounded by guards and not permitted to leave.

We waited there for a freight train. We were all searched in the meantime and then loaded 70 to a wagon and the train set off towards Baranowicze. I must stress that the wagons were screwed shut after we were loaded on. Some people tore open or broke the windows and jumped out of the train while it was moving. The Bolshevik bullies shot at them like dogs from the breaches in the wagons. I saw through a break in the wagon how they killed two and wounded another near Baranowicze. They led us as if to our execution all the way to the station in Negoreloe where we were separated into groups according to our rank and then subject to another search. Next, we were hounded back into the wagons and the train continued its journey. I must point out that we were given no food until we finally received one roll of bread to share between ten people, two pieces of sugar, a tiny piece of soap, some tobacco and two buckets of cold water at a small station on the way. We reached Minsk in the evening and were given dinner: thin soup (from cabbage) with no bread. We travelled in an unknown direction until we stopped in Bryansk where we also received a thin soup (pea) and no bread in the evening. We continued like that until we reached a station near Moscow. I do not remember its name. They unloaded us and marched us 35 kilometers along "Napoleon's road" to the camp in Pavlishchev Bor and then transferred us to Yukhnovo. Some people were losing their strength on the way and they were beaten with rifle butts and had the dogs set on them whenever they lagged behind.

We reached the camp in which 12,800 people were gathered, including: a general, staff officers, junior officers, police commissioners and privates of all arms. They stuffed us like sardines in a can into various buildings: stone ones, wooden ones and stables. We faced difficult moments of misery in the camp. Once a day we were given thin soup cooked on meat and maybe 200 grams of almost raw bread. Illnesses like dysentery and typhoid fever began to run rife. A lot of people died and the Bolsheviks carried them away at night, burying the swaddled bodies without our help. Once, they pulled one out from beneath the bunk – it had been lying there for three days. The soldiers retrieved nearly rotten cattle offal from the refuse and cooked it out of hunger in order to save themselves from the specter of death. Our names were read out every day and we were warned: whoever has a weapon should give it up, otherwise he will be sentenced to death if it is found. On – I think – 26 October 1939, we were summoned according to our prisoner numbers.

They let us through the gate where the searches were still ongoing and then drove us under escort, LMGs ahead, dogs behind, to a train station. We were loaded and transported to the steel foundry in Krivoy Rog. Several wagons were unloaded and the remained travelled on in an unknown direction.

Hard labor, still under guard, began in the factory and the sewage system. A few days later we left for the "Bolshevik" mine. The journey was more than 26 kilometers, we marched at night and in heavy rain; we were soaked to the skin when we arrived. In the morning, we were all taken for various work in the mine, regardless of age (and without medical examinations), after being told those who worked would receive food. Those who did nothing would receive 100 grams of bread and three portions of soup – the same applied to those who were unable to work because of illness. There were searches every few days in the barracks, and suspects were summoned for various interrogations.

Christmas came round. We organized a joint Christmas Eve on 24 December 1939 – some specially chosen people would break bread instead of a wafer and we sang carols. The Bolshevik authorities were informed of this by one Feliks Masłowski, who had previously said he came from Baranowicze. The political commissars came in the evening, rounded up everyone in building No. 24 (brick) and summoned me from the ranks. It was announced that I was arrested for being the leader of a conspiracy – an assassination attempt on the Soviet authorities – and for agitation. I was arrested and put in custody, where I found my colleagues in a tiny cell: Platoon-leader Gurczak, Platoon-leader Stefan Boroś and Officer Cadet Wereszczakow. That is how we all spent Christmas and New Year. We were called from the cell alternately, mostly at night, for questioning carried out by the political commissars and investigating judges. During the interrogation, we were threatened with being taken away to the "white bears" and rewards were offered – [e.g.] I was offered 500 rubles and the freedom to write home for revealing the officers and priests among us. I note, however, that I myself was not beaten during the Bolshevik interrogation, but others were. I was released on 5 January 1940 on the condition that I remain prepared for further questioning at any moment. On 20 May 1940, they carried out a thorough search, taking razors, knives, blades, spoons and sharp tools, and drove us far to the north like wild cattle. After arriving in Kotlas, they unloaded us and fed us soup and one bread roll for six people (on the way, four times they gave one bread roll for ten people, one dried fish, two pieces of sugar, a packet of tobacco and a bucket of cold water). It was in Kotlas that I happened to see how the dead from the other transports were being stored in the cemetery without coffins in a grave maybe a quarter of a meter deep. I saw half the last corpse over the top. We were pushed further on to Urdoma, camp No. 55, and then to Tyva – work began on the construction of the Kotlas–Arkhangelsk railway line: tearing up tree trunks, trimming trees, leveling the marshes wetlands, clearing stony hills (150–250 meters high), removing earth in wheelbarrows up mounds up to 130 meters, in temperatures of up to minus 60. They continued to work us to camp 54 and then to the Shiyes train station near Mezhog. The labor was hard, the ground was cold and food was provided according to the standard of work. It was very difficult even for the strongest to meet the set quotas, which is why a lot of our compatriots remained in the Far North. I remember the names of some: a certain Sroka, a young boy, was all swollen and yet he was driven to work – he could not hold out and died in the hospital of prisoner camp No. 55 in Urdoma; and Platoon-leader Stefan Boroś (resident of Hajnówka, Białystok Voivodeship before 1 September 1939), whom they drove to exhaustion and who died of tuberculosis in the aforementioned hospital. I was considered by a medical commission to be unable to work as a result of exhaustion (leg and tooth illnesses, scurvy). I could barely even walk with a cane and yet the head of the camp ordered me to boil water day and night, because the work was being carried out in two shifts during the midnight sun. I had a great help from my friends who took their time to fell and tear up trees and cut wood.

And so the days went by until we received the news that we would be leaving. And leave we did – we were released and transported to the camp in Vyazniki. After a parade of POWs organized by Colonel Nikodem Sulik[-Sarnowski], I joined the Polish Army.

Encampment, 13 March 1943

Collection of the Hoover Institution Library & Archives at the disposal of the Central Archives of Modern Records, Władysław Anders Collection. Reports, 800/1/0/-/46, account no. 360.

CZESŁAW KOŚCIELNY

Personal data (name, surname, rank, age, occupation and marital status):
Czesław Kościelny, second lieutenant, 37 years old, elementary school teacher, unmarried.

Date and circumstances of arrest:

On 17 September 1939 I was captured by the Bolsheviks in Tarnopol.

Name of the camp, prison or forced labor site:

a) Krivoy Rog, "Szylman's Mineshaft" and "Kaganowicz's Mineshaft";
b) The Komi Autonomous Soviet Socialist Republic – the 28th Colony, located 60 kilometers west of Kozhva (Pechora).

Description of the camp or prison (grounds, buildings, housing conditions, hygiene):

a) cramped barracks for workers, e.g. 40 people in a room 5 by 6 meters. Mud around the barracks was up to our ankles, the barracks were not well heated during winter, we were responsible for keeping them in order. Sanitary conditions were terrible, there was plenty of lice. We would hand over underwear for washing in private and in secret. We had to beg to be allowed to bathe.
b) taiga – tents. About 200 people lived in each tent. We sometimes had to sleep in the open air for several weeks. We would build shelters on our own, for example by the Ukhta River (so-called point 24). This is how we created "settlements" which we named Moscow, Leningrad etc. The Bolsheviks, the so-called *Vokhra* [armed guard], were furious when they found out about it. Housing conditions improved later, for it was we ourselves who built the barracks. Those in the 28th Colony were designed by our builder and built in accordance with his plans. After the barracks were finished, various Bolshevik commissions came by and could not believe how they turned out ("What a crafty bunch of Poles"). At first, sanitary conditions were terrible – lice were everywhere. Later, when the barracks and washroom were complete, hygiene was at a decent level. We changed our underwear once a week.

Social composition of POWs, prisoners, exiles (nationality, type of crimes, intellectual and moral standing, mutual relations, etc.):

a) Poles, Belarusians, and Ukrainians – the latter were in the majority. Many Poles changed their nationality, because the Bolsheviks said that Belarusians and Ukrainians would be released from the camp. In some cases the NKVD men talked people into changing their nationality. The intellectual level of the prisoners of war was very low. Only several out of about 800 had a secondary or university education. Moral standing – high. Only a couple of individuals served the Bolshevik cause. Others kept them at arm's length. This is why protests and hunger strikes went well. Despite their efforts, the Bolsheviks weren't able to identify the leaders of these operations. In order to scare us, they transported several people from our camp to another one, claiming that they would be prosecuted, while others would be sent to Siberia.
b) mutual relations between the Poles and Belarusians deteriorated – they distrusted each other and stuck to their own groups; then the Bolsheviks mixed them together – one could not plot against another, for there were informers among the prisoners.

Life in the camp or prison (daily routine, working conditions, quotas, wages, food, clothes, social and cultural life, etc.):

a) there were three shifts in the mine: the 1st from 7.00 a.m. to 3.00 p.m., 2nd from 3.00 p.m. to 11.00 p.m., and 3rd from 11.00 p.m. to 7.00 a.m. Everyone worked each shift for three days. Working conditions were difficult. A doctor segregated people based on what kind of work they were fit for. We were provided with mining clothes for work. These were often wet, because in some parts of the mine one had to go through water. We were given no other kind of clothing. The food was lousy, mostly without meat. No one met the quotas. We didn't want to accept money. Such was the situation from 15 October to 1 December 1939. Then we organized a strike which lasted nearly two months. The Bolsheviks tried to convince us to sign their so-called *dogovor* [a contract], but they failed. We were visited by various commissions and subjected to interrogations. They used delicate terms: "You must forget Poland", "Poland will exist, but only as a Soviet state" – and then they would insult President Mościcki and Marshal Piłsudski. The talks and interrogations did not succeed. They started putting people in punishment cells. I witnessed one half dead prisoner of war being carried outside after 20 days spent in the punishment cell (in the winter). It was impossible to even think about social and cultural life – the fenced-off barracks were separated so that we couldn't communicate with one another. We communicated in the toilet. The Bolsheviks organized assemblies of sorts, during which they praised their authorities – the speakers were booed. On one occasion prisoners started throwing shoes at their heads.

b) the quota and *payok* of bread prevailed.

Attitude of the NKVD towards Poles (interrogation methods, torture and other forms of punishment, communist propaganda, information about Poland, etc.):

Evident from the previous points.

Medical assistance, hospitals, mortality rate (provide the names of the deceased):

a) there was some medical care, but doctors would send the sick to work.
b) the prisoner-doctors did a lot to improve the POWs' health. For instance, no death occurred in the 28th Colony.

Was it at all possible to get in contact with one's home country and family?

We were allowed to send one letter a month. I received six postcards from the home country, sent by family and friends. We were not allowed to read newspapers. We communicated in an informal way.

When were you released and how did you manage to join the Polish Army?

On 24 August 1941 I was released from the camp in Talitsy, near Ivanovo, and in this camp I joined the Polish Army on 25 August. I handed my application for the Polish Army to Col. Sulik-Sarnowski.

Comments:

If the need should arise, I can provide some details in addition to the points discussed in the questionnaire.

Encampment, 16 February 1943

Collection of the Hoover Institution Library & Archives at the disposal of the Central Archives of Modern Records, Władysław Anders Collection. Reports, 800/1/0/-/47, account no. 586.

MOWKA MILIKOWSKI

Mowka Milikowski, born in 1911, Polish citizen, Jewish, manual worker, married.

I was detained on 24 September 1939 in Kowel.

We were put to hard work in the POW camp. The set quota was so high that it was impossible to meet, which resulted in very nasty consequences, namely, such a minimal food ration that people simply could not stand on their feet due to hunger. After two weeks, along with others, I was transported to Krivoy Rog, where we mined iron ore.

By working eight hours a day, I was able to earn 700–800 rubles a month, which was enough for me to eat, and even occasionally send money to my wife, who lived in Wołkowysk at the time. I received letters from my wife.

The housing conditions were good, we lived in wooden barracks. There was agreement and harmony among us, we helped each other, and when the Russians guarding us would tell us that there would be no Poland and that we would never return to our homeland, we all – be it a Belarusian, Pole, Ukrainian or Jew – refuted it, laughed in their faces, and awaited the moment of liberation.

We had good medical care.

I had stayed in eight camps before the amnesty. The hardest moments were those when I was transported from camp to camp. We often went on foot for several days or for more than a week with only a small piece of bread. The escorting soldiers were so inhumane that they were capable of kicking, beating, and slandering people just because a fainting person had drunk some water handed to him by a merciful woman.

I was released at the end of August 1941 in Starobelsk, where I immediately joined the Polish Army, 6th Division.

Collection of the Hoover Institution Library & Archives at the disposal of the Central Archives of Modern Records, Władysław Anders Collection. Reports, 800/1/0/-/48, account no. 2332.

MIKOŁAJ CZAJKOWSKI

Mikołaj Czajkowski, rifleman, 21 years old, Polish.

I was disarmed by the Soviets on 17 September in the town of Borszczów, in the square by the barracks, among a group of 15 infantrymen and three senior non-commissioned officers: Cadet Sergeant Jabłoński, Sergeant Świtajło, and Sergeant Głogowiec, the company head. We were immediately marched 30 kilometers into Russian territory, to Kamenets-Podolskyi. We had only carrots to eat, and only when someone was clever enough to get them at that, and boiled water. We spent three days there, and when more people were gathered, we were loaded onto train cars. Our transport comprised some 800 people, locked inside sealed cars without water, and with two kilograms of bread per five people a day. The journey to Tiotkino lasted eight days. We were placed in some summer barracks, although the cold had already settled in. The barracks were dirty, cold, and shabby, and we didn't receive any medical assistance. We had to survive three weeks in such conditions. On 25 October we were loaded onto a train at the Tiotkino station, and the transport left for Krivoy Rog. We travelled for ten days in sealed cars and received food only once a day, just to ensure that we wouldn't die.

In Krivoy Rog I worked in an iron mine. The daily quota was as follows: 18 tons had to be brought to the wagons, for which we were paid 5 rubles, and we had to survive the whole day on that. It was like this until 10 May. On 20 May we were again loaded onto cars and transported to Ostra Góra in Poland. I worked at road construction there. On 20 April 1941 I was taken to Czerlany, to an airfield. There were 1,500 people in that labor camp, and I worked there until 21 June 1941, that is, until the outbreak of the Soviet-German War. On 22 June we were marched on foot from Czerlany to Volochysk; the whole camp – 1,500 people – marched day and night, suffering from hunger. In Volochysk we were loaded onto a train and spent the next seven days in sealed cars, 80 people in an 18-ton car. We suffered terrible hunger; it was a deadly journey. We were taken to Starobelsk. 10,000 people were placed in the labor camp there. We weren't forced to work, but we also didn't receive any food, only water. We were starving until 10 August 1941.

On 26 August 1941 I joined the Polish Army.

Collection of the Hoover Institution Library & Archives at the disposal of the Central Archives of Modern Records, Władysław Anders Collection. Reports, 800/1/0/-/48, account no. 2292.

JÓZEF LIS

Personal data:

Testimony of Józef Lis, bombardier, II/5LAR platoon staff [2nd Division, 5th Light Artillery Regiment].

Name of the camp:

Labor camp in Olenovka, approximately 30 kilometers from Stalingrad (Donbas) [Donetsk, formerly Stalino], formed from several divisions.

Social composition of POWs:

Privates, police, Border Guards.

Number of prisoners:

960 per division.

Period of the camp's existence:

From 30 October 1939 to 22 May 1940, when everyone was transferred to the Komi ASSR.

Description of the camp:

The camp was located by a river in the mountains. Muddy terrain in autumn. Single-story buildings made of stone. The prisoners slept in beds, eight to a room. Food fairly decent during the initial period: 1 kilogram of bread, two-course dinner. The prisoners used a cafeteria which was kept clean.

Life in the camp:

The labor was very difficult, in quarries (quota: four people had eight hours to load a 60-ton wagon). The prisoners were so exhausted and weak after a few months that they could no longer work. That is when the persecutions and punishments began. Prisoners were arrested and thrown into a punishment cell where they were starved, or they were kept outside in the snow all day or subjected to interrogation. There was solidarity between the prisoners, who fought for better conditions. The orders to strike affected the whole Donbas area (around 6,000 Polish POWs). No cultural life.

Attitude of the NKVD towards Poles:

Very detailed inspections which included the theft of valuable items and religious iconography. Persecution in the case of refusal or inability to work. Highly developed propaganda campaign concerning the entirety of state and social life (agitators held propaganda lectures on a daily basis).

Deceased in the camp:

One prisoner was shot (I do not remember his name).

Collection of the Hoover Institution Library & Archives at the disposal of the Central Archives of Modern Records, Władysław Anders Collection. Reports, 800/1/0/-/46, account no. 16.

ELIASZ MACHNACZ

Eliasz Machnacz, rifleman, born in 1900, civilian occupation: farmer. Address in Poland: the commune and village of Dokudowo, Lida District, post office in Dokudowo.

I was taken prisoner by the Russians on 18 September 1939 together with my entire unit (military supply column no. 333) in Nowojelnia, district and voivodeship of Nowogródek.

On the evening of the same day we were sent to Nowogródek; we stayed there for one day and were then sent to Stołpce, where we arrived after two days of marching with nothing to eat. Two people who collapsed during the march due to exhaustion and hunger were shot. I don't remember their surnames.

In Stołpce, where we stopped for two days, we once got buckwheat soup, without bread. After these two days we were loaded onto a train and sent to a POW camp in Kozelsk. During the journey, which took some six days, each of us received 400 grams of bread, some salty fish and some water each day.

When we arrived in Kozelsk, the officers and policemen were put aside and placed together in separate barracks, which were fenced off with barbed wire and more carefully guarded than ours; we were forbidden to have any contact with them.

The living conditions in Kozelsk were very hard. The barracks were cramped, and lice and bugs pestered us all the time. Food was also scarce, as the place was severely overcrowded. Two times a day we received soup and 800 grams of bread, which resembled grey mud. In the morning we got our soup at about 10.00 a.m., and the evening ration was issued at about midnight. During our three-week stay in Kozelsk, almost everyone was summoned some 10 times for various investigations. They asked us about our occupation, economic position, membership in various social organizations etc. After these investigations and interrogations, a few privates were sent to the camp for officers and policemen.

After three weeks in Kozelsk, we – the privates – were transported for work in ore mines in Krivoy Rog. In the barrack in which I lived, one half was occupied by 500 of our people, POWs. Out of 500 people, 400 worked underground in ore mines. I spent six months in Krivoy Rog. Throughout this period, trains with ore were regularly sent to Vinnytsia, usually two trains per day.

Remuneration for work depended on the percentage of the work quota that one met. During the first month we received food regardless of our work efficiency, but later food depended on meeting the work quota. This led our group to stage a strike, which lasted for about two weeks. During the strike, people were summoned individually and given money in order to induce them to end the strike. Some took the money but did nothing to break the strike, but since we were destitute, after two weeks we had to accept the imposed conditions and resume work.

The strike was followed with arrests, which took place gradually: every day, a few people were arrested and placed in separate barracks, where they stayed under heavy guard and didn't go to work.

Some time later we were deported to the north, to the vicinity of Vorkuta, where the majority of us were forced to build roads and the railway. The last stage of our journey to Vorkuta was a two-week march, during which we often received food once every three days, and it was only moldy bread. During the first month of my stay near Vorkuta, we received only 300 grams of bread per day. There wasn't any salt, and the drinking water was unhealthy, as it was muddy.

I spent 13 months in the vicinity of Vorkuta. As for cases of death that are known to me, eight people died in my group – most of them because of diarrhea.

In close vicinity of our camp, there was another camp for civilian exiles from Poland (who were sent for forced labor in [illegible]). The mortality rate in that camp was very high, and almost each day two, three or four corpses were taken out, and they often lay for several hours on the ground in front of our barrack, in plain sight. Platoon-leader Hoszyk (currently in the 5th Infantry Division) was the commandant of my barrack: he harassed the POWs, pulling them by their legs from the pallets and driving them out to work, which was witnessed also by my colleague Jan Kopenich, currently serving with me in the same unit.

We wrote letters to our families, but we were forbidden to write where we were, and as our address we had to give: Moscow, no...

We were released on 17 July 1942 and escorted to Kotlas. There we were handed over to the NKVD, and they sent us to the Polish Army in Vyazniki.

In Kotlas, before we were sent to the Army, we were thoroughly searched. In Vyazniki we were divided according to branches of service and appeared before the draft board, and then we were sent to Tatishchevo, where we were enlisted into the 5th Infantry Division.

Encampment, 9 March 1943

Collection of the Hoover Institution Library & Archives at the disposal of the Central Archives of Modern Records, Władysław Anders Collection. Reports, 800/1/0/-/48, account no. 1748.

WIKTOR KOSTRO

Wiktor Kostro, senior rifleman, born in 1913, farmer, bachelor.

I was taken into captivity on 17 September 1939 along with the entire division and its commander, weapons in hand, in the little town of Dworzec in the Nowogródek region. The Soviet troops immediately forced us to lay down our arms and then took us to the Stołpce station. The name of the company commander was Captain Mac.

On 23 September 1939, they loaded us 80 at a time onto freight carriages and took us to the camp in Kozelsk. The food we received on the journey amounted to 200 grams of bread and a little water, but not every day. The carriages were locked, the windows barricaded, and we were forbidden to talk to one another, something which the convoy really paid attention to.

We arrived at the camp on 28 September 1939 and they put us up in an old Orthodox church. The buildings were brick, there was no light at all; 3,000 of us were gathered and allowed to sleep on the concrete floor, but there was no space left for anyone else and so the other 10,000 had to sleep outdoors. They put the wounded in hospital. The camp guards were very severe with us, especially with the officers. We were all registered after a few days and then the officers and non-commissioned officers were separated from us and fenced in with barbed wire. We riflemen were allowed to move about within the camp but we were not permitted to approach the officers and non-commissioned officers on the other side of the barbed wire. Officers and non-commissioned officers who needed to sort something at the camp office were surrounded by an escort.

Most of the prisoners were Poles and Jews, but there were also Ukrainians and Belarusians. There was no hygiene at all. Social life was good.

Machine guns were set up all around the camp grounds.

Food in the camp amounted to 600 grams of bread and little bit of boiled cabbage, those were the rations we were given every two days. After registration, they took us into a field that was surrounded by machineguns and called out groups according to region of origin. They said the riflemen would go home and that the officers and non-commissioned officers would remain in the camp. There were cases of riflemen handing over the officers who were trying to hide among our ranks. After the separation, we returned to camp. After five weeks in the camp, the began to send transports to Poland. I was directed to the iron ore mine in Krivoy Rog in Ukraine. We travelled in open carriages for two weeks with an escort, we had only a guide. We were convinced that we really were going home; there was plenty of food and we used the military cafeteria at the larger stations.

Upon arrival at the destination, they unloaded us and led us to the cinema. After the cinema, they led us naked to the bathhouse. After bathing in groups, we went to the canteen to have a hearty dinner. The tables were covered with white bread, dinner consisted of three courses. After dinner, they took us down to a two-story brick building for 570 people; the others went to other buildings. They kept telling us that we would rest here a few days, fill out the documents and go home. After a few days, a political commissar came and explained that we had to go to work for a few days, and in the meantime they began to register again, wanting to weed out the officers hiding among us. Once more, some of the riflemen began to hand over the officers who were then escorted to a penal camp. Some riflemen did not want to speak Polish anymore, only Russian, such as rifleman Piotr Oduszko from Zelwa.

Instead of several days of labor, we regularly went to work in the iron ore mine until 6 May 1940. We went there under an escort. The work was very hard, quotas were rarely met over 8 hours of work. Living conditions were quite tolerable; we received 1 kilogram of bread and three two-course meals a day. The monthly salary was 700–800 rubles for good workers. The Stakhanovites received bonuses of [illegible digit]00 rubles.

Medical aid was good, there was also a hospital. There were several fatal accidents during work, but I do not recall the names of the victims.

I maintained contact with home, I was even allowed to transfer money, parcels were forbidden. On 6 May 1940, they tightened the escort and did not send us to work for five days. In the meantime, the NKVD appeared, led us to an area where a thorough search was carried out, and even found hidden weapons. The next day, we were loaded into wagons which were then locked; the windows were barred. They stripped us naked and carried out a thorough search in the wagons. 40 people were placed in each wagon. They drove us deep into Russia instead of home. We stopped at the station in Moscow for 24 hours; they did not let us out of the transport and five NKVD-soldiers stood in front of the door with weapons ready to fire. Food consisted of 600 grams of bread and cold water.

On 16 May 1940, we arrived at the Kotlas station, where they unloaded us from the train, put us onto boats and took us north along the Dvina. We arrived five days later and they unloaded us and led us to a fenced-off area in the woods and told us to build barracks. The next day, some of us went to work on the construction of the railway, and some stayed behind to build the barracks. We did not agree when they wanted to send us to work, so they brought dogs to set on us – they tore at our clothes, so we were forced to go to the construction site, but we did not work. A machine gun was set up by each group. In the evening, we returned to that empty area, where we received a little boiled porridge without fat. The next day, we were taken to our places of work. Some were forced and some refused to work. After returning from work, those who did not work were stripped naked and put away in an isolation cell. The next day, we were forced to work, and we could not meet the quota. In return, we were punished with a foregoing of 300 grams of bread. I worked for a month. Seeing the tragedy around us, I decided to make a run for it; there were four of us:

1) Władysław Szczepko from Białystok,
2) Kazimierz Siennicki, Kostry-Noski village, Masovian District,
3) Bronisław Czaban, Wyliny village, Masovian District,
4) Senior Rifleman Wiktor Kostro.

We crawled under the fence after sundown and, in spite of the powerful spotlights with sentries placed in the corners, retreated into the forest. We headed southwards using a map and compass. We marched through forests for 13 days, eating blueberries and mushrooms.

After 13 days, we reached Kotlas and went to the station on our last legs. We found a freight wagon and hid inside. A thorough search of the train was conducted at the time it was scheduled to leave and we were discovered by the police. We were taken to the police station, where they interrogated us and immediately called the camp we had escaped from to inform them that they had caught the fugitives. After the interrogation, we were loaded onto a ship heading north towards Knyazhpogost and put in an interrogation cell. After the interrogation, which lasted seven months, our sentence was announced: three years. After a few days, we were sent to the Izhma base, where we worked on loading and unloading products. After seven months of work, we were given an amnesty.

I was released on 8 September 1941 and sent to Buzuluk. We were directed to Kogan due to overcrowding, where the Polish mission sent us to the kolkhoz in [illegible], where I stayed for two months before going to Lugovoy, where I joined the ranks of the Polish army.

Collection of the Hoover Institution Library & Archives at the disposal of the Central Archives of Modern Records, Władysław Anders Collection. Reports, 800/1/0/-/46, account no. 178.

THE FATE OF THE INTERNEES IN LITHUANIA AND LATVIA

By the end of September 1939, approximately 14,500 Polish soldiers crossed the borders with Lithuania and Latvia, where they were disarmed and interned. They found themselves in Soviet captivity in 1940, after the Baltic states were incorporated into the USSR.
In the photograph: reception of the officers of the Latvian Naval Forces at the Main Railway Station in Warsaw, July 1933.

Photo. National Digital Archives

ZYGMUNT GLEZNER

Zygmunt Glezner, second lieutenant of the reserve, born on 17 September 1911 in Warsaw, a roadway and construction technician by profession (Polish State Railways), married.

After crossing the border in Zawiasy, I was detained in the internee camp in Palanga and from there to Kalvarija in Lithuania. In June 1940 I was deported to Russia. Forced to endure exceptionally difficult conditions, I and the other internees finally arrived in Kozelsk (USSR).

The camp had been set up only recently and was located some 10 kilometers from the city of the same name, relatively close to a river, the name of which I don't remember [annotation: the Zhizdra River]. The area was more hilly than flat, and sparsely forested – I seem to recollect that only when passing the entrance to the camp did we walk between trees. Obviously, the whole camp was surrounded by a wire fence, with watchtowers at the corners. The buildings had once housed an Orthodox monastery; some were made of brick, and some of wood, however practically all required repairs and were infested with bugs. Only after we fixed them up ourselves, and also constructed bunk beds and repeatedly disinfected the place, did our living conditions become tolerable. There was a pump in close proximity, and this provided us with water for cooking and personal hygiene. Initially, there was only one primitive bath, which we were forced to use to both wash ourselves and do the laundry. Later on, however, we readied a second bath, using it exclusively for washing; the first then functioned as a laundry.

There were some 5,000 internees altogether: officers, officer cadets, privates and policemen. Generally speaking, these were intelligent people of a satisfactory moral caliber (a considerable number of men would go to confession, of course in secret), with relatively strong patriotic feelings; there were a few misfits, but they formed their own, numerically small groups. The largest was the group of the "reds" (that is what they were called), while I also heard of a few Ukrainian and Belarusian nationalists, and some German sympathizers who praised the strength and organization of our age-old enemy. Luckily, there weren't many of them in total – at most 1–2% of the whole camp population. I must add, with considerable sadness, that the majority of the "reds" were officers. Most unfortunately, I don't remember any surnames.

Mutual relations were correct, however conversations on political issues with men from any of the smaller groupings would often lead to a heated exchange of words.

Life in the camp was monotonous, for each day was similar to that before. We would be woken up at around 7.00 a.m. (some got up earlier, while others later) and eat breakfast – groats or herrings, and tea. We would spend the time till dinner reading books, learning foreign languages, playing chess, talking, or just walking about the camp. At around 1.00 p.m. we would be given dinner – usually fluffy or thickly-boiled kasha. Sometimes they gave us fried fish or a piece of meat. Indeed, our detention in the camp can be broken down into "food periods." There was a period when we ate kasha, then there was the "cabbage period", the "mangel-wurzel period", and the "fish period" (the fish would be of various kinds). After dinner we would continue to pass the time, with the difference being that we would sometimes go to the kitchen to peel potatoes or gut fish. Following supper, which comprised tea and bread, we would take a walk. The day ended with a bugle call. Sometimes, if I received a ticket, I would go to the cinema, which was located in the camp, or to a performance that we ourselves had organized. In order to give a complete picture, I must say that we would receive a *payok* containing tobacco, cigarette paper, matches, and sugar mixed with tea. Obviously, the quantities that we were given were small and never lasted until the next ration packets were handed out. In principle, we were not ordered to perform labor, occupying ourselves with maintenance work around the camp and assisting in the kitchen.

Each one of us was examined at least once by NKVD functionaries, and they were very interested in our life stories. In consequence of these examinations, certain number of our colleagues would be taken from the camp to unknown destinations. Thus, the population of our camp melted away, until – after nearly all the officer cadets and policemen were deported to the Kola Peninsula (as I later learned) – only one half or so of us remained. A political commissar was assigned to practically each living block, and his role was to disseminate communist propaganda, sound out our feelings, and generally to report on us to his superiors.

As regards medical care, it was organized more or less effectively. There was a hospital, and it was staffed by our doctors. The number of patients was relatively small, and – thank God – the mortality rate amongst them was low. There were a few instances of suicide, caused in all probability by our recent experiences. Some men lost control of themselves and went mad. Unfortunately, I don't remember the names of the deceased.

Towards the end of November 1940, we were allowed to write letters to our families back home, and also receive return correspondence. Until the outbreak of the Russian-German war, nearly everyone managed to send and get at least a few letters, even though we were permitted to write only once a month. A few days after the aforementioned war started, we were transferred to Gryazovets. Life in this camp followed a rhythm similar to that in Kozelsk. It was situated nearly 15 kilometers from the train station of the same name, by a river (the name of which I don't know) and near a forest, on slightly hilly land. In the main, the buildings were made of wood, but since they were few, we had to construct additional barracks. The food was worse than in Kozelsk, especially towards the end. Because our files accompanied us, only some of us were summoned for interrogation. Nearly all those from the "red" group were taken away in an unknown direction, and I have met not one of them to date. I heard that before their departure they signed declarations to the effect that they would assume Soviet citizenship.

On 29 August 1941, following the conclusion of the Polish-Soviet agreement, I reported to the Polish Army in the USSR and was soon summoned before a committee that had been established in the then former internee camp in Gryazovets. We left this township for Tatishchevo, where I began life as a Polish soldier.

Encampment, 7 March 1943

Collection of the Hoover Institution Library & Archives at the disposal of the Central Archives of Modern Records, Władysław Anders Collection. Reports, 800/1/0/-/48, account no. 2386.

LUDWIK KOWALSKI

Ludwik Kowalski, second lieutenant, 42 years old, accounting inspector, married.

After the Soviet troops took over Lithuania on 10 July, all the internees in the Kalvarija camp were surrounded by guards and taken to the USSR. They led us through the city as if to be tortured, with luggage on our backs, as far as 6 kilometers to the station, allowing us to rest only once, which was tantamount to superhuman effort and exhaustion, given the fact that we had already been nine months imprisoned in Lithuania and had almost nothing to eat. The carts which were supposed to take our luggage were chased away by the Soviets.

At the station we were forced into the wagons, 40 persons in each, with no access to air. Three of the four available windows were boarded up and one of them would be open, but only outside the station. With the temperature reaching 45 degrees, we were practically unable to breathe, which resulted in some of us developing emphysema. We were allowed to relieve ourselves after two days in the field, guarded by furious wolfhounds kept on a leash and a soldier with a rifle at the ready. No wonder that many of us could not fulfil their physiological needs. During the journey we were fed with bread, sugar, canned vegetables and dried fish, but people locked without access to air were saved by the water brought in buckets at designated stations.

After three days we were unloaded in Kozelsk. The average number of officers was about one thousand, plus 800 policemen who arrived later. The records of our predecessors indicated that until 15 May 1940, in this place there had been 5,500 officers – POWs who had been deported from Starobelsk to Kozelsk, and on 15 May 1940 from Kozelsk to an unknown destination. We were given a haircut and bath, and were waiting for the unknown.

Our predecessors left the buildings infested with bedbugs, so we spent long weeks trying to disinfect them. The site and buildings were previously occupied by Orthodox monks. We were to sleep on terribly dirty three-tiered bunks, which were later planed and cleaned. Works were not performed by interned officers, who were used for internal and cleaning activities only. Only policemen worked.

Among all those staying in the camp, morale was good, except for a few people whom we knew by sight and whom we avoided. Everyone strongly believed that it would soon come to an end. Help provided in the form of exchange, although prohibited by the camp authorities, made up for the deficiencies and fulfilled everyday needs. Relations between the inmates were friendly with mutual understanding of cultural needs. We exchanged various Polish books brought secretly from Lithuania. Local libraries were quietly boycotted and the theories of political commissars were ridiculed, however in such a way as to prevent them from using repressive measures. We did not provide them with any reasons or grounds.

We were interrogated on request, and having testified, were told to sign a report. When I was asked which political system was the best, I replied evasively that for every state the existing political system is the best, for example for Russians – the Communist system, for other nations – that chosen thereby; also the United States system is different than the Communist system, and the cultural development and prosperity is better than in other countries. Following this declaration, the political commissar got scared and interrupted the interrogation. Since then I was not interrogated anymore and as generally assumed by my inmates, we were all sentenced in absentia to eight years. After the interrogations, 40 prisoners were sent to the Butyrka prison in Moscow, the rest of us remained in the camp.

Medical assistance: hospitals, although not quite good, were satisfactory, since those remained in the camp were supposed to serve as a living advertisement for the good handling of prisoners, and the authorities used us to cover up the 5,500 of our officers deported in an unknown direction. I don't remember exactly the names of the deceased. I managed to remember that two of them went insane, one hanged himself and two died – among them was Lieutenant Góra.

Meetings and masses were prohibited. They allowed cinema and political review of global situation, which were eagerly attended by the internees, since this was the only way for us to find out what was happening outside the camp.

Information from the country was scarce, since not all letters were delivered. They delivered only those letters which contained tragic news, which they enjoyed, hoping to win the depressed individuals over.

The Germans attacked. The internees were happy to be most probably in the army again. A week after the declaration of war, we were sent from Kozelsk to Gryazovets, this time also in closed wagons, with a gutter to relieve ourselves, and one small window open, but our "guardians" already sent us to the North. On the way a message was delivered to keep us in Gryazovets. General Bohusz-Szyszko arrived in Gryazovets from London, where he was enthusiastically welcomed. At that time, on 24 August 1941, everybody joined the Polish Army to serve commendably.

I joined the 5th Infantry Division in Tatishchevo, later in Jalal-Abad, and on 10 February 1942, I was appointed the food officer in the Karasuu Artillery Training Center. Working conditions were terrible, we had to fight for everything that was needed for the army – horses, hay, equipment, food, water and fuel. There was nothing. Keeping books and personnel training, food and material assistance to civilian refugees – given poor health and exhaustion – required superhuman effort and persistence to avoid being affected by the wide-spread diseases, such as epidemic typhus, typhoid fever, dysentery, scurvy, night-blindness, malaria, pappataci fever, etc. It was then when I became convinced of my own strength, as I managed not to give up and fall ill, did not stop working for the army, military academy, testing grounds, where everything had to be provided on time. The course ended. The school left the encampment on 14 August 1942; I was appointed to be part of the liquidation committee, where in two weeks of painstaking and hard work we finished what we had initially set up. With the liquidation material, I went together with Major to Yangiyul, where we announced the completed liquidation.

There, I met a Polish delegate who had a list signed by the NKVD, allowing Poles to leave his district, but at the last moment the Soviet authorities refused to send Polish refugees, explaining that there were no wagons available. The army command intervened in Tashkent, however with no effect. The Polish delegate was beaten by local dregs of society, and the Polish community delivered thereby was arrested. I served as an inspection officer and at the last moment a poor woman came and said: "I sold everything, ruined myself, I want to go, and you are leaving and abandoning us to die." Her belongings were at the station and I told her to go back there, but she – instead of going to Bukhara, which was the destination intended for the rest of people – went further at her own risk with her family (husband, son and daughter) to Ashgabat, which she left later. In Ashgabat, everybody was surprised that so few refugees arrived. In Yangiyul and Tashkent, the provided contingent of wagons and [illegible] was purposefully so small, in order for the largest possible number of Poles to remain in Russia. Those who were brave, went straight to Ashgabat and although they were not included in the general list, were able to get outside the borders, as the cars had to be completely filled. The Soviet authorities did not tendentiously appoint Mr. Jubok [?], the delegate remained in Yangiyul, who had military storages of the departed army, to have an excuse to arrest him, take the food intended for the civilians, give it to their own army, and to chase people away. We received these messages from Tehran, from the rest of the people who arrived.

I went back from Tehran to my own unit, where I continue to serve as a food officer.

Collection of the Hoover Institution Library & Archives at the disposal of the Central Archives of Modern Records, Anders Collection. Reports, 800/1/0/-/46, account no. 104.

LUDWIK LATAWIEC

Ludwik Latawiec, sergeant major, born in 1897, sergeant of the State Police, commandant of the police station in Żyrowicze, Słonim District, Nowogródek Voivodeship, married; 104th Transport Company [illegible].

On 23 September 1939, I crossed the Lithuanian border, where I was interned in Ukmergė. On 12 July 1940, following the occupation of Lithuania by the Soviet army, we were deported to Kozelsk (approximately 160 kilometers south of Moscow). The conditions of our transport from Lithuania to Kozelsk were very difficult, we were treated like criminals. After the Lithuanian authorities picked us up in Lithuania, we were subjected to a body search, during which our personal belongings were stolen. They took my razor, penknife, electric torch, woolen gloves and a few other small things that were never returned to me. On the way to Russia, the wagon was checked several times at night, and its walls and roof were tapped with a hammer at every station. In each wagon intended for 40 people, there were 60 of us. The doors were locked, and there was only a small gap through which you could barely move your hand. During the transport, we were fed once a day. Due to the lack of water and air people in the wagon would pass out.

After the arrival in Kozelsk, we were locked in a camp (former Orthodox monastery), where the food and hygienic conditions were tolerable, because we renovated the ruined monastery a few months later. The camp consisted of: 900 officers, 1,400 non-commissioned officers of the police, gendarmerie, Border Guard and Border Protection Corps. The number of policemen amounted to approximately 50%. All internees were between 25 and 60 years of age, of a fairly high intellectual standing. Mutual relations were good. We worked on overhauling the former monastery buildings, which had not been renovated for 25 years. We were prohibited from performing cultural work and reading Polish books, which were taken from us. General health was good owing to our doctors who worked in the camp hospital. During our stay in Kozelsk from 15 July 1940 to 15 May 1941, six people died, two committed suicide. I don't remember their names.

In Kozelsk, we were interrogated day and night, in connection with the military and police service in Poland. During the interrogations, the NKVD officers referred to the subjects abusively and insultingly, Lieutenant Petrov was particularly rude and malicious. Both officers and policemen were often deported from Kozelsk to the prison in Moscow. Therefore, some internees were living in a constant state of anxiety. In addition to interrogations, communist propaganda was conducted among them through newspapers and readings.

For the first four months we weren't allowed to write letters. Afterwards they allowed us to write once a month, but when a reply was about to arrive, the letters would not be delivered, however they informed us that such letters had been received. This was aimed at tormenting us and winning over informers.

On 15 May 1941, I was deported (together with 1,800 other people) to Murmansk, where we were imprisoned in a Soviet prisoner camp. The food conditions were similar to those in Kozelsk, since we were still considered internees.

On 4 June 1941, I was arrested together with Senior Sergeant Major Wacław Rytwiński, Sergeant Major Antoni Drozdowicz, Michał Miernicki, Mieleniewski, Fuks and Brzozowski, and imprisoned in the NKVD prison in Murmansk. Hygienic conditions were terrible. The cell was damp, full of mold and infested with a multitude of bedbugs: we removed them by hands. Rats were circulating in the cell in herds of 30. Meals: watery soup and 300 grams of bread twice a day.

On 13 June [1941], we were transported to the NKVD "Shpalerka" prison in Leningrad. We were imprisoned (seven people) in two single-cells in the basement. I shared my cell with Sergeant Major Miernicki, Mieleniewski and Fuks from Nowogródek. Contrary to the prison regulations, we were not allowed to go for 15-minute walks or open the small window under the ceiling for 15 minutes a day. After two weeks I developed an eye disease and my legs were swollen due to hunger – food ration consisted of 300 grams of bread and watery soup for dinner and supper – like in Murmansk. Interrogations were not conducted.

On 18 July [1941], seven of us were deported to Tomsk. We were loaded on a wagon transporting Soviet prisoners. During the journey, which lasted three weeks, we were fed every day: 250 grams of bread, 20 grams of raw fish and a quarter liter of unboiled water. They treated us the same as the Soviet criminals accompanying us. In the prison in Leningrad they took our belongings and valuables, approximately 1580 zlotys.

After the arrival in Tomsk, Siberia, on 9 August [1941], I was imprisoned together with Sergeant Major Rytwiński, Drozdowicz, Miernicki, Mieleniewski, Fuks and Brzozowski in a NKVD prison cell intended for 40 people, but already occupied by 100 prisoners. There were 107 people including us, 50% Poles, Ruthenians from Romania, Slovakia and several Soviet citizens. The cell was located above the prison bathhouse and since the bathhouse was heated every day, the temperature in our cell was so high due to the heated floor and overcrowding that we were all sitting undressed. Interrogations were not conducted as all of us were sentenced to 8–15 years of prison for anti-Communist activities (serving in the Polish

Army or office). Nearly everyone suffered from dysentery and was covered with ulcers all over their body. I suffered from scurvy and swelling. Medical assistance was practically non-existent.

Starting from Murmansk, we were not allowed to communicate by mail with our families or home country.

After the amnesty at the end of August 1941, nearly 50% of Poles from this cell died. Several engineers from Warsaw, officers and policemen from the Lwów and Tarnopol voivodeships. According to verbal information from the head of the Tomsk prison, I was sentenced to eight years of prison by a secret Soviet court – *osoboye soveshchaniye*. However, the verdict was not read neither to me nor to other Poles from this cell.

As a result of the amnesty, on 28 August 1941, I was released from prison. On 23 October [1941], I arrived in Buzuluk, from where I was transported to Tashkent and there allocated to the kolkhoz. On 11 February 1942, I was called up into the 9th Infantry Division.

Collection of the Hoover Institution Library & Archives at the disposal of the Central Archives of Modern Records, Władysław Anders Collection. Reports, 800/1/0/-/48, account no. 1735.

BOHDAN ŚWIĘCICKI

Bohdan Święcicki, captain, born in 1893, regular army officer.

Deported on 11 July 1940 from the internment camp in Kalvarija, Lithuania, to Kozelsk.

Camp site – destroyed former monastery garden. POWs located partially in chapels and Orthodox churches, partially in former residential buildings. Three-tiered bunks made of raw, rough wood. Bedding – jute mattresses and cotton blankets. Allocation of straw for one hundred people – three bales of 50 kilograms. The straw was wet and mostly rotten.

Prisoners: officers, officer cadets, gendarmerie and police. Moral standing generally high. Mutual relations based on solidarity.

Food poor, although sufficient. After the POWs took over the kitchens and administration, the quality and quantity of food improved significantly.

Officers were not required to work; they worked voluntarily in the kitchen, chopped wood, etc. On weekdays, the gendarmerie and policemen assigned about 50% of prisoners for administrative works. The attitude of privates towards officers generally good, based on trust.

Medical assistance was provided by our doctors working very devotedly, in good facilities, however due to being supervised by semi-skilled Soviet doctors and the lack of necessary medicines, they could not always perform their tasks. From the three-month stay I remember three prisoners who went insane and two who died.

Bathhouse – untidy and primitive facility. Baths – irregular, but there were no lice. On the other hand, there was a plague of bedbugs.

The attitude of NKVD authorities and guards – indelicately proprietorial. Interrogation methods very tiring and exhausting, but I haven't heard of anyone being beaten. Propaganda institutions to be obligatorily attended: the communist club and cinema which many of us did not visit. The foolish propaganda, unadopted to the level of listeners, had often the opposite effect. Untrue information about life in the country was provided too naively.

In October, we were allowed to correspond with our home country, but I don't know in which form, as on 11 October 1940, I was deported together with 21 officers to the Butyrka prison in Moscow, where the level of housing conditions, hygiene, food and medical assistance was high. The prison regime was arduous and strict, however I did not experience major excesses or lawlessness. The personnel teased us under their rights and regulations, e.g. when I suffered from severe bladder neurosis, they would not let me out two to three hours, explaining that the closet was occupied (used by approx. 40 people). Interrogations were exhausting and lengthy, with attempted blackmailing, intimidating, promises, etc. Life and all activities were carried out at night. After three months, they ordered us to write to our home country. The content of letters and surnames were used later during interrogations. I sent several letters, but received only one postcard and part of one letter in reply.

In April 1941, we were transported to the isolated camp in Putyvl′, were the living conditions were quite satisfactory. In general, we were treated appropriately. However, they announced that they would never unite us with our friends, as in the prison we had talked about our attitude towards Germans, the alleged war with Germans, etc.

On 15 June 1941, I was transported, together with the remaining isolated POWs, to the isolated camp in Gryazovets. The conditions were primitive; however we were able to provide our own internal administration, which allowed for a generally tolerable living. After the announcement of the Polish-Bolshevik agreement, we joined the main camp in Gryazovets, where the living conditions were difficult as a result of the administration of Bolshevik, thieves from the Świętokrzyskie prison and, unfortunately, those rejected from our army.

As a result of the agreement, the said regime softened considerably, although until the last day, a dozen or so people were called to investigations and subjected to propaganda every day.

On 25 August 1941, we registered as soldiers of the Polish Armed Forces and on 2 September 1941 went to the designated forming locations.

Encampment, 28 February 1943

Collection of the Hoover Institution Library & Archives at the disposal of the Central Archives of Modern Records, Władysław Anders Collection. Reports, 800/1/0/-/46, account no. 200.

BOLESŁAW BIŃCZAK

Personal data (name, surname, rank, age, occupation and marital status):
Bolesław Bińczak, lieutenant, 34 years old, teacher, married.

Date and circumstances of arrest:

On 10 July 1940 I was deported from the internment camp in Kalvarija (Lithuania).

Name of the camp, prison or forced labor site:

Camps in Kozelsk and Gryazovets.

Description of the camp or prison (grounds, buildings, housing conditions, hygiene):

Former monastery buildings – generally warm, dark, cramped and damp (police?). The internees killed many bugs. We had baths often enough.

Social composition of POWs, prisoners, exiles (nationality, type of crimes, intellectual and moral standing, mutual relations, etc.):

Up to 1,000 officers, 1,400 non-commissioned officers and police officers, 200 gendarmes and approx. 200 civilians. Poles, Jews.

Life in the camp or prison (daily routine, working conditions, quotas, wages, food, clothes, social and cultural life, etc.):

We were counted twice a day, in the morning and in the evening. Wake-up was at 6.00 a.m., curfew at 10.30 p.m. Food twice a day, boiled water in the evening. The food which we received from July to November 1940 was bearable – a lot of herrings, which we couldn't eat in the summer; from November 1940 to March 1941 the food was worse – we had beetroot soup five times a week. We received 800 grams of bread. We ate the same kind of groats for months. As for clothes, they were issued mainly to those who worked in the bathhouse or kitchen, to pavers, carpenters, etc.

The work was compulsory for the privates and voluntary for the officers – in the kitchen, bathhouse, or carpenter's workshop. From May 1941 on, the officers also had to perform some compulsory labor. The cooks and shoemakers received payment; tailors and physical laborers received better food, and the tailors were additionally paid – but I don't know how much. Officers up to the rank of captain cleaned potatoes and fish for their own use in the kitchen.

Social life was limited to our own circles.

The groups of communists in particular wards had a negative effect on developing close relations.

Polish books – few. Bolshevik books, both in Polish and Russian – quite numerous. We had rather a lot of newspapers (Russian only). Cinema, lectures – all about communism, three foreign movies.

Attitude of the NKVD towards Poles (interrogation methods, torture and other forms of punishment, communist propaganda, information about Poland, etc.):

Interrogations during the day – or more often at night – lasted for three to four or six hours. Officers from the 2nd Department, policemen, political and social activists were very often interrogated, and virtually everyone was interrogated at least two or three times. We were threatened with deportation to Solovki, imprisonment of our families, execution by shooting, etc.

Propaganda: cinema, books, newspapers, lectures delivered by political commissars – the latter we barely listened to, as they were mainly almost illiterate ignoramuses whom we laughed at. They claimed that Poland would never be reborn. Our Commander-in-Chief and the Polish authorities were mocked. Communist Poland was propagated.

Medical assistance, hospitals, mortality rate (provide the names of the deceased):

Poor medical assistance. Shortage of medicaments. The X-ray machine, repaired by our engineers (like many other things), had to be dismantled. Poles worked as doctors. We were quite often vaccinated. There was a flu epidemic, cases of typhoid fever – two or three. Up to eight people died: Second Lieutenant Dłuski, Cavalry Captain Słapa and others. Five went insane. There were two suicides, but I don't remember the surnames.

Was it at all possible to get in contact with one's home country and family?

We were allowed to write letters for the first time in November 1940. We rarely got any answers, as they were kept for a long time by the NKVD. They were delivered after a long delay, either to the wards or sometimes during interrogations. We could write one letter per month. The internees received food and other packages from the Soviet and German-occupied territories.

When were you released and how did you manage to join the Polish Army?

I was released on 22 or 28 August in Gryazovets. On 29 August I was admitted to the Polish army.

Collection of the Hoover Institution Archives at the disposal of the Archives of Modern Records, Władysław Anders Collection. Reports, 800/1/0/-/48, reference no. 2298.

IGNACY ŻYŁA

[lieutenant]

Name of the camp:

a) Kozelsk,
b) Gryazovets near Vologda.

Social composition of POWs:

a) officers, privates, police,
b) officers, privates, police.

Number of POWs:

a) approx. 2,400,
b) approx. 1,500.

Period of the camp's existence:

a) from July 1940 to June 1941,
b) from May 1940 to August 1941.

Description of the camp:

a) former Orthodox church buildings and buildings of the former administrative office of the Orthodox church,
b) former Orthodox church buildings and buildings of the former administrative office of the Orthodox church.

Life in the camp:

a) arrangement of a choir by Second Lieutenant Edward Kwiatkowski, concerts – by two officers-pianists; facilities organized by Bolshevists for propaganda purposes: the club, cinema, library with communist propaganda books; Polish books (mandatory reading books) were confiscated by Bolshevik authorities. The camp was divided into blocks and companies. Radio messages – Polish translation was provided by Józef Pitneja, Captain of the Polish Army, being constantly exposed to repressions by Soviet camp authorities.

b) division into companies, organization of scientific lectures by Second Lieutenant Felsztyn; the lectures [were] arranged and carried out by the individual officers as lecturers. The large and very good choir organized by Second Lieutenant Edward Kwiatkowski quite often performed Polish compositions regarding soldiers, patriotism, Polish opera compositions or religious compositions. From time to time, artistic shows were performed in the open air by amateur comedians – interned officers.

Attitude of the NKVD towards Poles:

a) agitation by talks in groups in the blocks, long interrogations aimed at intimidating, terrorizing or winning over informers among the internees for the NKVD.
b) long interrogations and organization of intelligence among the internees for the local NKVD.

POWs who stood out either positively or negatively:

Positively: Captain Józef Pitras, Second Lieutenant Dyliga and many others whose surnames I don't remember.

Negatively: Lieutenant Colonel Podwysocki, Captain Kołaczkowski, Major Łoziński, Captain Smolański, Arciszewski with the appropriated rank of Captain, First Lieutenant Eugeniusz Mimikiel and many others whose surnames I don't remember. I heard that Lieutenant Colonel Podwysocki wished to become a German citizen at all costs, and therefore wanted to win the recognition of the Soviet camp authorities and NKVD, being loyal and helpful at the position of the commandant of the camp in Kozelsk. The rest of them were declared followers of the communist propaganda. Point b) – as in a).

Deceased:

0.08 to 0.1%, largely due to mental disorders, one suicide by hanging in Kozelsk: Captain Józef Wasilewski.

Notes:

The short time to complete this questionnaire does not allow for more accurate presentation of the material.

Encampment, 15 December 1942

Collection of the Hoover Institution Library & Archives at the disposal of the Central Archives of Modern Records, Władysław Anders Collection. Reports, 800/1/0/-/46, account no. 64.

WALDEMAR LEY

Personal data (name and surname, rank, age, occupation marital status):
Waldemar Ley, second lieutenant, 27 years old, Regular Army Officer.

Date and circumstances of arrest:

Arrested in June 1940 in Kalvarija (Lithuania). Transported from the internment camp to Kozelsk together with all Polish officers. Traveling conditions very bad! Three buckets of water were provided for a wagon of 50 people per day, three salty, dry fish and some bread. The guard was very strong, and the attitude of the convoy members was very bad (beating with rifle butts, insulting, etc.).

Name of the camp, prison or forced labor site; description of the camp or prison (grounds, buildings, housing conditions, hygiene):

The camp was located in Kozelsk, in an old monastery, and consisted of two large Orthodox churches and 10 wooden buildings, surrounded with a high wall with corner towers. The entire facility was densely fenced in with barbed wire and searchlights. Around the camp there were swamps and a stinking river, which wasn't moving, resulting in mosquito plagues. Housing conditions were terrible. A very small room, intended for four people, accommodated up to thirteen. Several hundred policemen, non-commissioned officers and some of the officers lived in the churches, with three-tiered bunks and literally 50 centimeters of lying space. Permanent dampness, darkness and bedbug plague. Owing to frequent baths, beating the blankets and laundering, lice were uncommon. Hygiene was generally maintained. All internees were meticulously vaccinated against typhus and pox! Medical assistance provided by Polish and partially by Soviet doctors was very good. Permanently open bathhouse.

Social composition of POWs, prisoners, exiles (nationality, type of crimes, intellectual and moral standing, mutual relations, etc.):

Those deported to Kozelsk comprised: a) officers – approximately 700–800; b) non-commissioned officers, mainly of the Border Protection

Corps and 300–400 gendarmes; c) police, approximately 1,500 people. Mainly Poles, except for a few Jews. Intellectual standing very high, owing to foreign language courses, choirs and orchestra. In addition, due to very frequent contacts with highly intelligent people, the intellectual standing increased significantly. Very high morale. Except for a small group of the Communist system supporters, such as Captain Mikołaj Arciszewski, Captain Smoleński from Lida, Second Lieutenant (Air Force) Ziółkowski, Second Lieutenant (Air Force) Romanowski, Cavalry Lieutenant Levis, Second Lieutenant Juszkiewicz, Second Lieutenant Konieczny, Second Lieutenant Buła, Second Lieutenant Żbikowski, Lieutenant Mielnikow from Warsaw (was in Russia in the 7th Infantry Division), all others were estimable Poles.

The intrigues of Bolsheviks, who treated officers better than others, initially resulted in antagonisms between the officers and police and non-commissioned officers, which were however eliminated afterwards. In general, relations were very friendly.

Life in the camp or prison (daily routine, working conditions, quotas, wages, food, clothes, social and cultural life, etc.):

Wake up at 7.00 a.m. Attendance check and breakfast. Forced labor for policemen and non-commissioned officers until dinner. Officers did not work. Foreign language learning, volleyball, basketball and sports. After dinner, choir and orchestra practice at the cinema (club). After supper – films. Propaganda films were displayed. At first, attendance very high, later – minimum. Food generally quite good. Underwear was provided from the storage facility.

Attitude of the NKVD towards Poles (interrogation methods, torture and other forms of punishment, communist propaganda, information about Poland, etc.):

Constant interrogations by the NKVD, lasting several hours, at the units, threatening that they would shoot us and the rest would be deported to Siberia. Regular subject of talks – attempts to find out the surnames of people working in the 2nd Division or working therefor, collapse of Poland, gentry representatives as executioners, prospected life in the future Soviet Poland. Soviet Russia as a liberator of oppressed Ukrainians and Belarusians in eastern Poland; Lwów and Wilno – everlasting Soviet towns, etc. Afterwards: proposals of serving Russia by reporting the subjects of inmates' talks, joining the Red Army, threats of deporting the family, etc. In a word: very hostile attitude.

Medical assistance, hospitals, mortality rate
(provide the names of the deceased):

Owing to permanent medical help and hygiene supervision, mortality rate very low. The deceased: 1) Second Lieutenant Wacław Dłuski from Lida, 2) Lieutenant Góra, 3) district head Pełczyński; Captain Wasilewski hanged himself due to a mental disorder and Second Lieutenant Krzeczkowski went insane.

Was it at all possible to get in contact with one's home country and family?

We communicated with our country and family by mail. Money orders and parcels were delivered. We were allowed to send letters once a month.

When were you released and how did you manage to join the Polish Army?

Following the outbreak of the German-Russian war, the entire camp was transported to the North. Partly to Arkhangelsk, partly to Gryazovets near Vologda. After the amnesty in August 1941, the internees were transported by rail to Totskoye and Tatishchevo.

Collection of the Hoover Institution Library & Archives at the disposal of the Central Archives of Modern Records, Władysław Anders Collection. Reports, 800/1/0/-/48, account no. 2094.

MICHAŁ BOJAR

Personal data:
Michał Bojar, corporal, 43 years old, married.

Date and circumstances of arrest:

On 11 July 1940, while detained in an internment camp in Ukmergė in Lithuania, I and some 5,000 other internees were deported by the Soviet authorities to a camp in Russia.

Name of the camp:

Kozelsk, from 14 July 1940 until 15 May 1941, and then the Kola Peninsula, until 12 July 1941.

Description of the camp or prison:

The area was forested, while the buildings in which we were kept were made of both brick and wood – in the main they were former Orthodox churches; the living conditions and hygienic conditions were passable.

Social composition of POWs, prisoners, exiles:

The prisoners were Poles who had been interned in Lithuania and Latvia, namely officers of the State Police, non-commissioned officers of the gendarmerie, the Border Protection Corps, and the Border Guard, and also court officials and employees of the civil administration.

Life in the camp or prison:

Our normal daily work was focused on ensuring the functioning of the camp; we would busy ourselves in the kitchen, and clean the sanitary facilities and buildings. The interned professors organized language courses – English, French and German – which were attended by many of the prisoners. We had our own clothes, and the food was passable; our mutual relations were good.

Attitude of the NKVD towards Poles:

The attitude of the NKVD towards us Poles was bad, they would interrogate us for days and nights on end, threaten us with the death penalty; they would also drag internees from their cells in the middle of the night and take them away to unspecified locations.

Medical assistance, hospitals, mortality rate:

Passable, the doctors were Polish internees, and there was a hospital on the spot.

Was it at all possible to get in contact with one's home country and family?

No.

When were you released and how did you manage to join the Polish Army?

On 24 March 1941, while in the camp in Suzdal, we started registering for enlistment in the Polish Army.

Collection of the Hoover Institution Library & Archives at the disposal of the Central Archives of Modern Records, Władysław Anders Collection. Reports, 800/1/0/-/48, account no. 2298.

BERNARD CHODOFF

Personal data (name, surname, rank, age, occupation and marital status):
Bernard Chodoff, senior sergeant, born in 1891, regular non-commissioned officer, married.

Date and circumstances of arrest:

Acting on orders, on 19 September 1939 I crossed the border between Poland and Lithuania. On 18 September 1939 at 5.00 p.m. the company which I headed was manning a defensive section stretching from a transmitter to the Rossa cemetery in Wilno. At 7.15 p.m. a messenger came to my company with a letter from the battalion commander, Lieutenant Colonel Szyłejko, ordering me to take my company and march to the Wilno–Grodno highway. 75% of my company consisted of Belarusians, who refused to go to Grodno, abandoned their weapons and went in the direction of Oszmiana, their home town. I gathered a small group of soldiers and marched as ordered. The soldiers who went with me were inhabitants of Wilno. At Legionowa Street they declared that they wouldn't go with me either, but would go home instead. At Legionowa Street I met Captain Mickiewicz, an officer from my battalion. He told me that an order had been issued to cross the Polish-Lithuanian border.

Captain Mickiewicz hailed a taxi which was going in the direction of the border, we got in and went to the Lithuanian border. On 19 September 1939 at 4.00 a.m. we crossed the border in Zawiasy, and the same car took us to the Lithuanian camp, Kulautuva. On the following day I was assigned to the group of Lieutenant Colonel Cymer. I stayed in that camp until 19 March 1940, and then I was transferred to the camp in Vilkaviškis. On 12 July 1940 Soviet troops arrived at the camp and took us all to the USSR.

Name of the camp, prison or forced labor site:

We were transported in sealed cattle wagons with barred windows, and for two days and nights we received neither water nor food. After 48 hours, when we arrived at some station, two buckets of dried fish and black biscuits were thrown into our wagon; at the next station we received water, but it was stale and dirty.

On 16 July 1940 the train stopped at the Nitochnaya station, located 240 kilometers from Smolensk. At 8.00 a.m. we were ordered to get out and arrange ourselves in fours. The NKVD soldiers, armed with light machine guns, surrounded us; a second line was composed of soldiers with dogs on long leashes, and a third of cavalry. In this sort of column we were marched to the camp, which was located 34 kilometers from the station. At 5.30 p.m. we reached the camp, where we spent three hours lying in front of the entrance gate, waiting for the soldiers to collect the rest of our soldiers left on the road. When we were finally admitted to the camp courtyard, we were thoroughly searched and herded to the bathhouse. The bathing of 3,800 people lasted for three and a half hours. There were 20 showers in the bathhouse, and each had to accommodate from 8 to 10 people. After the bath we were taken to buildings that could house up to 400 people, but 700 or more people had to live there.

Description of the camp or prison (grounds, buildings, housing conditions, hygiene):

The camp was situated in the woods – it was on the property of a former tsarist prince, Orlov. It was a pleasant location, surrounded with a pine forest and with a river flowing nearby, but it was also surrounded with three rows of barbed wire and had no exit.

As for the hygiene, it left much to be desired: underwear was washed by the inmates, and conditions for performing this task were awful, especially in winter, when water would freeze in the washing tubs, as the barn where the washing was done was not heated. In order to wash the underwear of one company, composed of 100 people of whom everyone was given one change of underwear and a towel, ten people from the company had to go to the washing room and wash the entire company's underwear from 9.00 a.m. to 2.00 p.m.

Social composition of POWs, prisoners, exiles (nationality, type of crimes, intellectual and moral standing, mutual relations, etc.):

3,800 non-commissioned officers and privates were detained in the camp. The majority of them were Roman Catholics.

Life in the camp or prison (daily routine, working conditions, quotas, wages, food, clothes, social and cultural life, etc.):

Every day at 8.00 a.m. a trumpet call summoned us to assemble in the courtyard and arrange ourselves in fours, each company separately. Then a Bolshevik officer would count us and take us for work on the camp premises, where we were erecting a building that was to house a theater. We worked from 8.00 a.m. to 4.00 p.m., without remuneration and regardless of weather. As for clothing, the Bolsheviks issued the foremen who supervised our work with boots and padded jackets, but the rest had to make crude shoes out of wood covered with cloth, which had to last them the whole winter; we used to wrap our feet in rags. As late as in the spring of 1941 the Soviet authorities began to distribute boots, padded jackets and underwear, but they were given only to those who worked as specialists; those who worked irregularly were told by the Bolsheviks that they didn't need these articles, as they worked very little.

Cultural life in the camp: every other day the Bolsheviks screened a propaganda movie about life in the Soviet Union, in villages and factories, and about private life. A balalaika prisoners' orchestra, conducted by a platoon-leader from the 1st Uhlan Regiment, was set up in the camp. There were talks each Tuesday, delivered by Bolshevik political commissars, on a variety of topics related to politics, economy, and state matters. In February 1941 one of the inmates, Józef Dobrowolski, a former headmaster of an elementary school in Mołodeczno, began to form Bolshevik cells and recruit inmates; about a hundred people of various backgrounds volunteered, including even regular non-commissioned officers. The course lasted for three months, with lectures every day after 6.00 p.m., and political commissars took turns delivering them. At the end of the course, the chief political commissar himself examined the participants.

Attitude of the NKVD towards Poles (interrogation methods, torture and other forms of punishment, communist propaganda, information about Poland, etc.):

As for the Soviet authorities' attitude towards inmates, some of them were quite decent, but some were dogs. One could sense that many Bolsheviks were in fact Poles from the Soviet city of Minsk, but they didn't reveal their nationality; these were the worst.

Medical assistance, hospitals, mortality rate (provide the names of the deceased):

As for medical assistance, some of the inmates were renowned physicians, famous in Poland, but unfortunately we were short on medications. The emergency room was supplied only with aspirin, quinine, ricin, and a few types of ointment; even bandages to make a dressing were lacking. We always heard the same answer: "Moscow hasn't sent them yet."

Was it at all possible to get in contact with one's home country and family?

When we arrived at the camp, the Bolsheviks told us that once we were registered – which would take up to four weeks – we would be released home. Six weeks later we were informed that we could write one letter of

25 words to our families. They used our letters to get to know what was going on in our country. During 14 months I wrote four letters and received three letters from home. These three letters resembled net curtains – a Bolshevik cut out the parts he didn't like with scissors.

When were you released and how did you manage to join the Polish Army?

On 26 August 1941, General Władysław Anders and General Bohusz-Szyszko arrived at the camp in Gryazovets, near Vologda, and told us that if we wanted to, we could join the Polish Army. Three days after the general's departure, the delegate of the Polish Government, Lieutenant Colonel Stanisław Pstrokoński, came to the camp and established a District Draft Office at the camp for conscripting us into the army. On 2 September 1941, at 3.00 p.m. the Bolsheviks opened up the camp gate and more than 1,600 officers and over 400 privates marched off to the train station in Gryazovets. On 7 September 1941 I was in the camp in Totskoye, where I was appointed head of the 1st Rifle Company in the 19th Infantry Regiment.

21 January 1943

Collection of the Hoover Institution Library & Archives at the disposal of the Central Archives of Modern Records, Władysław Anders Collection. Reports, 800/1/0/-/48, account no. 1673.

KONSTANTY LECH

Personal data (name and surname, rank,
age, occupation marital status):
Konstanty Lech, platoon-leader, born on 2 March 1902, official of the Telecommunications Office in Warsaw, married, one child; Staging Areas Communications Battalion.

Date and circumstances of arrest:

On 19 September 1939, having crossed the Polish-Lithuanian border, I was interned in Palanga (Lithuania) until 31 January 1940 and afterwards in a closed Vilkaviškis camp until 12 July 1940.

Name of the camp, prison or forced labor site:

On 12 July 1940, I was deported together with other inmates (more than 1,200 people) to the Yukhnovo camp in the USSR; the police, gendarmes and officers were deported to Kozelsk.

Description of the camp or prison (grounds, buildings, housing conditions, hygiene):

The Yukhnovo camp was located in the middle of a large pine forest. Housing conditions in two blocks were acceptable. The other two blocks were overcrowded, damp and infested with vermin, although the sanitary services did their best to provide the appropriate condition of the buildings. Hygiene – cleanliness in the kitchen and buildings was ensured. The kitchen and sanitary personnel, and doctors were appointed from among the internees, initially under the supervision of the NKVD and then under the supervision of our inmates.

Social composition of POWs, prisoners, exiles (nationality, type of crimes, intellectual and moral standing, mutual relations, etc.):

Internees from Lithuania and Latvia. Mostly Poles, a few Jews. All social groups: officials, teachers, farmers and craftsmen from all parts of Poland. Relations between inmates good.

Life in the camp or prison (daily routine, working conditions, quotas, wages, food, clothes, social and cultural life, etc.):

Life in the Yukhnovo camp: assembly every day at 8.30 a.m. – morning roll-call, afterwards breakfast. The internees were divided into units, each numbered one hundred people and was managed by a commandant. Commandants were designated from among our inmates who spoke Russian. After a few weeks, some of the commandants, such as Senior Private Stanisław Styczeń and Senior Private Bronisław Rutkowski, adhered to the policies of the NKVD. I don't remember the surnames of the others, they generally behaved well.

As for work, we were employed only within the region, for permanent and cleaning works. Permanent works were performed voluntarily by craftsmen: carpenters – built buildings for our own use; tailors and shoemakers – mended uniforms and shoes, bakers – baked bread; cooks – worked in the kitchen. We didn't yet know the quotas applicable here, we knew them only from newspapers. We weren't paid for permanent work, but we were given better food, additional 400 grams of bread per day and dry groats for dinner. Others worked on certain days – the duty company performed internal works. Except for underwear, we weren't given any clothing in Yukhnovo.

Mutual relations were good, with a few exceptions. Cultural life: the choir and camp orchestra conducted by the internees often gave Polish concerts, however following censorship by the NKVD. Sometimes film screenings, but only those Bolshevik. There was also a library with books by Lenin, Marx, etc. Initially, the internees used these books eagerly, removing pages from them to be used as rolling paper for tobacco, as no other paper could be purchased. Later, following our insistence, rolling paper was issued, and each unit received newspapers every day, but nobody was interested in reading them; it was only important for them to be fairly distributed.

Food was acceptable for Soviet conditions. Those who did not work received 700 grams of bread per day. Breakfast – soup and tea, dinner – thick soup and groats, supper – sometimes soup, usually tea. Meat – heads, livers and other meat waste only. Fat – olive oil. In general, it was bearable, we were not starving. For those who worked – as above, plus 400 grams of bread and groats for supper.

At the end of May 1941, after being examined by the Soviet and Polish doctors, vaccinated, bathed, given a haircut, provided with underwear, footcloths, jackets and padded trousers, all those qualified by the commission as healthy and able to work, were sent via Murmansk to the Kola Peninsula. Having arrived in Murmansk, I fell ill and lay 20 days in the hospital for prisoners. Care, meals and conditions in the hospital were good. On 21 June 1941, we were all transported to the Kola Peninsula.

The Kola Peninsula – a marshy area, tundra. Living in the open air, no kitchen. Unbearable conditions. Work for 10–15 hours. Quotas were so high that I don't think those strongest and healthiest could meet them. Fortunately, the English-Polish-Soviet agreement was concluded. Without telling us about it, they loaded us onto ships on 12 July 1941, and we returned to the camp in Talitsy near Vyazniki via Arkhangelsk.

On the way there, on both the ship and wagons, despite the agreement, we were treated worse than dogs. They fed us herrings and practically no water. The wagons were of course locked, windows open only on one side and barred, physical needs were satisfied in the wagon with 40 people present. Conditions were terrible, considering the July heat. People fainted. On the second day of the journey, we started shouting: "water, water, water" at a large railway station, the phrase was repeated by people in the second and third wagon and in all wagons to the end of the train and again from the beginning. After threefold repeating, the effect was immediate, the train was directed to the side track, we were given as much water as we needed, and an investigation was carried out. We were threatened to bear consequences, but this did not scare us; as soon as the water was running out, we started shouting again: "water, water, water," this time the effect was immediate as well, and we managed to arrive in Vyazniki, from which we had to go 40 kilometers on foot to the camp in Talitsy, where after a few days the content of the Polish-Soviet agreement was officially reported to us and a new life began.

Attitude of the NKVD towards Poles (interrogation methods, torture and other forms of punishment, communist propaganda, information about Poland, etc.):

The interrogation methods were relatively mild, limited to several calls by day and night. I heard that some were proposed to report everything they heard to the so-called first corps. He mentioned that even to me when he called me for the NKVD interrogation, but I pretended that I didn't understand (throughout my stay in Russia, I didn't admit that I spoke Russian). I talked to the NKVD only in Polish, which they detested and ended the conversations quickly.

The communist propaganda was present in all the talks in the individual rooms. The NKVD appointed those responsible for education, they visited each "corps" building every day. In my building there was the reservist Vereshchagin, a teacher from Smolensk. He was an exceptionally decent person for an NKVD man; you could tell that he would not say what he really thought. We conducted such fierce discussions that if somebody overheard them for the first time, they would be convinced that he was one of us, purposefully substituted.

Once, the deputy commandant of the camp, a political NKVD commissar, called England an "old whore." Although when he was speaking we weren't allowed to interrupt, one of the internees, a platoon-leader from Wilno (I don't remember his surname), stood up, asked for a permission to speak and politely requested the commissar to refrain from referring to England with such words, and the deputy commandant asked him whether this offended us and why. The platoon-leader replied: "This hurts all of us very much. England is our only ally who had stood by our side from the very beginning, and there are no grounds for us to doubt that it will keep its promises." Then, the commissar said: "If I offended any of you by saying that, I apologize and assure you that from today on, neither I nor any other NKVD officer in this camp will use any inappropriate expressions when addressing England and Poland." In fact, he kept his word in this case. I think this happened at the end of November or at the beginning of December 1940, maybe earlier, I don't remember the exact date, in the Yukhnovo camp, also known as Pavlishchev Bor.

Medical assistance, hospitals, mortality rate (provide the names of the deceased):

In the Yukhnovo camp: medical assistance on site. Infirmary: doctors from among the internees, independently thereof – a Soviet doctor and his deputy. Less severe diseases – outpatient treatment, more severe diseases – in the infirmary on site, good care and food there, everyday visits by a Soviet doctor. Only those whose condition was severe were sent to the hospital; there were a few cases of appendicitis, almost all of the patients returned healthy and said that the conditions had been very good. At that time there was still a lot of medicines. One of the internees died – due to a long-term disease. I don't remember his surname.

Was it at all possible to get in contact with one's home country and family?

From 16 July 1940 to mid-January 1941, we had absolutely no contact with the world. Later, we were allowed to write one letter a month. Nearly everyone received replies from their families or friends. The correspondence was handed over by the NKVD in the so-called first corps.

When were you released and how did you manage to join the Polish Army?

I was released from the Kola Peninsula together with others (about 5,000 people) and transported to the Vyazniki railway station at the Klyazma River, to the Talitsy camp, where more than 10,000 people were gathered. Here, the content of the Polish-Soviet agreement was announced to us, we were enrolled to the army. Afterwards, we were transported as free men to our individual divisions. I left Talitsy on 4 September 1941, joined the 5th Infantry Division and was allocated to the 5th Communications Battalion.

Encampment, 9 March 1943

Collection of the Hoover Institution Library & Archives at the disposal of the Central Archives of Modern Records, Władysław Anders Collection. Reports, 800/1/0/-/48, account no. 1736.

JULIAN CICHOWSKI

Personal data:

Julian Cichowski, Signal Corps captain on permanent active duty, 43 years old, unmarried, city commander of Jerusalem.

Date and circumstances of arrest:

I was deported from Kalvarija, Lithuania, on 10 June 1940.

Name of the camp:

Kozelsk and Gryazovets.

Description of the camp:

Kozelsk: A former monastery. A number of Orthodox church buildings and residential buildings were surrounded by a several-meters-high wall that formed an approx. 250-meter-sided square. Some buildings were made of bricks and some of wood. Inside were pallets made of rough wood, from one to several stories high (depending on the building). The buildings were rather dirty and bug-infested. During my stay in the camp we debugged the buildings several times with Lysol provided by the Soviet authorities, and towards the end of our stay we whitewashed the walls in some buildings and planed the pallet boards. It was quite warm in building no. 14, where I lived.

At first I had a bath every two weeks, and later, when the new bathhouse was furnished, every week. Many repair and maintenance works (paving, lawns) were conducted by the inmates under the guidance of Polish engineers. For this purpose the Bolsheviks were setting up volunteer work groups. Nobody was forced to work, but once one volunteered it was difficult to withdraw. At first we had to wash our underwear ourselves, in the bathhouse. Later, the officers' underwear was washed in town, and the underwear of the policemen and the privates was washed by a designated work group in the old bathhouse.

Shortly after our arrival at the camp we were vaccinated against typhoid fever I think, and later against smallpox. A barbershop was organized, where – having waited one's turn – we could get shaved for free by our policemen. I preferred to grow a beard.

The food was sufficient, but strangely insubstantial. We got mainly groats. In theory, we were entitled to 75 grams of meat per person a day, but in fact we received meat offal, such as heads, legs, and tails, the weight of hoofs, horns and bones included, so in effect there was virtually no meat at all. It was slightly better in the periods when salted meat was being distributed. The officers and the privates had separate kitchens. The officers received slightly bigger rations. They also received more sugar and, I think, meat and fat, and besides they received a scrap of toilet soap once a month. All detainees were issued a bar of washing soap, as well as shag tobacco, cigarette paper and matches (five packages of each of these three items per month). We were also issued blankets. At first we slept directly on the pallets. Later we received mattresses, straw, and sheets. We also got underwear and footwraps, and those who had no uniforms were also issued some.

Gryazovets: also a monastery. The Orthodox church had been demolished. Only one brick building survived, and about 300 Polish POWs were placed in it. We arrived in Gryazovets at the end of June 1940. For lack of space in the building, we had to live in makeshift barracks without outer walls (the roof was supported by posts). It was very cold in there and we were horribly pestered by mosquitoes. The food was worse than in Kozelsk. Later the food rations were drastically reduced, so for some three weeks before the agreement between the Soviet Union and Poland we suffered from hunger. As we didn't receive any straw for the mattresses, we picked and dried some grass to fill them with. Later on some hay was brought to us.

The Gryazovets camp was rather large, fenced with barbed wire, and wooded; there was also a river on the camp premises. When it was warm, we were taking baths in the river, and later on in a bathhouse, which was very small. The drinking water, as well as water for cooking and washing, was transported in barrels.

Social composition of POWs:

There were officers (about 1,000), policemen (about 2,000) and a number of privates in the camp. Apart from these, a few officers were brought in from prisons and POW camps at a later time. We didn't trust the latter, as we suspected that they were sent as spies. I think that our suspicions were partially justified.

The so-called 'reddies' were our greatest worry. They were communist sympathizers, and unfortunately recruited mainly (or even exclusively) from among the officers. The most active members of that group were: Captain Arciszewski (at least that was the name he gave), Captain Smoleński, Lieutenant Adrian and Lieutenant Rolewski. Others, especially young airmen, followed their example. As I gathered, in Kozelsk they used to meet in the kitchen. Some intrigues were being carried on in the kitchen, as the post of kitchen commandant (appointed from among the detainees) often changed hands. Apart from those open sympathizers there must have been some informers, as the Soviet authorities knew about many things that happened in the camp. Nevertheless, some decidedly anti-communist books also circulated in the camp.

When the Polish-Soviet agreement was proclaimed, the most active reddies were separated from us and sent somewhere else. It was said that they were to be used as saboteurs or paratroopers. As a farewell, they denounced a number of officers, mostly the ones with German surnames, for allegedly working with the fifth column. As I learned later, these officers were deported to Vologda. Later they were released and joined the army.

Life in the camp:

Wake-up was before 7.00 a.m., and was followed by a roll-call. There was another roll-call at the end of the day. It consisted of checking the number of detainees. At first, the roll-calls were conducted by commandants of particular buildings, appointed from among the detainees, but later the roll-calls were handled by NKVD functionaries. Once a month the lists of surnames were read out. The food from the kitchen was brought to the buildings in buckets by designated men, one for each room (we were taking turns in a set order). The same men also cleaned the rooms and kept guard.

All works in the Kozelsk camp, such as paving the grounds, repairs to buildings, kitchen work, chopping wood for the kitchen, all work in the shoemaker's and tailor's workshops and the barber shop were performed by permanent work brigades composed of volunteers. Those who worked received better food, but it was at the cost of everyone else; as far as I know, the Soviet authorities didn't provide any additional foodstuffs for the workers. All detainees were required to peel potatoes and skin the fish. However, there was a tacit agreement that staff officers wouldn't perform these tasks. They spent their time in learning foreign languages, reading, making musical instruments, knives, razors, and wooden items (such as tobacco boxes). Some of them were executed with real artistry. I saw beautiful chess sets, artistically carved boxes and skillfully made razors.

In Gryazovets, apart from the permanent staff in the kitchen, bakery, boiler room and bathhouse, there were no permanent work brigades, so we had to take turns chopping wood for the kitchen, bringing water, etc.

Mutual relations were generally good. The detainees grew close and helped one another in various matters. The policemen visited us and we returned their visits. I heard about some fights, even between officers, but in our building there was only one brawl.

There was an amateur orchestra that put on some revue and orchestra performances. I didn't see any of them, as I didn't get a ticket. However, it was no great loss as the orchestra members lived in our building and held rehearsals there all the time, so I knew their repertoire by heart.

There was a recreation room, known as the club, where chess tournaments were organized.

Attitude of the NKVD towards Poles:

As soon as we arrived in Kozelsk, we were all searched. I heard that the first groups had to strip naked. Later, due to the great number of detainees, the searches were less thorough. Identity papers, money, sharp and valuable objects were taken away from us. I managed to save all the documents that I had on me. However, I had to part with my camera, an alarm clock, and a few other items, including some Lithuanian and Polish money. During a search before our departure from Kozelsk I was also divested of a silver-plated drop-action pencil and a few other things. Although I had deposit receipts for these things, none of them was returned to me despite my repeated requests.

Once we were searched and quartered in the camp, we were summoned one by one and carefully registered. Later we were also called to the office at various times – some of us more, some of us less often – for the so-called *dopros*. Generally, those who were interrogated spoke unwillingly or not at all about what had been said during their interrogation. I gathered from what they were saying that those who took part in political or social life were summoned most often. The authorities were eagerly enquiring after all informers, both of the police and the 2nd Unit, who were still active.

Shortly after our arrival at the camp, Colonel Dąbrowski and all the officers from the 2nd Unit were separated from us. Of the latter, I knew only Captain Wojciechowski from the branch office of the Independent Office of Information of the 3rd Corps District Command in Lida, where I served during the war. All of them were deported in an unknown direction and I haven't heard of them since. Apart from them, Cavalry Captain Chludziński was also deported, because he told the political commissars too openly what he thought about their country and its political system. I heard that he was released and joined the army.

I was summoned only once after the register was drawn up. At the time, for two or three days, a few men from our building were called every day, so I thought that they were going to interrogate all of us. However, they interrogated 10 or 12 men and that was it. I was asked about a number of things that I had already provided during registration, so I had the impression that they wanted to determine whether I had given correct information the previous time and to catch me giving contradictory statements. I was also asked what I wanted to do if I were released from the camp. Of course I wanted to go abroad, but I couldn't say so. Besides, I considered the question rhetorical, as I didn't believe that they would release me. Therefore,

I told them that I wanted to settle down in some town and go to work. They replied that as a specialist (radio engineer) I would easily find a job. And that was all.

I had the impression that when the NKVD wanted to interrogate someone who was of special interest to them, at the same time they would summon a number of "unimportant" persons to make a "smoke screen" and divert attention away from the individual or informer in question. I would like to note that all those summoned were interrogated separately.

The interrogators were rather unintelligent and had little to no knowledge about our relations. The Bolsheviks despised satire. One of the detainees drew a number of caricatures about everyday camp life. When the Bolsheviks learned about this, they confiscated all his works, called them "political hooliganism" and strictly forbade carrying on such activities. Frankly, I don't know what is political about a drawing which depicts, for instance, a detainee taking care of his bodily needs in a makeshift camp latrine.

Propaganda was spread through newspapers, movies, and lectures, the so-called *doklady*. I rarely went to the cinema or attended the lectures. The movies were of course propaganda pictures of very poor quality. The lectures that I attended aimed to present an overview of the current political situation, but they were mediocre and merely repeated newspaper stories. It all boiled down to a declaration that the Soviets had good neighborly relations with the Germans, and England and the US were their worst enemies. They did mention that a war with the Germans would probably break out, but no sooner than "in a few years." I don't recall any direct attacks on Poland. Should they have happened, they would have sparked protests, or at the least the majority of those present would have left the room. The newspapers, in turn, published tall stories about the situation in Poland before and after the entry of the Soviet Army. For instance, I remember an article about Polish officers who were escaping to Romania across the Dniester River and plucked out the eyes of a fisherman's daughter who had helped them cross the river.

The NKVD camp authorities treated us decently and were rather kind. For instance, they never addressed us informally. On the other hand, the escorting units that were responsible for the transport of prisoners were real slave traders. They behaved in a cruel and ruthless manner.

Medical assistance, hospitals, mortality rate:

I didn't use any medical assistance, so I cannot say anything about that matter. Anyway, there was a hospital in Kozelsk. I know about two lieutenants who died, but I don't remember their surnames. Besides that, two men hanged themselves and a few – four, I think – went insane.

Was it at all possible to get in contact with one's home country and family?

If I remember correctly, we received "coupons" for writing letters once a month. I didn't have anyone to write to, so I wasn't really interested.

When were you released and how did you manage to join the Polish Army?

I joined the army in Gryazovets on 27 August 1941, and towards the end of that month I went with the others to Totskoye.

Jerusalem, 24 January 1943

Collection of the Hoover Institution Library & Archives at the disposal of the Central Archives of Modern Records, Władysław Anders Collection. Reports, 800/1/0/-/48, account no. 1620.

WITOLD KULIKOWSKI

Personal data:

Witold Kulikowski, lieutenant of the reserve, 44 years old, economist, married.

Date and circumstances of arrest:

In August 1940 I was deported from the internment camp for officers in Latvia (Ulbroka) to the camp in Kozelsk, USSR.

Name of the camp, prison or forced labor site:

Kozelsk – a camp for officers in the USSR – a former monastery situated some 200 kilometers from Moscow.

Description of the camp or prison:

A dilapidated monastery, which could house about 5,000 people. A few ruined Orthodox church buildings: in some, kitchens were organized, and in others they placed pallets. Plenty of bugs. In the former church buildings the pallets were arranged three stories high, and in other buildings two. The buildings were heated in winter, so the living conditions were bearable. The bathhouse was quite decent, and we took a bath every 10 days. Food was passable. We ran the kitchen ourselves, using products delivered by the NKVD authorities.

Social composition of POWs, prisoners, exiles:

The composition of internees: officers deported from Lithuania and Latvia, gendarmes and policemen. About 5,000 men in total. Mutual relations were rather good, with the exception of a dozen or so officers with communist leanings, who were generally avoided (Major Henryk Kowalowski, Captain Rozen-Zawadzki).

Life in the camp, prison:

Life in the camp: wake-up, cleaning, a walk, language classes in small groups, sometimes clandestine lectures on military knowledge. A radio, or rather a loudspeaker, with Soviet announcements. Roll-call from time to time.

Attitude of the NKVD towards Poles:

The NKVD's attitude was generally hostile, though on the surface correct. Those who had families in the Bolshevik-occupied territories and had themselves worked there before the war were often summoned for interrogations. The Soviets knew almost all details pertaining to such individuals. If they requested some information, they would threaten the person in question, also threatening repressive measures against his family. Officers from the Second Department of Polish General Staff were all gradually deported. Very few of them returned later to the Polish Army. Like this, for instance, several dozen of them were deported from Kozelsk, and only a few returned. Those who did return were in a very bad state of health – they were starved and morally exhausted. They were changed so much that when I met three of them, I barely recognized them as the same men with whom I had spent almost an entire year in Latvia. These were Cavalry Captain Tchorzewski, Captain Susicki and Cavalry Captain Chmielewski (who died of typhus).

Not everyone was interrogated in the same manner. Some were threatened with consequences and repressive measures against their families; others were interrogated kindly and superficially. They had the personal data of us all, as we had been divested of all documents. On top of that, they had local information (from officers who worked in the Eastern Borderlands).

Anyhow, it could be inferred from the conversations that our fates had already been decided. In addition to interrogations, communist propaganda was spread by so-called political commissars, who roamed the camp premises. However, these guys were pretty dumb and their work was rather detrimental of the idea of communism. Apart from that, from time to time we had to attend political lectures, during which the democratic states – mainly England, dubbed a political prostitute – were slighted and the wisdom of the Soviet policy and the alliance with the Germans were highly praised. All statistics provided during these lectures were very characteristic and even funny, as all the numbers given in comparison with other countries did not take into account the size and population of Russia.

The Polish government was ridiculed and criticized. They (the NKVD men) had an especially deep hatred for Marshal Piłsudski and the government after the May Coup d'État. They didn't recognize General Sikorski's government in London. Generally, in every word and every action of the NKVD men one could sense a hatred for Poland and Poles.

The library held communist works and some textbooks.

I have a very good command of Russian and I flipped through many books by Lenin, Stalin and other eminent Party leaders. Summing up, I believe that as long as Russia has a Communist government, no cooperation in any field is possible between that country and the Western states. No agreement will be honored, as their motto is that the end justifies the means. Both Lenin and his successors recommend entering into agreements and even alliances with Russia's chief enemies in order to attain a given goal, and then breaking them and finishing off the ally. They adhere closely to that principle.

Following the outbreak of the war with the Germans, we were deported north, to the vicinity of Vologda, to the camp in Gryazovets. There we were encouraged and even bullied into joining the Bolshevik Army. This lasted almost to the last minute before the amnesty was announced. A dozen or so officers, those with communist leanings, left, but unfortunately – with the exception of a few – all of them were later sent to the Army that was being raised under General Anders' command.

Medical assistance, hospitals, mortality rate:

We had good medical assistance, as our own doctors worked in the camp hospitals. Besides, their hospitals were clean and the patients were provided with tender, even apolitical care.

One officer (a captain) and one policeman took their own lives after returning from an interrogation, and three officers went mad (Artillery Lieutenant Dłuski went mad and died in Kozelsk).

Was it at all possible to get in contact with one's home country and family?

After a few months in the camp we were allowed to write to our families, and we then received answers. Parcels reached us in reasonable time.

When were you released and how did you manage to join the Polish Army?

After the amnesty was announced to us towards the end of August 1941, we were released and sent in transports to particular locations where our army was being raised.

My brother Jan, first imprisoned and then deported for hard labor to Komi ASSR, was released from the labor camp only on 20 June 1942, almost a year after the amnesty had been proclaimed. He returned in a very bad condition. He was on the brink of collapse; he spent six months in a hospital, insensible of where he was and what was going on around him.

Collection of the Hoover Institution Library & Archives at the disposal of the Central Archives of Modern Records, Władysław Anders Collection. Reports, 800/1/0/-/48, account no. 1630.

MARIAN GAJEWSKI

Marian Gajewski, platoon-leader, born on 15 August 1896, officer of the State Police, married.

On 17 September 1939, the district State Police was ordered to muster due to the Soviet Army crossing the border in Słonim District in the Nowogródek Voivodeship. After arriving in Orany, we were loaded onto trains along with the army and directed by the military authorities to defend Grodno. After the fight against the Soviets, we withdrew from Grodno to the town of Sopoćkinie on the orders of the commander of the "Grodno" Corps District Command, General Olszyna-Wilczyński. After entering the battle with Soviet tanks, General Olszyna-Wilczyński was killed on the field of glory in the battle of Sopoćkinie. On 24 September 1939, in Gromadziszki, we crossed the Polish-Lithuanian border and laid down our arms at the orders of the military authorities (issued by an unknown colonel). Then we were sent under escort to Kalvarija, and from Kalvarija to Vilkaviškis, where we were locked up in the camp. Life in the camp was sufficient, the Lithuanian authorities looked after us as much as possible.

On 12 July 1940, after the Soviets seized Lithuania, we were taken by the Soviets to the camp in Kozelsk in Russia. After taking us from Lithuania, the Soviet authorities loaded us into freight wagons, 48 people in each. The wagons were locked with padlocks during the journey, the windows were boarded up and we had only the wagons for our psychological needs as well. They did not give any water or food, and only after 48 hours did they give us one bucket of water and one salted fish per wagon.

After arriving at the Kozelsk camp, we were put up in the monastery. Housing, life and hygiene in the camp were bearable. The composition of the prisoners was 1,000 officers and 2,000 private police, gendarmerie, Border Protection Corps and Border Guards. Cultural and educational life was possible because it was organized by our officers: a choir and symphonic music group, and there was a chess, checkers and billiards club, and a propaganda library set up by the Soviets. At the same time, we had a very large number of Polish books from libraries in Wilno which the Soviets did not take from us during the searches. Relations between officers and privates were fraternal and the mood was good because the officers kept our spirits up. Radio loudspeakers were placed in the camp, from which we listened to news from the front of the fighting between England and Germany. We did not believe the Soviet propaganda (the messages were broadcast from Moscow).

The attitude of the NKVD authorities towards us was terrible – interrogations involved beatings, torture and insults that were enough to kill the spirit in every Pole, as well as curses on the Polish government and allied countries. The interrogations took place mostly at night. News about Poland was completely negligible; from time to time we only secretly received scanty news about the country and general politics from local civilians. In addition, we received very poor correspondence from families at home.

Hygienic conditions and medical aid were good, mortality negligible.

On 16 May 1941, we were separated from the officers and taken from the Kozelsk camp to the Kola Peninsula. Our journey took place in unbearable conditions. After arriving at our destination, we were thrown out of the ship and into the open. We set up tents in the mud, hungry and cold. We were quartered in these tents for two weeks, pushed to do hard labor, starving, lacking strength. The road to work was arduous and distant, up to ten kilometers. After returning from work to our living quarters, we received cooked food as well as 200 grams of bread and dry porridge, which we could not cook because there was no wood.

And so each day of tedious and arduous work passed in anticipation of a better tomorrow.

On 30 July 1941, intelligence was brought to us about the conclusion of an agreement between the Polish government and Soviet Russia, and from that moment we were counted as free Polish citizens. The Soviet authorities announced to us that a Polish army was being formed in the USSR.

On 22 August 1941, Colonel Sulik-Sarnowski came to Suzdal together with a representative of the Soviet authorities, and after reading the order of the Polish authorities, we were released from the camp. On that day I had a conscript commission and was drafted into the Polish army. After the commission, I was taken from Suzdal to Tatishchevo, where the 5th Infantry Division was formed.

Collection of the Hoover Institution Library & Archives at the disposal of the Central Archives of Modern Records, Władysław Anders Collection. Reports, 800/1/0/-/48, account no. 2298.

STEFAN KULESZA

Personal data:
Stefan Kulesza, platoon-leader, 39 years old, farmer, married.

Date and circumstances of arrest:

I was taken captive by the Germans in 1939, during the retreat from Ostrołęka. I was deported with a great many other POWs to East Prussia. After a few days we were sent to work on an estate. I didn't for one moment abandon my plan to escape, so I took the first opportunity and on 12 March 1940 I fled to Lithuania. After a dozen or so hours of walking around in Lithuania, I was arrested by a Lithuanian policeman and placed in the internee camp in Vilkaviškis, from where in the middle of July 1940 the Bolsheviks deported me together with the entire camp to Russia. We travelled 40 people to a wagon, with doors closed shut and windows barred.

Name of the camp, prison or forced labor site:

Pavlishchev Bor, called the Yukhnov camp. It had been the residence of Prince Orlov.

Description of the camp or prison (grounds. buildings, housing conditions, hygiene):

It was a pretty palace on the river, surrounded with a park, ponds and a pine forest. On the side of the road, there still stood a part of a brick wall and the entrance gate to the palace. Of course the palace was taken up by our guardians – political commissars, and we were quartered in stables, pigsties, and sheep pens that were converted to human abodes by cutting out window holes. The bigger coach house served as a club, and next to it was the infirmary. Just behind the barbed wire fence there was a bathhouse, a washroom and a power station. At each corner of the fence there were so-called dovecotes for the guards. Strong searchlights, which illuminated the area on both sides of the fence, were placed on posts. The dovecotes had telephone contact with the camp command, so they were able to alert them at any moment. The space between the wires was plowed and raked. The barracks were furnished with three-story pallets, and the lower ones with two-story pallets. They were overflowing with people. The barracks were stuffy, cramped and bug-infested. They had been previously occupied by POWs from 1939.

Social composition of POWs, prisoners, exiles (nationality, type of crimes, intellectual and moral standing, mutual relations, etc.):

There were mainly Poles there, non-commissioned officers and riflemen. Officers, policemen and gendarmes had already been sent to another camp from Mołodeczno.

Life in the camp or prison:

An hour after wake-up there was a roll-call – held every day regardless of weather – during which we were counted off. We performed various tasks and maintenance works on the camp premises, in the bathhouse or the garage. We received 700 grams of bread, some groats and all sorts of fish. The groups that worked received additional groats for supper. As for clothes, we wore our coats and military boots from Poland which were in quite a good condition. It was worse with uniforms and trousers, which had a lot of patches on elbows and knees. Those who enjoyed a privileged status and some of those who worked were issued padded jackets and quilted trousers.

In our free time, which we had in abundance, we made boots, played chess etc. We took walks ad nauseam, and read the books we ourselves had brought from the library in Vilkaviškis. At the camp there was a Soviet library, and Soviet newspapers and radio. Everything was filled with communist propaganda, not to mention the constant influence of the horde of political commissars. Under the strict supervision of the camp command, a camp choir was organized, which Corporal Dylong became the conductor of, and an orchestra was also established. From time to time, there were concerts and film screenings – usually featuring tractors, kolkhozes etc. Each organized event was preceded with a *beseda* given by a political commissar, as it was the only opportunity to address a larger group of people who had gathered of their own free will.

The period of my stay at the Yukhnov camp was the time during which the Soviets "developed" their friendship with the Germans, which was widely discussed in the press, the radio, and by the political commissars, who often got themselves into trouble on account of that during discussions, as questions posed by the bolder internees were usually beyond the comprehension of a political commissar, and when the internees told them "you'll be fighting the Germans anyway," the Soviets would be boiling with rage.

They also got on our nerves, constantly repeating "Poland will never be restored, there was never any Poland before, you don't have any history of your own" and a lot of other nonsense. All our holidays were preceded with a series of anti-religious talks. With regard to that, there was a split between the internees, and those who eagerly attended these talks were generally harassed by the believers. A so-called non-religious community functioned in the camp. Its members gathered in the evenings for communist talks. They studied Marx, Engels and others. Only those who the "I Corps" ascertained had been active in the communist movement back in Poland were admitted to the community, but there were also some who took leave of their senses as a result of the omnipresent propaganda.

Medical assistance, hospitals, mortality rate:

A Soviet doctor was the chief doctor of the camp. Our doctors were employed in the infirmary. The gravely ill were sent to the local hospital, and critical cases were taken to a civilian hospital in Yukhnov, where I heard the medical assistance was very good. From July 1940 to May 1941, there were three fatal accidents in the group of about 3,000 people.

Was it at all possible to get in contact with one's home country and family?

After six months at the camp we were allowed to write letters to our families. All my letters were delivered to my wife, but it took no less than five to six weeks for a letter to reach its addressee. The NKVD used the correspondence between the internees and their families to verify whether they had given true information concerning their place of residence and family members who remained in Poland. In view of that, some prisoners preferred not to write. All parcels were checked, but they were also delivered without delay.

When were you released and how did you manage to join the Polish Army?

When we arrived at our work site, that is, the Kola Peninsula, they dropped all pretense of treating us as internees. We travelled in train cars that were as overcrowded and as tightly shut [as previously], but it was a luxurious ride in comparison with the journey on board the "Klara Zetkin" from Murmansk to Ponoy. Hungry, cold, dirty and completely disheartened, we disembarked in the Far North.

We revived upon learning that the Germans had already begun fighting the Bolsheviks. We waited impatiently for further news, for any change in our fate. In the meantime, we were driven to work 12 hours per day, not counting the two hours we walked to work. We were to build an airport at the polar rocks. We no longer deluded ourselves: we had been brought there for extermination, for death, as the work quota surpassed the strength of even the sturdiest man, and 200 grams of bread and some flour couldn't give enough strength to survive this backbreaking toil. Nobody met the quota, not even those from the community, although they tried to accomplish this in the first days.

Finally, we got the news: the end of work – you're free. I have no words to describe the happiness and joy felt by the exiles.

The return journey by ship and by train was exactly like the previous one, the experience of which is known only to those who have "travelled" in the Soviet territory out of necessity. It was our last journey with barred windows.

On 27 July [1941] we returned to the camp in Vyazniki. Colonel Sulik[-Sarnowski], a delegate of the Polish government, came there to announce to us that we were again Polish soldiers, and that Polish Army was being raised and organized in the USSR. Having arrived in Tatishchevo on 15 September 1941, I was enlisted into the 13th Infantry Regiment.

12 January 1943

Collection of the Hoover Institution Library & Archives at the disposal of the Central Archives of Modern Records, Władysław Anders Collection. Reports, 800/1/0/-/48, account no. 2119.

FELICJAN HOFFMAN

Personal data (name, surname, rank, age, occupation and marital status):
Felicjan Hoffman, lieutenant, 34 years old, an officer with the Youth Labor Corps, married.

Date and circumstances of arrest:

On 10 June 1940, while I was detained at the camp for interned officers in Kalvarija in Lithuania.

Name of the camp, prison or forced labor site:

The first camp for internees in the USSR – Kozelsk.

Description of the camp or prison (grounds, buildings, housing conditions, hygiene):

Brick and wood buildings, formerly Orthodox churches. The level of hygiene was tolerable.

Social composition of POWs, prisoners, exiles (nationality, type of crimes, intellectual and moral standing, mutual relations, etc.):

Interned officers and privates.

Life in the camp or prison (daily routine, working conditions, quotas, wages, food, clothes, social and cultural life, etc.):

In principle, we were not forced to work, although some colleagues – considered as specialists – were purportedly made to perform certain jobs around the camp. There were, however, ceaseless and persistent proposals to engage in physical labor, and some of those who refused were even threatened. But there was no clear compulsion.

Attitude of the NKVD towards Poles (interrogation methods, torture and other forms of punishment, communist propaganda, information about Poland, etc.):

The way in which we were escorted by guard convoys from Kalvarija to the railway station. Our column, arranged four men across, was flanked by Soviet soldiers who were spaced every five to seven meters, bayonets fixed to their rifles. While marching to the station (6 kilometers), some of the officers – carrying their luggage on their backs – would fall and faint. The guards pushed them and hit them with rifle butts.

The doors of the train were sealed shut and the windows closed; they crowded us into cattle wagons, some 40–45 men to each. Many colleagues passed out due to the lack of air and water. During the first day of the transport there was absolutely no water. It was scorching hot. The only way we could quench our thirst was to catch some of the dirty rainwater which dribbled down from the wagon roof and in through the broken window. There were various inspections along the way, during which we were shoved around and showered with abuse. On three separate occasion in Kozelsk I was summoned for interrogation by a special NKVD representative from Moscow. Initially, he was polite and even made an effort to sound friendly, describing the utter hopelessness of the situation in which Poland had found itself. He tried to convince me that our current government was illegal and would not help us in any way. He further stressed that Russia would soon conquer all the nations and that any hopes we had of Poland regaining its independence were no more than a pipe-dream. A few times he asked for my opinion on the topic. Later, he put forward an offer of cooperation with the authorities of the USSR in combatting external and internal enemies, promising that he would have me set free and that my family would receive specific privileges. I refused categorically. In further discussions he strove to persuade me that since the camp would be dissolved, I should think about my future, for after all I had a wife.

But since I dug in my heels, he started blackmailing me, saying that my entire family would be arrested and deported, presenting the future fates of my wife, child and myself in the grimmest light possible. And since my wife's address was known to him, he gave me a piece of paper and ordered that I write her a letter in which I was to state that I was the sole reason for her deportation. Whereupon he placed a watch in front of me, saying that I had 15 minutes to make up my mind. I refused, stating that I would no longer reply to any of his questions. He continued to urge and pressure me for some two hours. Finally, seeing that he would not win me over, he ordered me to write a statement to the effect that I would not discuss the matters which he had talked about with me with anyone else. But a few days later it all started again from the beginning, only this time he threatened me, shouting that I had willfully brought myself and my family to ruin. In the meantime I talked to Lieutenant Walerian Charkiewicz and Lieutenant Doellinger, asking them for advice how to fend off these shameful proposals. From them I learned that many colleagues were in a situation similar to mine. If I remember correctly, this was in March 1941. Once the Soviet-German War broke out, the NKVD's attitude towards us improved considerably.

Medical assistance, hospitals, mortality rate
(provide the names of the deceased):

Medical care was passable. I am aware of a number of deaths which occurred. Captain Wasilewski committed suicide by hanging, and one of the policemen also hanged himself; this was all due to their difficult experiences [illegible]. They had been harassed and maybe even manipulated into doing things, or perhaps blackmailed in the way I have just described. A few men went mad: Second Lieutenant Dłuski, who later died, and two others, whose surnames I do not remember.

Was it at all possible to get in contact with one's home country and family?

Initially, I kept in touch with my family by mail, but later I ceased receiving letters.

When were you released and how did you manage to join the Polish Army?

I enlisted in the Polish Army together with all the other officers on the very day when the 5th Infantry Division was officially established in Tatishchevo.

Collection of the Hoover Institution Library & Archives at the disposal of the Central Archives of Modern Records, Władysław Anders Collection. Reports, 800/1/0/-/48, account no. 2024.

FLORIAN KUJAWA

Personal data (name, surname, rank, age, occupation and marital status):
Florian Kujawa, second lieutenant, 30 years old, elementary school teacher, bachelor.

Date and circumstances of arrest:

On 22 August 1940 I was deported from the internee camp in Ulbroka (Latvia).

Name of the camp, prison or forced labor site:

Kozelsk, Gryazovets.

Description of the camp or prison (grounds, buildings, housing conditions, hygiene):

In Kozelsk there were buildings of a former monastery, which – especially after some fixing up – were quite good. The housing conditions were bad due to lack of space and a great numbers of bugs, as the camp command did nothing to fight them. In comparison with other camps, the hygienic conditions were bearable, especially after February 1941. In Gryazovets – especially since it was summer – the conditions were slightly better.

Social composition of POWs, prisoners, exiles (nationality, type of crimes, intellectual and moral standing, mutual relations, etc.):

The internees were almost exclusively Poles. There were about 1,000 officers, 1,400 policemen, 400 non-commissioned officers and 200 civilians (in Kozelsk).

Life in the camp or prison (daily routine, working conditions, quotas, wages, food, clothes, social and cultural life, etc.):

In the morning and in the evening, roll-calls were held to check the number of inmates, building by building. Wake-up was at 6.00 a.m., curfew at 10.00 p.m. We had meals three times a day, but in the evening we received boiled water and made tea ourselves. All tasks were generally performed by privates, while officers up to and including captains peeled potatoes, cleaned fish and volunteered for work in the kitchen and the bathhouse.

Bread was the staple of our diet (800 grams). The worst food was between November and March. About five times a week we had soup made from beet leaves (pickled), which was very bland.

In December 1940, social life deteriorated significantly. The reason for this was the spread of communist views among the internees, which resulted in suspicion and often mistrust of people who didn't exactly waver, but were simply less active.

Cultural life was generally limited to reading a small number of Polish books that had been brought to the camp by those interned in Lithuania. The internees from Latvia had had their books taken away on the very first day after their arrival. A choir and an orchestra had to suspend their activities due to our unwillingness to sing Russian songs.

Only tailors received remuneration, and only for work done for the Bolsheviks (the camp crew). This was why they were so obliging towards them.

In Gryazovets, the food was much worse. For a few weeks before the signing of the Polish-Soviet agreement, the [daily] bread ration was 400 grams. The food was completely devoid of fat, and fish were usually half-rotten. In both these camps the sugar ration was 25–30 grams, but there were periods during which we didn't receive any sugar at all.

Attitude of the NKVD towards Poles (interrogation methods, torture and other forms of punishment, communist propaganda, information about Poland, etc.):

As a rule, they interrogated those who had worked in political organizations, or the Second Department [illegible], or those who were denounced by interned Communism sympathizers or simply Communists, who provided the Bolsheviks with incriminating information pertaining to attitudes towards Communism and concerning a particular prisoner in question. Interrogations were carried out usually at night, often until 6.00 a.m.; the interrogators used various tricks and threatened the prisoners with deportation to the north or imprisonment of family that had remained in the home country, which was why many inmates broke. In all probability, sophisticated torture wasn't used.

The communist propaganda was spread through movies, newspapers, books, radio broadcasts and talks which the political commissars organized in various blocks for small groups on an ad hoc basis. This method yielded meager results, as the intellectual level of the political commissars was low and they often made fools of themselves. The propagation of communism by interned communists was much worse for the internees. Many people lent their ears to them, and they managed to turn many Poles – seemingly decent individuals – into communist agitators, and even to talk them into joining the Red Army.

The information we received about Poland and the government were such as to undermine our faith in regaining our freedom and restoring the Polish State.

Medical assistance, hospitals, mortality rate (provide the names of the deceased):

The camp hospital functioned thanks to Polish doctors. It was poorly equipped: for instance, the first appendectomy was performed by a Polish doctor with the use of crude instruments and at great risk. There were only the most basic medicaments.

As for the medical assistance, my own experience can serve as a good example. Due to general exhaustion and avitaminosis, I suffered retinal hemorrhaging in the left eye. The tool indispensable for medical examination (a magnifying glass) was delivered to the doctor after five weeks, although the nearest hospital was located in a town that was only three kilometers away. Since the Polish doctor was unable to make a diagnosis and my condition was deteriorating (with a risk of blindness), he told the chief doctor, a Soviet woman, that I should be sent to Smolensk for a clinical examination. I appended my own request to the doctor's statement. The answer was a curt "no", accompanied by an ironic laugh and a waving of the hand. Then I understood that my request must have seemed like a pipe dream to this doctor. I was eventually sent to an ophthalmologist after eight months of illness, following the conclusion of the Polish-Soviet agreement.

Was it at all possible to get in contact with one's home country and family?

We were first allowed to write letters to our families after five months. We received only some letters from our families, and they were often delivered after two or three months. Usually the letters were distributed in batches. The letters were kept by the camp command so that they could compare them and learn detailed information about the internee.

When were you released and how did you manage to join the Polish Army?

I was released on 22 or 23 August [1941] in Gryazovets. On 25 August I was admitted to the Polish Army.

Collection of the Hoover Institution Library & Archives at the disposal of the Central Archives of Modern Records, Władysław Anders Collection. Reports, 800/1/0/-/48, account no. 2036.

WINCENTY HOFFMAN

Personal data:

Wincenty Hoffman, sergeant, 47 years old, farmer (military settler), unmarried.

Date and circumstances of arrest:

On 20 September 1939, I crossed the border with Latvia along with the "Brasław" National Defense Battalion. After laying down my arms, I was interned at the camps in Litene, Lilaste and Ulbroka. We were transported into the USSR after the Bolsheviks took Latvia on 22 August 1940.

Name of the camp:

Yukhnovo, Smolensk Oblast.

Description of the camp:

The camp was set up in the buildings of a dissolved estate 35 kilometers from the Babynino train station near Yukhnov. Condition of the buildings – ruins which were renovated by the prisoners. Living conditions made difficult by overcrowding and bug infestations.

Social composition of POWs:

Around 2,600 in total of which around 2,100 prisoners came from Lithuania and around 500 from Latvia. Nationality was 90% Polish, the rest were Belarusians, Ukrainians and a few Jews.

Life in the camp:

We built and renovated buildings in the confines of the camp and cleaned the surrounding area. Only trusted volunteers worked outside the camp. There were also around 150 people who worked constantly – the Stakhanovites. Those who were not working had to attend talks (*beseda*) held by political commissars. We received no wages for our labor. The Stakhanovites received an extra 200 grams of bread per day and groats for supper. The food was generally poor. Clothing was handed out to the workers, the rest just had their lives made difficult. Social life was good in groups, of which there were two. The first were loyal Polish citizens; they were 96% of all the internees. The second group were those with broken spirits who had succumbed to the hostile conditions and worked to Poland's detriment by announcing that Poland would no longer exist, etc. These latter took part in classes – lectures of a communist and anti-religious nature. We were permitted to borrow books but few people ever did as there was only communist doctrine available. We were allowed to put on shows but we were forbidden from saying a word about anything that was Polish or brought Poland to mind.

Attitude of the NKVD towards Poles:

There were always at least four political commissars in the camp constantly occupied with giving lectures on the history of communism and the Soviet system. Everything Polish was condemned, they claimed that Poland would never exist, etc.

There were also many anti-religious lectures. The greatest ordeal were the interrogations. Everyone was divided into two partitions – German and Bolshevik. I told them that I lived in Pabianice even though I had a military settlement in the Wilno region and so I was considered as someone from the German partition. However, a few weeks later, Leonard Puzinowski, a former clerk of the "Połtawa" Draft Office [?] (currently serving in the army as a senior accountant at the Repository of Chancellery and Publishing Materials Of the State Archives in the East), informed on me and I was consequently questioned many times. I was asked how I came into possession of the settlement, how many Bolsheviks I had killed during that war, if – as a military settler – I was an informant for the police and intelligence ("2"). I was threatened during interrogation with a revolver, forced to stand motionless for several hours. All of these interrogations were generally carried out at night. I was forced to sign a declaration which said I was to be imprisoned for having given a false place of residence and not having confessed my alleged guilt.

During this entire period, around 150 people were transported from Yukhnov to other camps or prisons. On 31 May 1941, I was taken to Ponoy on the Kola Peninsula. The trip to Murmansk took five days, during which time we were given some warm soup only once. The journey by ship lasted nine days, during which we received no food for three days. When we started shouting: "Give us bread!", the exit and hatches were covered with boards and we nearly suffocated. There were 3,500 people on the ship. We were forced to live in the open air after reaching Ponoy. Several tents were set up later, but not enough for everyone. Work on constructing the airbase lasted 12 hours [per day]. Initially, about 100 grams of bread was given daily, then 200 grams and a little soup. There were 4,500 of us, including about 1,000 policemen. Were it not for the Polish-Bolshevik agreement, hardly anyone would have endured there, because, as we were unofficially told, we had been sentenced to indefinite labor for being dangerous and unreliable elements.

On 17 July [1941] we were transported to Arkhangelsk, and on 25 July to the Vyazniki camp, Ivanovo Oblast.

Medical assistance, hospitals, mortality rate:

There was a medical point at the camp in Yukhnov where aid was provided by prisoner-doctors. There was a lack of proper medicine, however. Around 12 people died in the period between 25 August 1940 and 31 May 1941.

Was it at all possible to get in contact with one's home country and family?

We were allowed to write to our immediate family, but it was more difficult to get a response, as the incoming letters were used by the NKVD during the interrogations. For instance, they would show us a letter and say that we would get it only if we confessed to a crime we had not committed.

When were you released?

Colonel Sulik[-Sarnowski] arrived in the camp on 27 August 1941 and read out an order from the commander-in-chief regarding the organization of a Polish Army in the USSR. After the colonel had read this out and made a speech, a cheer went up for Poland, the president and the commander-in-chief, after which the 12,000 POWs in the camp paraded before the colonel. The medical commission began their work the next day. I was deemed fit for military service on 29 August 1941. Immediately following my medical inspection, I reported to the colonel that I wanted to serve in the army (everybody did the same). There were a few among us who declared that they did not want to serve and the Soviets took care of them. I arrived at Tatishchevo with the others on 7 September 1941 and was assigned to the 5th Infantry Division.

I would like to add to the above that, during my time in Yukhnov, I had hung a picture above my bunk and after three [illegible] I was forced to hide it. We were not permitted to pray together, to sing Christmas carols or Easter songs. The political commissars lectured constantly that there would be no more Poland, or, if it would be a Communist state supervised by the USSR. Nobody listened, however. On the contrary, we laughed at their agitation. In a word, we lived in the hope of a brighter tomorrow and we were not disappointed.

Encampment, 25 February 1943

Collection of the Hoover Institution Library & Archives at the disposal of the Central Archives of Modern Records, Władysław Anders Collection. Reports, 800/1/0/-/46, account no. 114.

CZESŁAW KRÓL

Personal data:

Czesław Król, platoon-leader, regular non-commissioned officer with the Border Protection Corps, born in 1902, married.

How did you end up in Russia:

Acting upon an order given by Colonel Świątkowski, commander of the "Głębokie" Border Protection Corps, together with my regiment, on 21 September 1939 I crossed the Polish-Latvian border in Zemgale. The Latvian authorities disarmed and interned us. On 28 August 1940, after they had occupied Latvia, the Soviet authorities deported us to the Smolensk Oblast, Yukhnov District. We were kept in stables there, and we were promptly taken for interrogation.

Methods of interrogation and torture during investigation:

I was interrogated by the NKVD authorities from Yukhnov, who used the following methods: appealing to the prisoner to tell the truth, which would diminish his "guilt" or even result in release; interrogating at night: the prisoner was woken up and interrogated for a few hours, during which he had to remain standing under a bright electrical light (about 300 Watts), which quickly led to exhaustion; punching in the face with fists – this is how I lost two teeth.

Ruling in absentia, means of delivering verdicts:

I wasn't served an indictment and there was no trial, but a ruling in absentia was given and I was sentenced to eight years of hard labor for serving in the Polish army. I didn't receive a copy of the ruling nor had I any access to the "incriminating" material.

Life in forced labor camps:

Location and grounds: Yukhnov, Murmansk, Kola Peninsula, Arkhangelsk and Suzdal. Tundra, with rocky desert in some places (Kola Peninsula); everywhere there were billions of mosquitoes and virulent midges.

Living conditions: In Yukhnov we lived in a stable, and in other places in the open air. We slept on the ground, on beds made of heather, with our own clothes for cover.

Food: In Yukhnov – 700 grams of bread and three fourths of a liter of soup twice a day. The soup was either with groats or potatoes, boiled from fish. In the Kola Peninsula – 200 grams of bread and soup twice a day, made either of wholemeal flour or bran.

Working conditions: We worked at road construction on rocky ground (Kola Peninsula) or swampy ground (Yukhnov), with no rest (no days off) and regardless of rain, sleet, blizzard or frost.

Work quotas: There were no quotas.

Working time: In Yukhnov 8 hours, in the Kola Peninsula 12 hours per day.

Clothing: I received one change of underwear, a padded jacket, quilted trousers and a quilted cap with ear flaps. I didn't get any shoes.

Hygienic and sanitary conditions: Medical assistance was provided by good specialists, Polish citizens, but they didn't have enough medicaments at their disposal, either for treating or preventing diseases, and disinfectants were missing as well. We didn't take baths, which resulted in filth and lice.

Entertainment and cultural life: None.

Contact with the home country: I had none, because my family had been deported.

Remuneration: None.

The guards treated Poles badly and were generally hostile towards us.

Mortality at the camp: At first it was rather low, but then it increased significantly; it was at its highest after we were released.

Communist propaganda: Every second day, a communist propaganda movie was screened, and there were meetings three times a week during which the power of the USSR was juxtaposed with the "powerlessness" of the Polish state, the audience was presented with the "torments" which the national minorities had suffered at the hands of the Polish authorities, and the "unfairness" of the Polish government towards Ukrainians, Belarusians and Jews was emphasized; a number of other issues were also addressed. They tried to prove that Poland would never be restored, and moreover they criticized the former government of the Polish Republic. By way of example, a brochure was published in which there was the following picture: General Sikorski, having left his shoes and saber in Warsaw, and his gloves and cap in France, runs away down some other road; the caption read, "Where to now?" Or another illustrated brochure: Churchill in the official gallery, surrounded by his staff and generals; next to them, English soldiers are beaten and impaled with the bayonets of the Soviet troops.

Collection of the Hoover Institution Library & Archives at the disposal of the Central Archives of Modern Records, Władysław Anders Collection. Reports, 800/1/0/-/48, account no. 1392.

EUGENIUSZ JACKOWSKI

Personal data:

Eugeniusz Jackowski, lieutenant of the reserve,
born on 12 December 1901,
a judge at the regional court, married.

Date and circumstances of arrest:

I was arrested on 19 September 1939 as I was crossing the Polish-Lithuanian border in Zawiasy. I was interned in Lithuania at the camp in Kulautuva until 11 November 1939 and at Kalvarija until 10 July 1940. After the USSR entered Lithuania, the NKVD took over the camp in Kalvarija on 10 July 1940 and transported the prisoners into the USSR.

Name of camp, prison or forced labor site:

I was interned in the USSR in the Kozelsk camp until 29 June and then in Gryazovets until 28 August 1941.

Description of the camp or prison (grounds, buildings, housing conditions, hygiene):

The internment camp in Kozelsk was located in a monastery at the edge of a forest. It was mostly in ruin and had earlier been earmarked for a *detskiy dom*. The buildings were only suitable for living after we completed renovations. The lice-infested brick church buildings and wooden houses equipped with two- and three-level bunks in particular only became bearable after a renovation of the interior, which we made using tools and materials provided to us by the camp authorities. The renovation of the buildings, the setting up of a hospital, laundry building and bathhouse created tolerable living conditions.

The camp in Gryazovets had several similarly semi-dilapidated church buildings large enough only to hold the 300 POWs who were already there. We -- more than 1,000 new arrivals at the camp -- had to live outdoors at first. The barracks we then built from wooden planks only partly protected us from the hordes of mosquitos and the cold weather. By a stroke of luck, the afternoons were warm and a small river ran by the camp.

Social composition of POWs, prisoners, exiles (nationality, type of crimes, intellectual and moral standing, mutual relations, etc.):

The vast majority of internees at both camps were officers of the Polish Army and officers and privates from the State Police. Mentality and morale – fairly high. Mutual relations in the Kozelsk camp – good until the end of 1941. Mistrust crept in then, caused by the appearance of a small group of people with "new", "modern" socio-political views concurrent with those of the USSR. Both as a consequence of this and as a result of the outbreak of the Russian-German war, that minority separated from the majority of prisoners who stuck closer together.

Life in the camp or prison (daily routine, working conditions, quotas, wages, food, clothes, social and cultural life, etc.):

Everyday life included a wake-up call, morning roll-call, breakfast, voluntary physical labor in the carpentry, tailoring and cobbling workshops, renovation of buildings and cleaning the camp, laundry building and bathhouse, then a break for lunch, more labor, dinner and evening roll-call.

Food – almost entirely lacking in meat but sufficient enough to stave off hunger. Clothing – primarily our own; repairing underwear and shoes was done in our own tailoring and cobbling workshops. Social life – fairly well developed. The camp library and our own supplies of books partly fulfilled our needs. Our choir and orchestra, partly using instruments of our own construction, earned deep gratitude in proportion to the number of viewers the camp cinema lost.

Attitude of the NKVD towards Poles (interrogation methods, torture and other forms of punishment, communist propaganda, information about Poland, etc.):

The comportment of the NKVD was almost proper; I do not know of any cases of torture. Propaganda – cinema and surveys, the level and contents of which matched those of the majority of Soviet daily newspapers.

Medical assistance, hospitals, mortality rate (provide the names of the deceased):

Medical aid thanks to the establishment of a hospital and the involvement of Polish doctors – sufficient. Mortality in the camp was low, as far as I know.

Was it at all possible to get in contact with one's home country and family?

We were first permitted to write home in mid-November 1941, and then once a month until the outbreak of the war with Germany. Throughout this whole period, however, I received only five cards and letters out of several dozen that were sent to me from Poland.

When were you released and how did you manage to join the Polish Army?

I was released on 28 August 1941 from the camp in Gryazovets, where I signed up for further service in the Polish Army on 29 August.

Collection of the Hoover Institution Library & Archives at the disposal of the Central Archives of Modern Records, Władysław Anders Collection. Reports, 800/1/0/-/46, account no. 347.

STANISŁAW KASZLIKOWSKI

Personal data (name, surname, rank, age, occupation and marital status):
Stanisław Kaszlikowski, second lieutenant, 34 years old, State Police officer (aspirant), widowed.

Date and circumstances of arrest:

On 11 July 1940, I was taken to the USSR by the NKVD along with all the internees of the camp in Vilkaviškis (Lithuania). At 6.00 a.m. on that day, having rallied together all of the internees, the NKVD officers conducted a search, ordering the prisoners to line up in groups of eight and sit in the middle of the road, as tightly as possible, not allowing them to talk or move. As a result, we were scorching, crowded in the sun. Acquiring water was out of question. Around 1.00 p.m., following the search, they led all of us to a railway station, hustling us to march faster and keep the formation tight. After arriving at the station around 2.00 p.m., we kept on waiting in the scorching sun next to the rails.

Around 6.00 p.m., we were loaded in groups of 45 onto medium-sized freight wagons and we soon departed. Our transport didn't get any water on that day. The wagon doors and two small windows were locked up. The big number of passengers and poor access to air caused incredible stuffiness. During the 4-day trip to Kozelsk, physiological needs had to be satisfied inside the wagon, except for one time. In the subsequent days, we received small amounts of water. We could wash ourselves only by sacrificing the drinking water. As for food, I was given one small can of meat, [illegible] of dark bread, and extremely salty, dried fish which made me thirsty. Neither me nor anyone else received any cooked meal. There were wooden bunks inside the wagons.

Starting from the station in Mołodeczno, where they separated officers, police, gendarmes, and the Border Guards from us, they transported us in smaller freight wagons, 36 people each. Other than that, the conditions were the same.

Name of the camp, prison or forced labor site:

In the USSR I stayed in the camps of Kozelsk and Gryazovets.

Description of the camp or prison (grounds, buildings, housing conditions, hygiene):

The Kozelsk camp was situated in a former monastery, located near a forest, surrounded with a wall and barbed wire. Buildings: large bricked Orthodox churches, as well as bricked and wooden houses for bygone priests – destroyed, shabby, dirty, infested with incredible amounts of bedbugs, and hard to heat. The latter might have been because we were given wet firewood from poplar, or fruit trees branches (which we had to collect ourselves from the snow, walking several hundred meters out of the camp), or nothing at all, which forced us to pick wood shavings from around the kitchen or to steal the wood prepared by the Bolsheviks for their office buildings. We slept on wooden bunk beds. I received a pallet and a blanket after around a month after arriving at the camp. I lived in block no. 15, situated near a large lavatory (the only one in the camp), whose stench often forced us to close the windows tight. There were 10 of us sleeping in rooms that were on average three-by-three meters, which made them utterly overcrowded, and the bed would also serve as a table, chair, etc.

The Gryazovets camp was also situated in an old monastery. Having arrived there on 2 July 1941, we encountered POWs who had already been living in the building. As this small and heavily infested with bedbugs building couldn't fit in the newcomers from Kozelsk, the vast majority of them slept under the stars, being cruelly bitten by swarms of mosquitoes and flies during bright nights. After three weeks or maybe a month, wooden barracks were built and everybody was able to find shelter. In the barracks, we slept on wooden bunk beds with no pallets.

Social composition of POWs, prisoners, exiles (nationality, type of crimes, intellectual and moral standing, mutual relations, etc.):

The prisoners in Kozelsk were mostly officers of the Polish Army, officers and privates of the State Police, Border Corps and several administrative or court clerks, etc. In Gryazovets, the composition was similar, but also included officer cadets. Among others, there were two individuals who reported Lithuanian nationality, sentenced for spying for Lithuania by the Polish authorities, as well as several Polish criminals: one of them sentenced for a murder, and another [illegible]. Apart from that, both in Kozelsk and Gryazovets, there was a certain percentage of Jews who collaborated with the NKVD authorities, and a small number of Polish citizens who were listed as Belarusian, Ukrainian, or even German nationality. In both camps there was also a large percentage of Polish citizens who were supporters of Communism. After the camps in Gryazovets merged, 28 of them left, voluntarily joining the Red Army. A significant percent of these proponents, as well as people who listed German nationality or the ones that didn't want to join the Polish army, stayed in Gryazovets following our departure. As a result of the above, mutual relations in the camps were unbearable. At every step, one had to beware of the NKVD's informants willing to share insights from the camp with the authorities.

Life in the camp or prison (daily routine, working conditions, quotas, wages, food, clothes, social and cultural life, etc.):

Daily routine in both camps: wake-up call, roll-call organized by the NKVD, breakfast, dinner, supper, another roll-call, and curfew. In Kozelsk, only privates were used for doing work outside the camp's premises. It happened once that officers were used for that purpose too, but due to protest raised by some, it was stopped.

Everybody, however, except for the staff officers, had to work in the kitchen, bathrooms, laundry, and cleaning and ordering in the camp's grounds. Those who worked on building renovations, in carpentry workshop, etc., would receive increased food rations with an extra portion of soup in the evening. They would also get some clothing pieces from time to time, most often padded jackets, while other people would only get underwear and footwraps, in case their old ones tore.

Cultural life was under close supervision of the authorities. There was a choir and makeshift orchestra concerts, lectures on foreign languages or on general topics, and these were the only signs of cultural life. Lack of support as well as insufficient amounts of paper and textbooks was limiting for those willing to self-educate.

Attitude of the NKVD towards Poles (interrogation methods, torture and other forms of punishment, communist propaganda, information about Poland, etc.):

The NKVD was hostile towards us throughout the whole time we stayed in the camps. Upon admittance to the camp, a thorough personal search was carried out. Shaving accessories and other sharp items, non--Russian currencies, any gold items, documents and photographs were ceased. Some of us never saw the confiscated belongings again, but often they would be given back before we were released from the Gryazovets camp in order to join the Polish army. I heard a lot about methods of interrogation, but I don't have anything to say myself. They questioned me in a strict manner, but with no swearing or beating.

The communist propaganda was spread with the aid of newspapers, books, films, lectures, and talks delivered by the political commissars inside each of the houses. I avoided entering any discussions with the Bolsheviks as a general rule, and I don't have anything specific to accuse them of. I heard from other companions that they would say Poland would never exist anymore. They recruited for the Red Army with the use of corrupted proxies, such as Arciszewski – supposedly a captain.

With regards to food, I need to say that in Kozelsk it was overall bearable, but in Gryazovets it worsened after the merge of the two camps resulted in a sharp increase of prisoners, which went beyond 1,000 people, while the kitchens had only a capacity of serving food to 600 people. On top of that, three or four weeks before the amnesty, they decreased our rations to 400 grams bread a day and a watery soup in the morning, with two or three tablespoons of groats for dinner and boiled water in the evening. By the end of this food restriction, real hunger ensued. We couldn't even dream of buying something to eat.

Medical assistance, hospitals, mortality rate (provide the names of the deceased):

Medical assistance was mostly provided by the Polish doctors in both camps. Mortality was relatively low. Only a few people died.

Was it at all possible to get in contact with one's home country and family?

From November 1940, we were allowed to write home or wherever we wanted. We could do so once a month until May 1941, when our writing options stopped. It was worse when it came to receiving the letters. Personally, I received one letter in May and it was only thanks to a great deal of effort our fellow Polish block elders had put in in response to many of the prisoners reporting that their correspondence wasn't getting through to them.

When were you released and how did you manage to join the Polish Army?

After the amnesty was announced and General Anders visited us on 2 September 1941, we left Gryazovets and went to Totskoye. We travelled the way to the Gryazovets railway station on foot, in the pouring rain. At the station, soaking wet and freezing, we waited till morning under the stars for the train, as the NKVD hadn't made any attempt to bring it earlier.

Encampment, 25 February 1943

Collection of the Hoover Institution Library & Archives at the disposal of the Central Archives of Modern Records, Władysław Anders Collection. Reports, 800/1/0/-/47, account no. 589.

ANTONI JANUCHOWSKI

Antoni Januchowski, born in 1900, Roman-Catholic, Polish nationality, a regular non-commissioned officer in the cavalry, previously in the 4th Uhlan Regiment in Wilno.

On 19 September 1939, my superiors and I were interned in Ukmergė and Palanga, Lithuania. In June 1940, I was deported along with the whole camp to Yukhnov, Babynino railway station, in roofed freight wagons. At Mołodeczno station, the transport was divided in such a way that chaplain priests, officers, gendarmes, policemen and border guards were separated by the NKVD and later placed in Kozelsk camp, to my knowledge. There were around 3,000 people in the Yukhnov camp, and all of them had been interned in Lithuania or Latvia. The labor was carried out mostly on the camp's premises, but no work quotas were imposed on us. Food rations – compared to what we ate back in Poland – were usually very poor and insufficient, with almost no fats. It's enough to say that during 10 months everybody lost from 20 to 35 kilos of weight.

It's hard to precisely determine the camp's composition in terms of nationality, however there were Ukrainians, Jews, Belarusians, and I also encountered Protestants born in Germany. I don't remember their surnames, but they strongly disapproved of Hitler and the Reich's politics. A very painful thing in the Yukhnov camp was that there was a so-called commune or a temple organized under directions of Corporal Dobrowolski (a teacher by profession) from Mołodeczno. The commune was attended mostly by intellectuals, such as teachers, clerks, officer cadets and regular non-commissioned officers. The lectures took place almost every evening, with the doors shut and windows covered. From my colleagues' accounts, I know that they were learning to become political workers and were taking an exam on that matter, and that they sent a card to Stalin thanking for having been freed, with signatures; they were painting posters with the slogan "through revolution to Soviet Poland"; they held anti-religious lectures, appointed a Communist government of the future Poland, and likely, they were judging our government in England. They were often visited by the NKVD men, and whenever they came, a joyful and happy atmosphere prevailed.

The Soviet propaganda in the camp was really active, but one-sided, anti-Polish and anti-democratic, shamelessly mendacious, done by political commissars and political workers. They would express themselves by saying that England was a prostitute and democracy was syphilis to the ground, that it was only to be lifted onto [illegible] and it would vanish, that officers and non-commissioned officers of the Polish Army used to beat their subordinates, that Poland existed just for 20 years and it would be no more, that Poland had one plow for every five farmers and that the Germans were fighting a just war. On our side, just out of curiosity, questions were posed and answers were given, which compromised all the blatant lies they were feeding us. In reaction, they asked for our surnames and noted them down – we often gave surnames of people who weren't even in the camp. We often responded with screams and whistles to their lies. It was at the beginning of our stay in the camp when they said that attending the lectures was mandatory. When it became clear that taking part was voluntary, the speaker was left surrounded only by a couple of listeners, who most probably were making fun of him. I should mention here that the senior lieutenant political worker used to read out the articles from their newspaper "Pravda" like a semi-literate person.

They also screened movies, but from what I'd heard it was all lies and mockery. A library was open and filled with books by Marx, Engels and Lenin. They were only read by the "commune-temple" goers.

Health care was really scrupulous, thanks to the fact that our doctors were performing the duties. Mortality was minimal. Lice appeared only out of negligence. Bathrooms and the disinfecting facility were open every day, so that your turn came every 10 days.

Cultural life and patriotism thrived day by day thanks to the loyal sons of Poland. Prayers often took place in hiding, in the attics of old buildings, in the bushes, or quietly on the fourth level of bunk beds. During movie screenings and during the breaks when the equipment failed, the audience would often sing patriotic songs like *Poland Is Not Yet Lost* etc., to protest against the ultra-blatant lies. In those cases, the political workers would tell us to disperse, screaming with anger. But it happened only after we finished the song. The commune participants willingly attended the screenings, showing their honest satisfaction. There were voices in the crowd that we should hang the commune-goers – traitors of the nation – and none of them would come back to the fatherland alive. But this didn't scare them; they blindly believed that there would never be free Poland.

I received four letters from my wife and children from Wilno, the last one in April 1941. In June 1941 the Yukhnov camp was deported to Murmansk, and then to the Kola Peninsula. A couple of days after the outbreak of the Soviet-German war, we were moved through Arkhangelsk to Vyazniki – for the first time, Polish internees and POWs were placed in the same camp. There were about 10,000 of us. Then a representative of the Republic of Poland, Colonel Sulik-Sarnowski, came to the camp and we were accepted into the Polish Army in the USSR. I was assigned to the "Tatishchevo" 5th Infantry Division.

In the Kola Peninsula, before the outbreak of the Soviet-German war, we suffered hunger and inhumane treatment – there was a total lack of food. We received 80 grams of bread a day and a flour soup with no fat twice a day. They wouldn't let us use water for washing ourselves or the dishes. There was a sense that we were truly brought there for extermination just because we were Poles.

13 February 1942

Collection of the Hoover Institution Library & Archives at the disposal of the Central Archives of Modern Records, Władysław Anders Collection. Reports, 800/1/0/-/48, account no. 2312.

ALFONS KARPOWICZ

Personal data (name, surname, rank, age, occupation and marital status):
Alfons Karpowicz, platoon-leader, born on 16 [?] September 1904, Border Guard functionary by profession, unmarried.

Date and circumstances of arrest:

I was crossing the Latvian border on 20 September 1939.

Name of the camp, prison or forced labor site:

I was incarcerated in the camp in Lilaste. In the spring of 1940 we left the camp to perform various kinds of forest labor. When the Soviets entered Latvia, I was arrested by the Latvian police and sent to the camp in Ulbroka, which had already been a Bolshevik camp at the time. On 2 September 1940 I was taken to the internment camp in Kozelsk. Next, on 9 June 1941, I was deported to the Kola Peninsula, from where on short notice I was transferred to Suzdal (on 27 July 1941).

Description of the camp or prison (grounds, buildings, housing conditions, hygiene):

The camp in Kozelsk – a former monastery; we lived in farm buildings and abandoned Orthodox churches. At first the housing and hygienic conditions were bad, and we were plagued by bugs. Later on, thanks to the energetic efforts and organization skills of the Polish camp administration, the conditions improved.

Social composition of POWs, prisoners, exiles (nationality, type of crimes, intellectual and moral standing, mutual relations, etc.):

There were approximately 2,700 internees in the camp, including about 950 officers; the rest were policemen, Border Guards and gendarmes, and there were a few local government officials. The majority of the internees were Poles, but there were also a few Jews, and I recall that there was one Ukrainian. The intellectual and moral standing was average. Mutual relations were good, with the exception of a few communists, of whom I remember Airman Sergeant Medard Konieczny from the 5th Air Force Regiment in Lida, Commander Second Lieutenant [surname missing].

Life in the camp or prison (daily routine, working conditions, quotas, wages, food, clothes, social and cultural life, etc.):

Daily routine: wake-up at 6.00 a.m., checking the number of prisoners by the Soviet authorities at 6.30 a.m., breakfast at 7.00 a.m., setting off for work for the service units (improving camp conditions, repairing buildings, cleaning the camp premises), dinner at noon, then work again, supper at 6.00 p.m., counting the prisoners at 8.30 p.m., curfew at 9.00 p.m. Permanent workers (blacksmiths, carpenters, laundry attendants, barbers) received better, more nourishing food. Food: soup with groats for breakfast; for dinner – soup (meat-based cabbage soup) and thick groats; for supper – soup and tea. We received 800 grams of bread per day. Generally, the food was sufficient. We received five 50-gram packages of shag tobacco and 5 matchboxes per month. Clothes and underwear were issued from Soviet warehouses only to those who didn't have any of their own. The officers had a separate kitchen, with bigger food rations. Mutual relations were generally good. Towards the end of our stay, radio loudspeakers were installed in the camp. We were short on books. The internees had about 200 of them; there was a Soviet library, but it was filled with propaganda books and therefore rarely used. There was a club in the camp, and plays were staged there; we also had a choir and a good orchestra. There was a piano in the club. Approximately once a week we could see a movie, and the same picture would be shown several times.

Attitude of the NKVD towards Poles (interrogation methods, torture and other forms of punishment, communist propaganda, information about Poland, etc.):

Tedious interrogations, but they didn't resort to physical violence. The frequency of interrogations varied and depended on the individual in question and the functions he had held back in Poland. We were constantly subjected to communist propaganda in the form of talks, lectures and movies. The speakers, however, represented a low intellectual level. Political commissars went from one block to the other and tried to initiate political, propagandist, anti-religious discussions. Poland was talked about in negative terms, and its political system and actualities were always denounced. I cannot provide any specific examples. The only Poland whose existence they were ready to allow for was a red Poland.

Medical assistance, hospitals, mortality rate (provide the names of the deceased):

There was a hospital in the camp. We received Polish medical assistance under Soviet supervision – and it was good. The mortality rate was low, I think that it didn't exceed 10 deaths. I know that the former Kutno district governor from Poznań Voivodeship died.

Was it at all possible to get in contact with one's home country and family?

We had poor contact by post with our country and our families, all the more so due to the fact that the NKVD used to intercept and keep our letters in order to harass the internees and force more confessions during interrogations.

When were you released and how did you manage to join the Polish Army?

I was released on 24 August 1941 in Suzdal, where I also appeared before the enlistment board of the Polish Army. On 8 September I came in a Polish transport to Tatishchevo, to the 5th Infantry Division.

Collection of the Hoover Institution Library & Archives at the disposal of the Central Archives of Modern Records, Władysław Anders Collection. Reports, 800/1/0/-/48, account no. 2113.

KAZIMIERZ JASIEŃSKI

Kazimierz Jasieński, captain, 47 years old, clerk, unmarried.

I crossed the Lithuanian border at Zawiasy on 20 September 1939 together with the 3rd Auxiliary Artillery Corps in Wilno. We were taken to Kulautuva – a summer resort near Kaunas. We lived in wooden buildings that lacked furnaces. It was only in the middle of November that they gave us iron furnaces and the only fuel we had were damp, rotten tree stumps that did not want to catch. On the rare occasion that we received better wood, the temperature in the room sometimes to five or seven degrees. The camp commander was Colonel Brazilius, a Pole. His name before 1920 was Brazulewicz. His attitude to us inmates was hostile.

A Soviet commission arrived at the camp around mid-December 1939 in order to record all the Polish citizens who came from countries under Soviet occupation. They were promised that they would be released if they voluntarily agreed to return home (a typical NKVD tactic). More than 200 people, including around 10 officers, agreed to go home. I don't know if they signed any declarations to this end but they were particularly reticent about the subject.

It later turned out that those people were indeed released only to be arrested and deported after some time. The rest were deported immediately. Relations in the camp worsened. Some of the officers and privates from Wilno and the Wilno Region started to add Lithuanian endings to their names and many tried to become Lithuanian serfs. In mid-December, we were taken to the camp in Vilkaviškis; some (mainly police and privates) were taken to Ukmergė. The camp commander was a major either of German or Latvian origin, but he behaved himself properly. We lived in a two-story brick buildings (former officers' quarters). Housing conditions were perfectly fine, as was the food. The officers were transported to Kalvarija at the beginning of April 1940. The camp commander was Major Jaksztas, a prison warden by profession. We occupied a building that was originally intended to be a madhouse. We reached the camp at around 10.00 a.m. (6–7 kilometers from the station). It began with basic search of our persons and affects which lasted until 4.00 a.m. the next morning.

We were treated exactly like prisoners. Wake-up call at 7.00, breakfast before 8.00 a.m., a walk in pairs around the small, rectangular courtyard between 8 a.m. and 9 a.m. Another hour or sometimes two walking after lunch. We declared a hunger strike for the insult to the Polish coat of arms but this was ended five days later, when a commission arrived from

Kaunas to put a stop to it. We were allowed to write a letter once a month, ten lines on a postcard.

I encountered the NKVD authorities on 2 July 1940. On that afternoon, the Lithuanian outposts were being reinforced by the Bolsheviks and it was announced in the evening that we would be deported on 10 July. Initially, an NKVD officer, the commander of the transport, agreed to take the goods to the station for us, but then, at 5.00 or 6.00 a.m. on the day of departure, he withdrew his promise. We stood in the courtyard from 6.00 to 11.00 a.m. and we went on foot to the station, carrying our things in the greatest heat-wave. We were been warned that the escort would shoot without warning if we left the road. We were led by General Przeździecki. We were walking for the first time surrounded by bayonets and dogs. Our bigger items were thrown out onto the road.

At around 4.00 p.m., after 45 people were loaded into each small freight car, we were given a bucket of water and the door was locked. We did not set off until the evening. We were not released from the wagons at all, so physiological needs had necessarily to be relieved in the wagon. At around At 2.00 a.m., Umiastowski (the son of Colonel Umiastowski) managed to slip out of the car through the window near Wilno. He was spotted, swept up with the help of a dog, and, of course, beaten in the face with a rifle butt. An roll-call was immediately carried out, which took place in the manner they usually used. They woke us up from the outside, opened the door, reprimanded us and ordered everyone to go to one side of the car and then walk to the other side one by one, insulting us all the time. Sometimes, as a result of inefficient counting or simply to harass us, the roll-call was repeated two or three times.

On 11 July at 12.00 p.m. in Mołodeczno, we were taken out of the station and we were released from the wagons for the first time in over 20 hours and given a few minutes to relieve ourselves. We switched to broad-gauge wagons and after a few roll-calls at night, which took place in a very similar way, we set off. Russian wagons were already prepared for similar transports and had small drains [?], so the hygienic conditions were much better.

We arrived in Kozelsk on 13 July 1940. We occupied around 10 buildings. The largest of them (a former Orthodox church), with three-level bunks, housed over 600 people; in my block, housing over 400 people, there were also three-level bunks. We slept for a whole month on floor-boards (the previous prisoners bad been taken away in May). Hygienic conditions were terrible. There were countless bugs in all the buildings. Two small light bulbs in the high ceiling cast a dim light on the room. There was no way that we could read anything.

I forgot to mention that we were searched before we were let into the camp. I do not mean the searches of our possessions that were carried out perfidiously, but I would like to mention how the prisoners themselves were searched. They were stripped naked, told to raise their hands; they even looked into the rectum. All personal belongings were taken without a receipt. Receipts were given for watches, especially gold ones, even though this meant nothing after the amnesty – Lieutenant Kowacz did not receive the watch, as far as I know, even he had a completely official receipt. He was told his watch had been sent to Moscow. A few days after arriving in Kozelsk, Colonel Jerzy Dąbrowski and Lieutenant Korkmaz of Turkish nationality – contract officer were [searched?], of course during night time.

A week later, the so-called *doprosy* – the interrogations – began. This involved a detail record of our lives with particular emphasis on voluntary service in Polish Army, not excluding any awards received, membership of a political party – Polish Socialist Party, Camp of National Unity, even the Nature Protection League [?] which was also considered a political party – as well as military settlement status. The political commissars, mostly Ukrainians, people of low intelligence, recorded these testimonies. The interrogations began once more a few months after this data was recorded; they lasted all day and night [and were led] by a special commission from Moscow. The interrogations sometimes went on uninterrupted for 8 hours (Lieutenant Roszkowski?). They asked almost identical questions: do we want to go home? What would we do if we went? What would our attitude towards the Soviet authorities be like? We were advised to think about it because we might remain in the camp a long time and, when the war was finished, Poland would disappear forever.

They acquired a new means of blackmail when we were permitted to write letters in November 1940 and when the replies came later. We were summoned to pick up letters which were shown to us from a distance and we were told that we could have them only after signing a declaration to become a confidant or join the army. When this did not work, they turned to threats. Abusive words were very often said about Poland and the government during the interrogations; they tried to prove that the Polish government was misleading its citizens and that the so-called current government could not be taken into serious consideration because nobody except England recognized it. They pointed to an article by Wanda Wasilewska to show that things were wrong in Poland. After all, it is our Polish writer Wanda Wasilewska who is writing about what is happening in Poland and you are sitting there lying to us.

As regards the communist propaganda, we were fed communist ideals by any means possible. They organized readings, gave us books – mostly the works of Lenin, Stalin and others – some reports from conventions. They set up a library of Polish books that only contained translations of Bolshevik propaganda brochures, screened specially selected films. The political commissars moved freely about the camp, happy to discuss at any moment under the pretext of friendship. It did not take long for this agitation to have an effect. Small groups began to form, usually made up of officers, who began to help the Bolshevik agitators. Very unpleasant relationships developed. We were afraid to speak freely because everything was immediately reported "beyond the gate," that is, at the camp's command center.

One of the largest and absolutely the most talented agitators who surpassed their teachers by a country mile was one particular Second Lieutenant Arciszewski, a deserter from the marine battalion from Gdynia, who still claimed to be a captain right up to the point he met his immediate superior Lieutenant [surname missing], the company commander. Arciszewski was [illegible] in Gdynia.

He was able to unite the younger inmates, especially the aviation lieutenants including Second Lieutenant Romanowski and Second Lieutenant Mickiewicz. Captain Smoliński and Lieutenant Rolewski from the 1st Wilno Brigade of the Polish Legions openly participated in the *krasnolyudki* group. The commander of the block was appointed by the Soviet authorities. His attitude towards the officers was sometimes worse than that of political commissars. Chemical engineer Second Lieutenant Pawłowski, Lieutenant Adrian from Łódź, the airman Sergeant Koneczny (Lida), Second Lieutenant Lewis from the 4th Battery of [?] Horse Artillery [?], Second Lieutenant Zieniuk (Belarusian) – a judge, Second Lieutenant Kukulski – a primary school teacher by profession, Second Lieutenant Królski – also a primary school teacher – and Second Lieutenant Żbikowski from Baranowicze, who belonged to a secret organization in the Kalvarija camp. He was probably the reason why General Przeździecki, Captain Bogdan Święcicki, Lieutenant Kłosiński and others (about 20 people in total) were deported to the Butyrka prison in Moscow.

These people agitated among officers and privates, mindlessly repeating the communist preaching of the Soviet agitators. They claimed that Poland would – thank God – be no more, and if it were, then it would only be a Soviet Poland, and that we should help in creating this new Poland by joining the ranks of the Red Army. Some of them volunteered as paratroopers; they were released from the camp for voluntary work. A corporal from the gendarmerie agitated among the non-commissioned officers (apparently he was seen in Quizil Ribat).

I can cite one more fact from our social life. When the block senior, the captain, currently Major Górnikowski, ordered a minute of silence during an evening roll-call on 11 November 1940, Second Lieutenant Mickiewicz (he was in Totskoye in the 19th Infantry Regiment) and Lieutenant Pawłowski (a chemical engineer who volunteered for the paratroops) said from the ranks: "Come on, let's go, enough of this farce, we are fed up with your bloody Poland." Pawłowski, a student named Bućko, Second Lieutenant Pieczyński, Captain Smoliński were the last leaders of this "club," handpicked by the Soviet authorities.

The most notable among the political commissars were NKVD Major Demidovich, Senior Lieutenant Fadej Król (a Pole), one Nesterov (in Kozelsk) and NKVD Captain Vasilevsky (Gryazovets).

I will mention one more march from the station to the camp. We had to walk on foot with our belongings about 6 kilometers, tired and starved, after a four-day trip in the heat, 50 people crammed into a wagon, where we were fed small fish (about 5 centimeters long) and one bucket of water per day. When the senior officer could no longer walk and fainted, the escort soldier reported to his supervisor and asked what he should do. He received a laconic response: "Don't you know what to do with him, you fool? Pick him up with the bayonet and you'll see how fast he goes!"

I will list the people with whom I was interned at Kozelsk that were deported and about whom I never heard anything again:

- Cavalry Lieutenant Jerzy Dąbrowski;
- Second Lieutenant Krzyczkowski, transferred to hospital in Moscow;
- Flight Captain Bruner;
- Captain Pilarski (Border Protection Corps), apparently he was imprisoned in Minsk or Borisov;
- Captain Chludziński;
- Cavalry Captain Chmielewski from the 4th Regiment;
- Major Sekunda;
- Sergeant Rozmysł.

Medical aid – sufficient, as we were treated by doctors, however it was worse with medicine. Around 10 people died, including:

- Second Lieutenant Dłuski, a geometrician by profession, around 30 years old (madness);
- Captain Wasilewski, a military settler, around 45 years old, hanged himself as he was unable to stand the constant interrogations;
- Policeman (chief? I do not recall his name), also hanged himself for this same reason;
- Lieutenant Marcinowski or Marcinkowski, around 40 years old, director of a school in Nowogródek, died in Gryazovets near Vologda;
- Major Müller, head of armaments for the 3rd Grodno Corps;
- District head Pełczyński.

Most illnesses regarded dysentery and dust blindness, lesser so scurvy.

From around 6 November 1940, we were permitted to write to our families once a month. The letters from home were mostly never delivered or arrived with a significant delay. In order to get them, we were summoned "beyond the gate," where the letters were used in the interrogations. Receiving a letter sometimes took longer than 1.5 hours.

We were read the so-called amnesty on 25 August 1941, released on 1 September and transported from Gryazovets to Totskoye via rail.

Encampment, 28 February 1943

Collection of the Hoover Institution Library & Archives at the disposal of the Central Archives of Modern Records, Władysław Anders Collection. Reports, 800/1/0/-/48, account no. 102.

JAN SZCZYGŁO

Personal data (name, surname, rank, age, occupation and marital status):
Jan Szczygło, born on 20 October 1895, senior officer of the State Police, married.

Date and circumstances of arrest:

I was interned in Lithuania from 19 September 1939 in the camp of Palanga and Vilkaviškis; there was no forced labor. I stayed in the USSR in the camp from 12 July 1940 to 24 August 1941.

Name of the camp, prison or forced labor site:

I did forced labor in the USSR in the camp of Kozelsk and on the Kola Peninsula.

Description of the camp or prison (grounds, buildings, housing conditions, hygiene):

In the Lithuanian camps, the accommodations, area and hygiene were good. The buildings where the internees lived were usually wooden and reasonably well heated in winter. In the USSR camps in Kozelsk, the housing conditions were very bad because there were at least 150 people living in wooden houses, while brick buildings – former Eastern Orthodox churches – were occupied by up to 500 people. The housing conditions and hygiene were completely neglected. On the Kola Peninsula, the housing conditions were completely impossible for people to live in because some of us had to sleep in tents and others under the open sky.

Social composition of POWs, prisoners, exiles (nationality, type of crimes, intellectual and moral standing, mutual relations, etc.):

There were about 2,000 internees in that camp, Polish soldiers and police officers. Their moral standing was depressing.

Life in the camp or prison (daily routine, working conditions, quotas, wages, food, clothes, social and cultural life, etc.):

The life in the USSR camps was as follows: 12 hours of work per day, without any rest or remuneration; food – from 60 to 150 grams of bread a day and soup twice a day, usually fish soup. Some prisoners received clothes and shoes, while others wore their own. There was no education or cultural life whatsoever.

Attitude of the NKVD towards Poles (interrogation methods, torture and other forms of punishment, communist propaganda, information about Poland, etc.):

The behavior of the NKVD towards Poles was simply terrible. They would summon Poles for interrogation (usually at night) and constantly ask why people in Poland were fighting Communism and beating people. They said that we would pay for it dearly and that Poland would never exist again. They demanded that we denounce agents and informers in the police service. They promised that if we did that, we would be released from the camp and go home. They also asked where and what positions people held.

Medical assistance, hospitals, mortality rate (provide the names of the deceased):

In the Lithuanian camps, the medical assistance was good. As for the USSR, the medical aid provided in Kozelsk was acceptable, while in other camps there was none. Several of the interned soldiers died in Kozelsk, but I don't remember their names or how many there were roughly.

Was it at all possible to get in contact with one's home country and family?

On 1 November 1940 in the Kozelsk camp, the NKVD allowed us to send letters to our families and I received several letters from my family.

When were you released and how did you manage to join the Polish Army?

On 8 August 1941, the USSR authorities transferred us from the Kozelsk camp to the camp in Suzdal, where on 24 August I appeared before a draft board and was declared fit for service. That day, I joined the 5th Division in Tatishchevo, and then on 5 January 1942, I was transferred to the 1st Krechowce Uhlan Regiment. On 1 April 1942, we arrived in Persia, while on 13 May we came to Palestine and made a stop in the Bashshit camp near Gedera. On 24 May 1942 together with the 1st Krechowce Uhlan Regiment, I was appointed to a gendarmerie school, and afterwards I stayed in the Gedera gendarmerie platoon, where I am currently serving as a gendarme.

Collection of the Hoover Institution Library & Archives at the disposal of the Central Archives of Modern Records, Władysław Anders Collection. Reports, 800/1/0/-/48, account no. 1827.

MARIAN JANICKI

Personal data (name, surname, rank, age, occupation and marital status):
Marian Janicki, lieutenant, 29 years old, permanent service officer, bachelor.

Date and circumstances of arrest:

Deported as an internee from Kalvarija in Lithuania on 12 July 1940 to Kozelsk in Russia.

Name of the camp, prison or forced labor site:

Kozelsk, Gryazovets.

Description of the camp or prison (grounds, buildings, housing conditions, hygiene):

The buildings were neglected (former monastery), 10 people living in a 2.5 × 4 meters room, sanitary conditions quite good.

Social composition of POWs, prisoners, exiles (nationality, type of crimes, intellectual and moral standing, mutual relations, etc.):

Poles and Jews (Kozelsk camp) – deported from Lithuania and Latvia, a lot of variety in terms of the intellectual standing: an illiterate man (rifleman), engineers, colonels. People lived in small groups, mutual relations worsened as many individuals decided to cooperate with the Soviets. In Gryazovets, we encountered POWs taken captive in 1939.

Life in the camp or prison (daily routine, working conditions, quotas, wages, food, clothes, social and cultural life, etc.):

They didn't force us to work, we were paid for voluntary work with an extra food ration (a portion of soup). Food rations sufficient as for the Soviet standards. Rationing got worse in Gryazovets (300 grams of bread a day). Clothes were very hard to obtain. Social life – as mentioned in the previous point. When it comes to cultural life, our leaders were not allowed to organize anything apart from concerts and a choir. Bolsheviks, on the other hand, set up a cinema, which was to function as one of the many communist propaganda centers. The same could be said of books and newspapers.

Attitude of the NKVD towards Poles (interrogation methods, torture and other forms of punishment, communist propaganda, information about Poland, etc.):

After my personal data was recorded, I was summoned to an interrogation once, but I can't understand what it was all about until this day. After 15 minutes of sitting in silence in front of an NKVD man, I was asked which year I graduated from Cadet Corps, and then I was released.

Communist propaganda was apparent at almost every step. Suffice it for three internees to stand on the square, and a political instructor would appear right away, starting a conversation on the situation in Russia and speaking critically of the conditions in Poland. They organized information talks (a review of recent developments), emphasizing their good relations with the Germans and complaining about England. They would come to dormitories, taking up various subjects, but always propagating communism. They spoke about Poland as if it was non-existent. They attempted to ridicule the Polish Army, using the campaign of 1939 as an example; Wanda Wasilewska's works were aiming to do the same.

The way of transporting from one camp to another was so horrible that only the Bolsheviks could have arranged it (people in overcrowded wagons, without a toilet for two days, with no water, windows and doors boarded).

Medical assistance, hospitals, mortality rate (provide the names of the deceased):

Good, thanks to our [Polish] doctors. Supply of medicines in the hospitals was very poor.

Deceased: Second Lieutenant Dłuski, Lieutenant Gór., Captain Wasilewski (hanged himself).

Was it at all possible to get in contact with one's home country and family?

We were able to contact our country and family by mail. During a year of my stay in Russia, I received one postcard.

When were you released and how did you manage to join the Polish Army?

I was released from the camp as a result of the Polish-Russian agreement. General Anders along with General Bohusz-Szyszko came to Gryazovetz camp and announced the formation of the Polish army on the Russian territory.

Collection of the Hoover Institution Library & Archives at the disposal of the Central Archives of Modern Records, Władysław Anders Collection. Reports, 800/1/0/-/48, account no. 2027.

IN THE FAR NORTH. POWS IN PONOY AND THE MURMANSK OBLAST

The Sikorski-Mayski Agreement of 30 July 1941 allowed the Polish citizens to escape Soviet hell. Hoping to survive, they travelled thousands of miles to join the forming units of the Polish Army. About 115,000 Poles left the USSR as part of Anders' Army. In the photograph: **General Władysław Anders** and his officers in Tehran, April 1942.

Photo. NN, Polish Institute and Sikorski Museum in London / KARTA Center

DO WARSZAWY 4371 km
CENTRUM
TEHERANU 3 km

JAN MISZEWSKI

Jan Miszewski, platoon-leader, 44 years old, senior sergeant of the Border Guard, married.

On 20 September 1939, at 2.00 a.m., along with the entire Grajewo police station, [illegible] Brasław command, and other army units, I crossed the Polish-Latvian border in Turmont and I was interned.

In Latvia, I stayed in the camps in Dyneburg, Litene, Ulbroka, and for three months I worked for a farmer. The treatment I received in Latvia was impeccable in all respects. The military authorities strictly followed the legal provisions on internees, and none of the officers, non-commissioned officers, or soldiers caused me the slightest unpleasantness, not even verbal. When the Soviets entered, relations exacerbated; however, despite this, the Latvian military authorities continued to show a lot of understanding and friendliness towards us.

Around 15 August 1940, several civilians arrived at the Ulbroka camp. They later turned out to be from the NKVD, and they started writing down some personal details, claiming that they were listing those who wanted to go to German-occupied Poland. A prison ambulance came three days later, onto which 13 officers were loaded, including Colonel Dukawicz [?], and taken away from the camp.

On 22 August 1940 at 11.00 a.m., several NKVD officers and dozens of soldiers with dogs, machine guns, and handguns, ran up to the camp and then dispersed.

Some NKVD man in civilian clothes first accused the Latvian commandant that he had let the Poles flee, that he would answer for it, that he'd make sure of it, etc., which did not even happen at all. Then, the officers, military police, the Border Guard, and the State Police were separated from the rest of the army; these units were detained in the yard, and the military units were taken to a vacant room. The NKVD man started talking down in a conceited voice that he had imagined that military police, the Border Guard and the State Police as strong, unshakable people, like those who used to be in Poland. Now, all he sees is little slouches; then he added that [illegible] would be better. After this, they started a personal search, which was just limited to taking away sharp tools like knives, forks, spoons, pocket knives, scissors, etc. We were supposed to be taken to the station, but the Latvians delivered trucks and we were driven there under heavy escort. The NKVD men were bragging that now relations have changed; that in 1920 they were barefoot, in shreds and hungry, but today they're strong and they can do whatever they like. We arrived at the station at 2.00 p.m. The small wagons with boarded up windows were loaded each with 48 people; the wagons were padlocked and quickly left for Russia.

We traveled three days. During this ride we were given bread and half a herring each, two times; once a day we were given water that was taken from a puddle near the tracks. When the transport commandant was reminded that the water was unfit to drink, he simply replied sarcastically that we didn't have to drink it.

On the third day of the journey, our transport was separated. The military units went to the Yukhnov camp, while the officers, military police, police and Border Guard went to Kozelsk, where we arrived on 25 August 1940.

At the railway station in Kozelsk, 35–40 people were loaded on each of the cars; we were ordered to pick up the luggage and sit down in a way that no one could move. After the warnings and the yelling of the guards, we set off to the camp, which was 7 kilometers away from the station. It was the first time in my life to experience such a hard journey. My limbs went completely numb, I couldn't move at all. Three people fainted during this short ride.

At the camp in Kozelsk, they first cut our hair and then a medical examination was carried out by women; each person was examined by three. Once the medical exam was over, they started personal searches. They were carried out with all the possible harassments. They stripped us naked, told us to bend over, do squats, dress and undress, while all sharp tools, civilian clothes, Latvian and Polish money, watches, wedding bands and rings were taken; religious objects were brutally destroyed.

I was interrogated only once. For the entire time there, I didn't get even one letter from my wife, even though she and my son were ill [?] in the Pavlodar Oblast for over half a year.

The camp had mostly Poles and about 10 people of Jewish nationality. They kept on setting up different informants, they often held talks about relations in the Bolshevik paradise; they even started setting up parties of godless people.

The food we got consisted of 800 grams of bread, groats, cabbage or beets, and fish. The former district head Pełczyński and one border guard died in the camp; one officer and a policeman committed suicide; four or five people died whose names I don't remember; and one officer, one police constable, and one [illegible] gendarme went crazy. The political commissars often said that they had formed an alliance with the Germans and now they don't fear the world, and that there'll come a time when they will deal with that whore, England.

On 9 February 1941, new revisions took place and preparations for a journey took place in the morning. The Border Guard, the police, military police, a few civilians, several officers, among them Major Aleksandrowski, district head Drożeński, were taken away and at 9.00 p.m. were brought to the railway station in Kozelsk. Once again they loaded 45–50 people into each wagon and deported them via Moscow, Volkovstroy [?], Kandalaksha to Murmansk, where we arrived on 15 June 1941.

During these five days we got two cups of soup, we weren't given medical care, the wagons were shut all the time, and we received water once a day with great difficulty.

On the way, we passed many areas of imprisonment camps; these people were emaciated, dirty, ragged, and covered with lice. We could see lines of figures that had been driven with all their assets in a bag on their backs. They never parted with their belongings; they worked and slept with them, otherwise it would have been stolen.

Nearly the entire Karelian Isthmus with Murmansk was one enormous camp of prisoners. From Murmansk we were led to the so-called "Weeping Valley," which was located 7 kilometers from the port. There, we were placed in a camp for civilians. They put us wherever it was possible – in tents, barracks, wherever anyone found room; many people slept outside. Even though this was in June, there was still snow in those areas. When we were led through Murmansk, I saw how on one side of the road there was a football game taking place, and right next to it there were women crushing rocks and repairing the road. There we worked for 16 hours, because at this time of the year in these areas, the sun practically doesn't set. It is still very cold though.

On 21 June 1941, we were led out of the camp to the port and about 4,000 people were loaded onto the "Klara Zetkin" ship, a cargo ship with a displacement of 8,000 tons. We were packed so tightly that no one could even dream about lying down. For seven days on board the ship, I sat on a wooden perch next to the stairs that led to the deck. The toilets were on the deck, where they let us go only one by one. If you wanted to get there, you had to stand in a queue for four hours, so out of necessity some would go on the spot. [illegible] getting through this tight mass of people to the other side of the ship was impossible. No one can stand on their feet for seven days, so the soldiers attached themselves with straps or rubber to the walls of the ship and they made it through the trip in a hanging position. You got the impression that these people were hanging.

On the first day the food was acceptable – we received 800 grams of bread and 400 grams of canned peas. On the second day they gave us half of this, on the third – a quarter, on the fourth day only a few crumbs of bread, and on the fifth, sixth and seventh days we didn't get any provisions, and we couldn't get anything by ourselves. In the last couple of days, few people went out to the toilet on the deck, plus the cold was taking its toll as we were traveling between ice caps. We were not served any hot food, tea, or water.

On 22 June, when we were at sea, we learned that our ship was stopped by a Finnish submarine and that the Germans were waging war with the Soviets. The war broke out when we were in the Murmansk Bay. None of us were terrified of this outbreak.

After three days of travelling, we arrived at the shores of the Kola Peninsula; we weren't unloaded until four days later, on 29 June. That day we were placed in a camp on the Ponoy River. There was still a lot of snow, and drinking water came from the puddles that were in the camp. There weren't enough tents, so people slept in the open. Finally, we were given one tent with holes that was meant to accommodate 70 people, but 460 people were placed in it; there was 14.5 centimeters per person to sleep in shifts. After a few days, the puddles had been exhausted; we had to supply the kitchen with water from the Ponoy River, which was about 200 meters down from us. At least 270 people were needed for this, who formed a chain and passed up the water in buckets. It took about 2.5 hours twice a day. The sea water was salty, there was no water for washing; food consisted of 300 grams of bread, soup, and fish.

We worked on building a road in this tundra 12 to 14 hours [a day], day and night in shifts (there was no night), without any remuneration. The second party of our people worked 12 kilometers away. As there was no road or access there, we had to deliver supplies there once a day on our backs. This line was made up of 70 to 100 people, and because everyone there was hungry, and there were very little provisions, a lot of it disappeared along the way, which made the food situation even worse. The people who worked further away from us didn't have any tents.

The NKVD men found many reasons to punish us for any committed offense. We were put in a barrel or, usually, in a hole dug in the ground: there, they'd sit the offender down without any trousers, on bare ground, and told them to keep their bare feet in water for many days.

On the second day after arriving in Ponoy, a political commissar ordered an assembly and told us that Nazi bandits had attacked their country and were murdering them; that an alliance with England had been made. He did not mention anything about Poland, he only stated that one day, perhaps it may come to an agreement, but there's no chance for this now.

Our luggage [was placed?] outside the camp and we were allowed to take it only after a few days. Due to a lack of nutrition and being without even the most primitive accommodation, we attained only 6–15% [of the quota]. They threatened us: "you will work, [or] we'll deal with you."

On 11 July 1941, work was stopped and we were ordered to prepare for departure. We were given a packed lunch, which consisted of boiled unpeeled potatoes cooked three days prior, half a herring, and about 10 grams of pork fat. During the night, we were loaded onto the "Andan" ship, and on 12 July at 6.30 p.m. we left the Kola Peninsula in the same conditions as on the "Klara Zetkin," the only difference being that they gave us sea water to drink in abundance. On 13 July at 5.00 p.m. we reached the port of Arkhangelsk. We weren't taken off the ship until three days later, that is, on 16 July at 4.00 p.m. We weren't given any provisions. So, for almost a whole week, I lived on boiled potatoes which didn't even fill my canteen, and 10 grams of bacon, and on the ship we were given one salt fish per two people. We were hungry and exhausted. The soldiers threw rotten fish through the hole in the ship floor for fun and enjoyed how some of the people threw themselves at this "dog's meat." We started singing patriotic songs and shouting as a sign of protest, but what good did it do – no one was released on the deck and our voices didn't go far.

We were led into the prepared camp in Arkhangelsk. In the section to where we were led (half of the transport – 2,000 people), the entire square covered an area of 45 by 48 steps; there were five barracks standing there, a latrine, and a brook that flowed through the middle with dirty, stinking water. There was no room to stand, let alone sleep. I was fortunate that someone gave me some space to sleep for 3–4 hours. We slept in shifts with district head Drożeński, Mangołowski, and others.

For two days we still weren't given anything to eat, nor could we see a doctor. Supposedly this was due to the fact that the NKVD transport unit hadn't yet handed us over to the guard unit. The camp had no water, so people drank from this stinking brook and two days later dysentery emerged to the extent that people couldn't make it to the latrine; anyway, there was no room there.

The living conditions in this camp were so hard that they cannot be described. We didn't count on anything, we brawled, shouted, sang – everything just to make these people with no heart or conscience ask for a doctor and give us food and water. Their response was that they set up double posts armed with machine guns. Despite this, we still believed that our liberation was coming soon. The political commissars began to show a certain helplessness, but also indifference towards us.

On the third day, we were given food, water was provided, and they ensured us that everything would get better, just as long as we would calm down. But what did this matter! The dysentery was spreading terribly.

On 21 July, we were given provisions for five days; quite abundant compared to those before, though only comprised of rusks baked in sea water, and on 22 July we left in closed wagons, each carrying 50 people. This time they didn't carry out any personal search. The transportation conditions didn't change a bit; we had many people suffering from dysentery in the wagon. For five days we begged and screamed for medical help every chance we got. We didn't get any; death came sooner, because these people showed no understanding. I lay on the very bottom of the wagon and looked through a small hole. A guard noticed this and suddenly he hit that spot with a bayonet; luckily he missed.

During the ride, we met masses of refugees who were riding on passenger freight trains, usually on the platforms, with their simple belongings. The guards would tell the civilians that we were Germans, and they wanted to place my few colleagues under arrest for disclosing the information that we weren't Germans, but Poles.

On 26 July 1941 at 4 p.m., we arrived in Vladimir. That evening, one of my colleagues asked me if anybody in our condition would be strong enough to do another 20 kilometers. He didn't need to wait long for the answer: the next day at 6.00 a.m. we were unloaded from the wagons, the entire transport was divided into four groups, the packages were collected onto carts, and we were led to Suzdal (40 kilometers away). On the way, people from the fields rushed up to see the German prisoners, and the guards in all seriousness told them how we were Germans, dressed without uniforms, ragged, and how elegant the Red Army soldiers looks compared to them. At the twentieth kilometer, they prepared a surprise: everyone was given half a liter of warm water.

After all these trips from Kozelsk via Murmansk, "Klara Zetkin," Kola Peninsula, and Arkhangelsk, people were so exhausted that they looked like wandering figures – emaciated, lean, and starved, so the walk was very slow.

The political commissars and guards hastened us with yelling and rifle butts. People would fall and lose consciousness from the fatigue. One of the NKVD officers right beside me tried to hasten a policeman who had fallen. He picked him up brutally, and when he fell again, the officer kicked him, raised him up and then threw him to the ground. I told him to keep [illegible] to himself, because this man couldn't go on. The officer told me to take him. I said that he should put him on the car or carry him on his back. He got angry, started cursing and shouting insults, and then began to shoot his gun. The entire march was full of such incidences. We couldn't go as fast as the escort, so every now and then they would point their LMGs at us.

6 hours 21 [sic] – we arrived in the town of Suzdal. One policeman died on the way and one on the third day. More unconscious people were brought. Anyway, at the end of the journey, even the guards were falling asleep when we stopped to rest. When we passed through Suzdal, the escort behaved quite well, they didn't even stop us from talking to the civilian population. The next day after arriving, I had a rather heated conversation with the commandant of the Suzdal camp. The commandant and two civilians were talking with our soldiers. The commandant, a major of the NKVD, told them that there were many illiterates in Poland. The soldier replied – yes, there were, but all countries have such illiterates, including the Soviets, America, England, etc.; they are people who are mentally completely unfit and they cannot be taught. At these words, the commandant asked why other languages were forbidden in Poland, especially Russian. I said

that it wasn't true, and the best proof was that he could communicate freely with almost all of us; besides, "You were on our territory, so you could see that it was not so, and Ukrainians even had their universities and no one bothered them; every library had books by foreign authors, including Soviet ones." He said it was not true, and that I didn't know a thing. At this I told him that he had just revealed to me how much he knew. Then he asked why there was such nationalism in Poland, and not internationalism like in their country; why was there no such freedom, liberty, and equality in Poland, as good as it was in their country. I said: "I don't know how you conceive liberty, equality, and a free life; why, after helping the Germans finish off Poland, did you take to exterminating the Poles; why did you deport the entire population to different prisons, camps, taigas and tundras? Unless you wanted to show us your freedom." At this he said: "Speak only for yourself!" "Well, why did you take my wife and 10-year-old boy – were you worried they would have overthrown your system?" He replied: "We had to defend them so that the local people would not hurt them." I said that it was a superfluous problem; on the contrary, after my departure, the people helped my family. Neither I nor my wife had to fear the local people. He asked: "And where were you?" I replied that I was being interned in Latvia. "And why did you run away?" I said that I didn't run away, but received such orders. He asked who gave us the order and who could have issued it on his own. I then asked if the freedom in their army was so advanced that every soldier could do what he liked without having to obey orders. He replied that that their situation was completely different. I said: "My wife was not running away, and she could have gone to the German partition; it was only a matter of being a *Volksdeutscher*, she wasn't running away from you; yet your freedom meant a kolkhoz in Kazakhstan!" At this he declared: "You were running away from us, so you and your family are our enemy." I said that we had been told something very different about their freedom. We were told that they had 40–45 million prisoners; we didn't believe it, we couldn't even fathom how it was possible to lock up a population of a country like England in prisons and camps. But after passing through Kalinin, Volkovstroy [?], Murmansk, Kola Peninsula, and Arkhangelsk, we could see for ourselves the sad truth about their freedom.

"Who told you that – Wyszyński?" He asked. I said that it was not Wyszyński, but a political commissar of the same rank as him. He responded to this with exultation that it was their army. I said: "My knowledge seems to fail me, I don't think you know your army, I still don't think so little of them; I won't believe that your army is enclosed behind barbed wire lines, that they are guarded by civilians in booths, with bayonets, or that they walk to work with bundles on their backs, with bayonets pointed at them, in dirty and disgusting rags, barefoot or in bast shoes, unwashed, etc. No, commissar, that's not your army – it's your citizens who, according to your concept, enjoy the greatest freedom in the world. And you [illegible] your army too much." At this, the commandant got completely irritated and said: "We'd need a long discussion with you, and there isn't any time." I said: "You talked for two years, and further talk is useless." They made me a fascist!

A week after we arrived in Suzdal, we were informed that we are free citizens of the Polish state. The conditions in this camp were much better than in the previous ones. Although we were given 500 grams of bread and a watery soup, our treatment improved. The political commissar conducted frequent lectures, he encouraged to cooperate, and threatened that they will detain those who are disloyal to them when the commanders come to the army.

On 24 August 1941, a Polish delegate arrived at the camp, Lieutenant Colonel Sulik-Sarnowski. That same day I was admitted to the Polish army. As the delegate of the Polish Republic was delivering his speech, the Soviets removed their posts from the camp. I received some 500 rubles as moral compensation. I could not buy anything for it, because a kilogram of tomatoes cost 10 rubles.

On 3 September, now without a convoy, we marched out from Suzdal to the railway station in Vladimir. Old women were making the sign of the cross and wept for us. On 4 September at 11.00 a.m., we left Vladimir and headed to Tashkent, where the transport arrived on 8 September. On 6 September, as the train departed, Senior Rifleman Gromadziński was run over. On 8 September, I joined the 5th Infantry Division in Tashkent. Due to poor health, during the first days of November I was assigned to the Tashkentan [?] company.

On 7 November, we were loaded into wagons and given provisions for 10 days. During this journey I got to know the delight of Soviet citizenship in all its glory. When we passed Engels station, our train was fired upon by a Bulgarian plane; outside the city of Aralsk, on 17 November, our transport's wagon caught fire, and seven people were totally incinerated before the train stopped, 12 who were seriously burned were taken to hospital, some jumped out from the moving train into the snow and thus saved their own lives. On 21 November, we arrived at Arys station. We weren't let into Tashkent because of overcrowding. After three days, we were directed to Almaty. On 25 November we arrived at Jambyl station. Someone had robbed a wagon with sugar, the NKVD carried out a search, a bag of sugar was found in our wagon, but the perpetrators were not there. They took me for the wagon commandant and they wanted to arrest me. Our transport was stopped at this station for three days and they interrogated me about the perpetrators; they were arguing that I must answer for it because sugar was stolen and there must be a perpetrator – that's their law. I said that even if it was so, people just wanted to eat; we were on the train for 25 days and we had received provisions for the first 10 days, but we had not received any provisions for the last 15 days, people were selling the last of their clothes to stay alive, and their duty was to give us subsistence. After detaining six people from the transport, they released four of our wagons and drove us to Almaty. On 28 November, our transport was turned back via Frunze to Tokmak, where we were unloaded on 5 December.

I sat on the train for a whole month, and we had received provisions for 10 days. For 20 days, everyone ate whatever they could, it depended on cleverness and luck. Until we departed from Tatishchevo, I had 32 rubles on me, this money was enough for only one day. Describing these hardships is simply impossible; one would have to experience it or have an incredible imagination that focused on the worst conditions that a person can only imagine. From there we were led to the Kyzylsay kolkhoz in Kazakhstan, near the Chu River; 150 people were placed in two mud huts, on dirty and tattered pallets that were looming with lice.

Food consisted of nothing more than 300 grams of [illegible] with bran flour, without any spices, bread, or even salt. The kolkhoz workers there were not much better off. Apart from the representative of the rural council of the kolkhoz, there practically wasn't anyone there who favored the Soviet system. One had to struggle to get even that 300 grams of flour, almost beg, scare [illegible], etc. The [illegible] NKVD came, they promised help, even [illegible], but nothing like that actually happened.

After less than three months in the kolkhoz, on 27 February 1942, I made it to the 10th Infantry Division in Lugovoy. I got there totally exhausted, blind, sick with jaundice. People in the kolkhozes were dying from typhus on a mass scale; Rifleman Warmiński died from jaundice in our kolkhoz. In the neighboring kolkhoz, seven Poles died of typhus on just one day. It was dangerous to remain in the kolkhoz, and there was no medical care.

When I came to Lugovoy, I met a friend whom I knew from Kozelsk, Second Lieutenant Blum. He gave me my family's address and I met up with them four days later. I was sure I'd never see them again, as despite my great efforts, I hadn't received any information from my family. Several days later I was lucky enough to be able to take my wife to Persia – the country that brought us back to life.

Collection of the Hoover Institution Library & Archives at the disposal of the Central Archives of Modern Records, Władysław Anders Collection. Reports, 800/1/0/-/48, account no. 1761.

JAN PYTLAK

Sent from Lithuania to the USSR as an internee.

Personal data (name, surname, rank, age, occupation and marital status):
Jan Pytlak, sergeant major, born in 1896, senior constable of the criminal investigation branch of the State Police, married, three children.

Date and circumstances of arrest:

On 12 July 1940, the authorities of the Soviet NKVD took me from the internment camp in Vilkaviškis, Lithuania, and deported me to the USSR. On 15 July 1940 I was incarcerated in the camp in Kozelsk. This camp was for politically dangerous persons.

On 15 May 1941, together with other privates, I was transported by train from Kozelsk to Murmansk, and on 22 May I was escorted on foot to a camp for prisoners, which was located 12 kilometers from Murmansk. The Poles called it the "Weeping Valley." On 6 June, after we were issued padded jackets, I was transported by ship to the Kola Peninsula, and on 13 June I was unloaded onto the land with no shelter. We were immediately driven to work at the quay, without any rest or food, and we toiled thus day and night until 30 June 1941.

On that day I was escorted a dozen or so kilometers across the swamp to another labor camp on the Ponoy River, which the Poles called the Valley of Death.

On 13 July I was taken by ship from the Kola Peninsula to Arkhangelsk, where they announced to us that the war with Germany had broken out. On 15 July, after I had arrived in Arkhangelsk, I was placed in a camp. On 22 July I was transported by train to the Vladimir station, and on 27 July I was escorted on foot to Suzdal and placed in a camp.

On 24 August in Suzdal, I appeared before a draft board chaired by a colonel of the Polish Army, Sulik-Sarnowski, and on 4 September 1941, as a free Polish citizen under the command of Polish officers, I was assigned to the 5th Infantry Division. On 8 September I arrived in a transport at Tatishchevo, where the Polish Army was.

We repeatedly asked the NKVD about our status at the camps. Were we internees? POWs? Prisoners? But they never gave us a definite answer, and in the Kola Peninsula they told us that everybody was treated equally there and that this place was our homeland, our home, our family – right up to our deaths. It follows that the verdicts were delivered in absentia.

Description of the camp or prison (grounds, buildings, housing conditions, hygiene):

From among the above-named camps, Kozelsk and Suzdal were the most decent ones – in terms of food, living conditions, medical assistance and the level of hygiene. However, we had to sleep on floorboards without straw.

Social composition of POWs, prisoners, exiles (nationality, type of crimes, intellectual and moral standing, mutual relations, etc.):

There were up to 4,000 Poles in the camp in Kozelsk, but only officers, gendarmes, policemen, border guards, prison guards, and priests. They were of various ages, mostly Polish. These people represented a high intellectual level and were of strong moral fiber, so the camp remained unbroken in spirit. We were able to keep our spirits up thanks to the devoted work of officers and priests; a choir and a musical ensemble were established at the camp and sports were also organized. A few Polish officers and privates from among those incarcerated at the camp broke and gave ear to the propaganda, becoming tools in the hands of the NKVD. I don't remember their surnames.

Life in the camp or prison (daily routine, working conditions, quotas, wages, food, clothes, social and cultural life, etc.):

Life in the camp – both in Kozelsk and Suzdal – was bearable, but when we were transported by train and by ship, there was hunger, thirst, and lack of air and of space for relieving oneself. Eventually we had to create makeshift air inlets, as everything was boarded up and people grew weak and fainted. There were over 40 people in small cargo wagons, the doors were sealed, and all pleas to the NKVD and their soldiers to give us water were to no avail; what is more, they made fun of us.

At the Kola Peninsula, we had to work day and night without food or shelter; everyone dug a hole in the ground for himself in order to get some rest. There was no medical assistance.

The NKVD imposed such work quotas on us that nobody was able to meet them, as we were issued only up to 200 grams of bread and some soup per day. When on 29 June 1941, on St. Peter and St. Paul's Day, we asked for a day off to wash our underwear, they refused and forced us to work the whole day without any food, and at 1.00 a.m. they organized a roll-call, surrounded us with guards, threatened us with death and ordered that everyone take a sack of flour (weighing 100 kilograms) and carry it on his back from the quay to the top of a rocky mountain, a few hundred meters or so uphill. We were so exhausted that we were collapsing under the heavy sacks, and the guards beat those who couldn't continue on with rifle butts.

As for food and the housing and working conditions at the Kola Peninsula, they were unbearable for everyone during the six months we spent there; it was a place of perdition for each of us Poles. In the camps in Kozelsk and Suzdal, the NKVD organized film screenings, but they showed us only propaganda pictures that were not much to our liking. Mutual relations were good, we warned one another and kept away from those who broke and who wanted to influence others, so that they couldn't do so.

Attitude of the NKVD towards Poles (interrogation methods, torture and other forms of punishment, communist propaganda, information about Poland, etc.):

The NKVD was hostile towards us Poles. The NKVD's behavior doesn't bear comparison with anything known to humanity at its present level of civilization. It was hard to believe – I myself found it difficult to acknowledge that people could be as bestial as they proved to be.

During the entire period of my stay in the camp in Kozelsk, at various times of day and night, I would be summoned to the office, where they tried to make me – an investigative officer of the State Police – give them the surnames of informers and so on. They threatened me with death and put me out in the cold in light clothes to make me rat on people who had helped the Polish authorities. The NKVD man showed me letters from my family and told me that if I said what he wanted me to say I would get the letter, and when I refused – he didn't give it to me. They tried to stir up hatred for my colleagues in the camp, saying that they had informed on me and had claimed that I knew a lot about the informers; they promised to release me from the camp should I prove to be of use. Finally they told me that my family was no longer my family, that I was in their care and that I would never see my family again. There were a few cases of suicide and mental breakdowns – it was such behavior that led to it.

When we were marched somewhere and someone fainted, he was beaten with rifle butts and poked with bayonets by the NKVD soldiers, as happened on 27 July 1941 during our journey from Vladimir to Suzdal: the sweltering heat, 40 kilometers to cover on foot, hunger and lack of water made us collapse on the road. They rifle-butted us and poked us with bayonets, and the officer who was the commandant of the escort would shoot with his revolver above the head of the weakened person. During transport by ship from the Kola Peninsula to Arkhangelsk, we didn't receive any food or water, and when we made a request for bread and water, the officer ordered us to keep quiet or he would shoot. In Arkhangelsk, a few thousands of us were put in a small, fenced off camp, where we had to sleep and relieve ourselves in the same place. The feces from the toilet overflowed into the camp square, and they kept us there without food and water for two days, which resulted in the deaths of several young soldiers whose surnames I don't remember. Many fell ill.

Communist propaganda was vigorously spread by the NKVD officers in Kozelsk. They claimed that no system other than the Communist one could exist in other countries, and that the USSR would take control of the whole world. They claimed that capitalist states were not good for the nation as a whole but only for individuals, and gave Poland as an example, saying that capitalism was one of the factors that had led to Poland's collapse. They spoke blasphemously about God, saying that there was no God, and forbade us to observe any religious practices. Information about Poland: the NKVD officers claimed that they had their people also in Poland, and that soon Warszawa would be taken over by the USSR, that Poland would never be restored and that we should stop thinking about the past and get used to their laws.

Medical assistance, hospitals, mortality rate (provide the names of the deceased):

From among the above-described camps, real medical assistance was provided only in the Kozelsk camp and in Suzdal, but there was a lack of medicaments. It was Polish doctors who worked tirelessly to save the lives of Polish soldiers. I remember neither the number of the dead nor their surnames.

Was it at all possible to get in contact with one's home country and family?

I didn't have any contact with our country; I received only two postcards from my family throughout the entire time, although they had sent several dozen. [...]

I would like to emphasize that everything that I have described above is nothing but the truth, but if I recollected and described every single fact, my account would take several volumes, not pages.

Encampment, 13 March 1943

Collection of the Hoover Institution Library & Archives at the disposal of the Central Archives of Modern Records, Władysław Anders Collection. Reports, 800/1/0/-/48, account no. 1784.

ANTONI BURJAN

[sergeant]

I would like to supplement my questionnaire for former prisoners and deportees to the USSR as follows.

I was interned in Lithuania, in a military camp. After they took over Lithuania, the Soviets also took Poles under their "care," and thus in the morning hours of 12 July 1940 NKVD soldiers carried out body searches and counted us. This occurred in the township of Vilkaviškis, where the camp for Poles was located. Next they led us on foot, in groups of one hundred, to the train station 4 kilometers away. Before we were marched off, they announced that if any of us made just one false step to the left or to the right, firearms would be used without any forewarning. The escort was numerous and behaved with great severity. At the train station I and the others were loaded onto freight wagons; the windows were boarded shut, so it was completely dark and extremely stuffy inside. People fainted. When we cried for the guards to give aid to the sick, they did not respond. We had to relieve ourselves in the wagon, and a terrible stench soon arose. We were transported in these conditions to Mołodeczno. In Mołodeczno they loaded us onto another wagon – similar to the first – and ferried us to Kozelsk.

On 15 February 1941, after the inquiries against all of us had been brought to a close (the Soviets considered us as politically suspect), I and the others were taken – as I have already stated – to Murmansk, traveling in an equally dark and stuffy wagon. Furthermore, when night fell the train would be halted a number of times, and during each stop NKVD soldiers would bang on the wagon walls with hammers. In all probability, they were worried that in spite of the strong guard and electric floodlights (which lit up the entire train) someone might try to escape.

On 5 June 1941 we were put on a ship in Murmansk. We were forced to wait outside for a whole day and night before they loaded us onto the vessel. A very strong wind blew gusts of snow at us, making the waiting all the more difficult to bear; in addition, we were all hungry. Finally, we were put on the ship; it was so cramped on board that we were unable to sit. A Soviet prosecutor boarded the ship, and we turned to him with a complaint as to how we were being treated. He responded that the conditions were not that bad, and added that as enemies of the people we were being sent to die. On 17 June 1941 they offloaded us on the Kola Peninsula, at the spot where the Ponoy River flows into the White Sea. They forced us to work every day. We toiled 12 hours daily, not counting the time it took to get to the place of work. It took two hours to get there and back. The sick also had to work. Everyone was forced to toil at gunpoint, and the guards said that they would readily shoot us, for the country was in a state of war.

On 13 July 1941 we were all loaded onto a ship and taken to Arkhangelsk. On 22 July 1941 they put us on a train heading for Vladimir. Conditions on the ship and the train were nearly the same as those which we had experienced previously. After arriving in Vladimir, we were driven on foot to Suzdal, some 40 kilometers distant. Those who couldn't walk were prodded with bayonets to keep moving. I was in this group, walking barefoot. Along the way one of the Poles, a policeman, wanted to draw some water from a well near the road. The commandant [illegible], an NKVD political commissar, shot at him from his revolver, but missed. A commotion broke out. The escort set up their weapons and announced that they would shoot us. A similar situation arose further along the route. Throughout this time we received no food or water. We were not informed of our sentences. One of the NKVD political officers who often came by the building in which I was detained in Kozelsk said that we had received sentences of 9 to 15 years in absentia.

Collection of the Hoover Institution Library & Archives at the disposal of the Central Archives of Modern Records, Władysław Anders Collection. Reports, 800/1/0/-/48, account no. 1371.

JÓZEF MAKOWSKI

Personal data (name, surname, rank, age, occupation and marital status):
Józef Makowski, 30 years old, locksmith and mechanic, unmarried, military brigadier.

In 1939, after the "Budsław" Battalion of the Border Protection Corps was scattered near Worniany, Wilno Voivodeship, I was stopped by the red patrol in Antokolskie Street in Wilno; I escaped and crossed the Lithuanian border on 23 September, where I was interned in the camps at Kulautuva, Ukmergė and Vilkaviškis.

Date and circumstances of arrest:

During the Russian occupation of Lithuania in July 1940.

Name of the camp, prison or forced labor site:

Yukhnov internment camp; the Kola Peninsula – Ponoy – Suzdal.

Description of the camp or prison (grounds, buildings, housing conditions, hygiene):

a) The camp was situated in Yukhnov, in the former tuberculosis sanatorium of Pavlishchev Bor, Smolensk Oblast. The area was about 200 by 400 meters, surrounded with three rows of barbed wire and watchtowers, lit with searchlights at night. There were around 2,7000 people in the camp. Kola Peninsula – Ponoy. Wet tundra.
b) Housing was very poor, initially I lived in a square-shaped park building, where the windows did not match the proportions of the area; in summer at 5.00 p.m., in order to reach one's bed – which didn't have any straw – you had to light matches. Apart from that, the room was really wet, with a moldy smell. Later I lived in a dry building, but there were 40 people living in an eight-meter cell without any way of controlling the heat in winter, so sudden changes of temperature caused toothaches and headaches. During the transport to the North I was in the surroundings of Murmansk – Mys Zelenyi) – in a room in a camp for prisoners. We had to sleep in turns due to lack of space.

Both in Yukhnov and in Murmansk there were millions of bedbugs. In Murmansk, together with the melting snow, the sewage flowed out from the latrines from beneath the floor of our quarters. While staying in the peninsula, lack of room forced us to dig holes that we covered with sheets, layering the bottom with moss.

c) In Yukhnov there was a bath, a disinfector and a laundry that we used every 10 days, with enough soap. Lice were a rarity in the camp.

Social composition of POWs, prisoners, exiles (nationality, type of crimes, intellectual and moral standing, mutual relations, etc.):

a) Nationalities: Poles with a few Jewish, Ukrainian and Belarussian individuals, everybody speaking Polish. We hadn't committed any crimes apart from not going along with the communist propaganda.

b) Intellectual standing among the majority was high, the rest – average; there was self-study through mutual aid in spite of tough conditions. Moral standing was high, especially in critical moments: the celebration of a National Holiday below decks on the ship "Klara Zetkin." We showed an unshakable faith in the victory of our allies, with a strong manifestation of joy before the radio speaker after the British triumphs in North Africa in 1940.

c) Mutual relations were generally very good, all class antagonisms between different social groups vanished behind bars. This assessment, however, does not apply to a few individuals, led by a teacher from Mołodeczno, Dobrowolski, who created their own community under the slogan "Through Red Poland to Freedom." I could give further details if need be, some of those people are actually serving in our army. Other than that, laborers of the 2nd Division from Baranowicze were snitching on each other. Besides this, members of the Dobrowolski's group stood out because of their rush to work, which forced us to work even when the authorities weren't making us do so. They called us "Polish pigs" on many occasions. They were using such methods to influence us.

Life in the camp or prison (daily routine, working conditions, quotas, wages, food, clothes, social and cultural life, etc.):

a) A day in the Yukhnov camp was organized in a military way, according to a trumpet signal: 6.00 a.m. – wake-up call; 7.00 a.m. – report, status check by the duty officer; 9.00 a.m. until noon – work on camp construction or other things; noon to 2.00 p.m. – lunch break; 2.00 to 5.00 p.m. – as before noon; 9.00 p.m. – curfew. When we were moved to the Kola Peninsula, all these patterns vanished. Work was from 6.00 a.m. until 6.00 p.m., or from 6.00 pm to 6.00 a.m. at an airfield construction site. Leaving and arriving at work, counting us a few times, took two more hours. At first, the labor would go on without any break, later a one-hour break after six hours of work was introduced. The work consisted of collecting turf, collecting and removing rocks and stones; twelve hours of night shift, often accompanied by constant drizzling, with no way of warming oneself or drying one's clothes, or having a hot drink, gave our faces an earthy color. The quotas for every two people were: cutting out 76 square meters of turf, sometimes up to 0.5 a meter thick, with a tremendous amount of dwarf birch roots, and taking it out of the worksite, or removing stones and putting them in piles. The tools we were equipped with were absolutely unfit for this kind of work (gigantic shovels and crowbars) and allowed us, in the best case scenario, to fulfill 30% of the quota. All the work had to be done without any remuneration, it wasn't until our dismissal that we were paid 500 rubles each, thanks to reaching an agreement.

The question of clothing was an exceptional burden for us. At the beginning, during the disinfection with hot air, some of our clothes were burned and others damaged so badly that they fell apart after a few weeks. Supplies came only on special occasions; the cadets who had left Poland with inappropriate clothes would lie on the bunks only in their underwear and go to the lavatory in a borrowed coat. Footwear was initially not provided and not mended at all, we made soles from military belts, or we wore clogs. After arriving on the peninsula we were supplied with quilted clothes, shoes were provided only in some cases. Sometimes on the way to work we had to walk through marshes where the water was ankle deep.

Throughout my whole time in Russia, food rations caused constant starvation. In the Yukhnov camp we were given 800 grams of bread (although baked in such a way that it consisted of water to a large extent), twice a day half a liter of soup made from millet groats, oat or potatoes with salted fish in such a condition that the odor didn't permit eating it. Meat (available only in exceptional cases) was either past its time or consisted of meat scraps from heads and legs of cattle. Oil was used as a fat so scarcely that it's not worth mentioning. Lack of vegetables was one of the reasons that night-blindness became widespread in the camp. My worksite on the Kola Peninsula did not have a kitchen at all, so after 14 hours of work you had to cook in a small flask, over the green branches of a birch brought from the site. Our food supplies were delivered on the backs of our cadets – each carried 30 kilograms through the rough, pathless terrain of the tundra. The bread rations we received were around 300–800 grams, depending on how much they had baked in the nearby kolkhoz. Dry provisions, which we received for cooking, were [fragment missing] scarce, for example: seven raw potatoes, 500 grams of canned food, peas with bone marrow, 80 grams of meat, and 800 grams of bread for three days.

Overall nourishment was poor – especially during transports. While being deported from Lithuania, after we had been loaded on a hot July day, after going a few kilometers on foot, being loaded and locked up in the wagons in the scorching sun, we were given the first drop of muddy water far beyond the former Polish-Russian border. And the rations at that time consisted of salty and dried fish. During the journey over the Barents Sea from Murmansk to Ponoy (the Kola Peninsula), we received very small portions of water and food consisting of rusks and canned peas, and by the end of a 10- day journey there were 2 days of absolute starvation diet (we hadn't been provided anything, the supplies had been loaded off ship and a storm broke in the meantime). Next, on our way across the White Sea to Arkhangelsk, very poor nutrition – raw salty fish and sea water to drink. After getting off the ship, the hunger and lack of water provoked a violent demonstration within the camps. During transport by rail from Arkhangelsk to Vladimir (Russia), in response to demands for water, one of our fellow inmates was beaten up and locked in an isolation cell. After reaching Suzdal, we were given rations of 400 grams of bread and a very thin soup twice a day.

c) Cultural life in the camp, during our stay in Yukhnov, was quite active. We had a choir of 120 people and an orchestra, which – led by conductors Dylong and Klauden – gave very good performances, more or less every two weeks. The program consisted of our folk and military songs as well as melodies of Polish composers, sometimes Russian and Ukrainian, but without a taste of propaganda. The choir conductor, our colleague Dylong, was working in difficult conditions, as the program had to undergo censorship and the words "God" or "homeland" were rejected. Sometimes he would change the words, but the audiences filled them in, giving the performers thunderous applause and throwing the NKVD into confusion. There were libraries on the camp's premises: an official one with Russian works and propaganda magazines, and the one consisting of Polish books brought by us from Lithuania and exchanged amongst ourselves. We could listen to the radio, but only from Moscow. Besides that, there were newspapers on display in the camp: "Krasnaya Zvezda", "Izvestia", "Rabochyi Put´" and "Pravda."

Attitude of the NKVD towards Poles (interrogation methods, torture and other forms of punishment, communist propaganda, information about Poland, etc.):

Their propaganda was an attempt to transform us – representatives of various social classes – into an avant-garde of the new movement, but the longer we were in the camp, the more oppositional our response was, contrary to what had been expected from us. Even initially hesitant individuals turned into fierce proponents of our principles. The attempts began right after our arrival. During a speech one of the NKVD officers was trying to prove that England had betrayed us, he even used the word "prostitute." The response was unexpected by the NKVD: whistling and dispersion of the crowd. That topic was never discussed again publicly. There were lots of propaganda movies depicting the achievements of the Communist system in all fields. Before the screening of a film, a propaganda speech was given to take advantage of the gathered crowd – not enthusiasts, but curious people and commentators. As a result, the next day, when a political commissar assigned to the campaign came and brought up the subject, we asked him a few down-to-earth questions concerning the movie we'd seen and the numbers and slogans that came with it – as these were the usual means of conveying the message – then a colleague of ours would give him a true depiction of who a Soviet citizen was, or how their economic system worked, based on their own national press. Then the political commissar wouldn't show up for a few days. By debating with them, you could realize that these people had no idea about international relations. At first they took all the denial of their nonsense as a sign of propaganda, but gradually their interest started increasing. While being in Russia, we didn't get any information about Poland and about our army after the fall of France.

Medical assistance, hospitals, mortality rate (provide the names of the deceased):

Medical care was very limited. There were a couple of nurses in the camp with very limited treatments. Dental aid, due to lack of proper tools, consisted solely in removing teeth. There were seven cases of death within the camp premises. The hopelessly sick were taken to a hospital on a cart with no suspension, on a tuft of straw, during heavy frost, over a dozen kilometers away. There were fatalities on the way.

Was it at all possible to get in contact with one's home country and family?

Correspondence was officially allowed once a month; in reality it was one letter per 11 months. Until the Russian-German war, I was able to send only four letters and I received three. They allowed correspondence using encrypted addresses. Moreover, letters were subject to censorship.

When were you released and how did you manage to join the Polish Army?

I was released from the NKVD's supervision in the camp in Suzdal after the proclamation of the Polish-Soviet agreement. I arrived in Tatishchevo together with a transport of a few thousand other inmates.

Collection of the Hoover Institution Library & Archives at the disposal of the Central Archives of Modern Records, Władysław Anders Collection. Reports, 800/1/0/-/48, account no. 2047.

WINCENTY BUBEN

Wincenty Buben, regular senior artillery sergeant, Artillery Training Center, Artillery Reserve Officer Cadet School.

After the arrival of Bolshevik troops in Wilno on 18 September 1939, I went towards the Lithuanian border in Zawiasy and crossed the Lithuanian border on 19 September 1939. I was interned. I stayed in the Kulautuva, Ukmergė and Vaitkuškis camps.

On 10 July 1940, in the evening, Bolshevik troops surrounded the camp of internees in Vaitkuškis. The next day we were all taken to the railway station in Ukmergė and deported to the Mołodeczno station. Officers, policemen and gendarmes were allocated to a separate transport, while I and the others were brought as line army to the POW camp in Yukhnov near Moscow.

Three days after we arrived in the camp, a detailed registration of personal origin was conducted. First, they registered those with the highest military rank, i.e. [starting] with a senior sergeant and equivalent ranks. During the several-hour-long registration, various sensitive questions were asked, such as: "Did you kill many Bolsheviks while being on the front 1919 and 1920?", etc.

During our stay in the camp, they agitated us with the benefits of communism, criticized Poland, America and England, and praised Germany and the USRR. They also distributed Bolshevik publications. The literature and agitation of the individual political commissars in the camp had little effect. It is true that there were a few individuals from among the Polish prisoners of war who insisted on agitation, but this was also in vain. The main agitators were: Dobrowolski – a school teacher from Mołodeczno, a cadet platoon-leader whose surname I don't remember, probably an employee of the Polish "Robotnik" newspaper editorial office and Senior Sergeant Major Szurpit from the 10th Uhlan Regiment in Białystok. They were employed in the camp administration office, where they hung a poster reading: "We are returning to the Soviet Poland through a revolution," showing a worker holding a hammer in his hand.

People were deported very often from the camp in Yukhnov in an unknown direction, even at night.

After 10 months in the Yukhnov camp, on 31 May 1941, we were deported to Murmansk and then to the Kola Peninsula on board of the "Klara Zetkin" ship. There, we were forced to perform works relating to airbase and road construction. We worked continuously 12 hours a day, being fed with 100 grams of bread and one millet soup per day, without any fat. In my opinion, Bolsheviks didn't care about the airbase and the road – they wanted to kill us, Poles, by means of hunger and cold. On the Kola Peninsula, where rainfall and hail occurred frequently, we stayed in the open air. When someone reported that he was sick and could not work, they replied: "Who does not work for us, does not eat," and "You can die."

On the Kola Peninsula, for some time the Bolshevists didn't admit that they were at war with the Germans. They did shortly after we had already seen the exploding shrapnel from the ships firing at each other in the White Sea.

On 18 July 1941, we were withdrawn to Arkhangelsk, from which we were transported to the POW camp in Yuzha, Ivanovo Oblast.

On 25 August 1941, we were notified that diplomatic relations had been established with the Polish government and that an agreement had been signed, under which we, as the Polish citizens, would be granted amnesty and the Polish Army would be formed in the USRR.

On 10 September 1941, we were released from the POW camp and announced free Polish citizens. We left for Tatishchevo, where I was assigned to the 5th Light Artillery Regiment of the Polish Army.

Encampment, 25 February 1943

Collection of the Hoover Institution Library & Archives at the disposal of the Central Archives of Modern Records, Władysław Anders Collection. Reports, 800/1/0/-/46, account no. 109.

JAN TYLMAN

Personal data (name and surname, rank, age, occupation marital status):
Jan Tylman, senior sergeant major, Pole, regular non-commissioned officer, married.

Date and circumstances of arrest:

On 14 July 1941, I was transported from the Vilkaviškis camp of internees in Lithuania to Yukhnov.

Name of the camp, prison or forced labor site:

In the Yukhnov camp, I worked within the camp whenever I was told to do so by the company senior and three times worked on removing snow from the road to the forest.

Description of the camp or prison (grounds, buildings, housing conditions, hygiene):

The camp comprised four residential buildings, very cramped, damp and dark, with little lighting. Hygienic conditions were barely satisfactory.

Social composition of POWs, prisoners, exiles (nationality, type of crimes, intellectual and moral standing, mutual relations, etc.):

There were about 2,000 internees, intellectual standing varied, moral standing – depressing at first, then good; the same goes for mutual relations.

Life in the camp or prison (daily routine, working conditions, quotas, wages, food, clothes, social and cultural life, etc.):

Life in the Yukhnov camp began at 6.00 a.m.: wake up, roll-call, breakfast, we worked in the camp from 8.00 a.m. until noon. From 12.00 p.m. to 2.00 p.m. dinner break. Work from 2.00 p.m. to 6.00 p.m., supper at 7.00 p.m. and at 11.00 p.m. – curfew. Remuneration for work: those who worked every day received additionally supper and 400 grams of bread, while regular meals comprised: 800 grams of bread, thin soup for breakfast, soup and grouts for dinner, tea. Soups included fish or meat waste with a very little fat. Clothing was provided only to those who voluntarily worked every day and it was very flimsy. In the camp, there was a room called club, where concerts and intensive Soviet propaganda were arranged; in addition, one could play billiards and chess. In the camp on the Kola Peninsula, the housing conditions and food were very bad, we were given a small amount of bread – 200 grams, soup twice a day – in the morning and in the evening. We worked for at least 12 hours, in wet and cold circumstances. During transport, wagons and ships were overcrowded. Food was very poor, there was not event water on the "Klara Zetkin" ship – they didn't give us bread or water for four days.

Attitude of the NKVD towards Poles (interrogation methods, torture and other forms of punishment, communist propaganda, information about Poland, etc.):

At the beginning, the attitude of the NKVD authorities was satisfactory, later very hostile. The initial propaganda was very extensive, information about Poland was very bad.

Medical assistance, hospitals, mortality rate (give the surnames of deceased persons):

Medical care – sufficient, there was a hospital. About 15 people died in Yukhnov, I don't remember their surnames.

Was it at all possible to get in contact with one's home country and family?

Communication with our home and country was very poor. We were allowed to write one letter a month and sometimes no letters at all.

When were you released and how did you manage to join the Polish Army?

I joined the Army on 27 August 1941 in the Yuzha camp.

Encampment, 13 February 1942

Collection of the Hoover Institution Library & Archives at the disposal of the Central Archives of Modern Records, Władysław Anders Collection. Reports, 800/1/0/-/46, account no. 277.

STEFAN FRELKA

[cavalryman]

Personal data:

Stefan Frelka, son of Franciszek and Julianna *née* Grzyl, born on 16 December in the village of Skrzetusz, Oborniki District, Poznań Voivodeship; a State Police Inspector, during the war in 1939 served at the State Police station in Prozoroki, Dzisna District, Wilno Voivodeship; currently a military police sergeant.

Date and circumstances of arrest:

From 20 September 1939 I was in Latvia as an internee. Recently I was in the farm in Lapaini, Lugaži Commune, Valka District. I was arrested on 24 August 1940 by Latvian police and remanded in custody in Valka. On the following day, I and twelve other internees from Valka were taken to the camp in Ulbroka, where the Soviet authorities set up a concentration camp for Polish internees arrested in Latvia.

On 2 September 1940 trucks arrived in the camp. We were loaded onto trucks in a standing position. It was such a tight squeeze that we couldn't move. This is how I was brought to the train station, the name of which I don't remember. There was a train with freight cars. The trucks drove up to the train and we were loaded into the cars, from 36 to 40 people per car. The cars weighed 15 tons and less. When the train was loaded, and the task had to be carried out with speed, the cars were locked up. Soviet soldiers were very harsh in their treatment of the internees, some of whom were brutally shoved around. On 5 September 1940, the whole transport arrived in the camp in Kozelsk.

Name of the camp:

The camp in Kozelsk: from 5 September 1940 to 15 May 1941.

On 15 May 1941, I was taken in a transport of over 1,000 people to Murmansk. After arriving there on 22 May 1941, we were placed in a camp 12 kilometers away from Murmansk, only to be transferred back, on 3 June, to the camp in Murmansk, in the vicinity of the harbor. On 5 June, we boarded a ship and sailed to Ponoy in the Kola Peninsula. Our ship arrived in Ponoy on 12 June. On 17 June it was unloaded and we were placed in the field, that is in some swampy area, 2 kilometers away from Ponoy.

Thin planks, which were only now brought over from the ship, were used to build tent frames over which we pulled tent canvas. Finally, after a few days of staying there in the open air, without being properly fed, we were accommodated in the newly built tents, from 100 to 200 people per tent. It was only at this point that we set up the camp proper. All of us were forcibly marched to work, also in rain and all kinds of bad weather. We worked 12 hours a day. The time spent assembling and marching didn't count towards working time. All of this amounted to between 12 and 16 hours a day. Along with a group of about 500 people I was sent from the camp in Ponoy, after it was partly organized, to another camp which, located about 12 kilometers in a straight line away from Ponoy, was just being set up. We were again left in the open air, in a swampy area. Relying on our own resources, we set up tent poles and covered them with canvas. The tents served as our home until 13 July 1941. On 14 July, we were loaded onto a ship called "Uzbezkin" and taken to the camp in Arkhangelsk. The camp was situated near the train station. We were there until 22 July 1941. That day we were loaded into a train and transported to Vladimir, from where we marched to a monastery in Suzdal. In Suzdal the whole transport was accommodated on the floors in the monastery buildings.

Description of the camp:

The camp in Kozelsk was set up in the buildings and churches of a monastery. Living and hygienic conditions were satisfactory.

The camps in Murmansk (I and II) and in Ponoy on the Kola Peninsula were set up in a swampy area, in tents. Because of the congestion in the tents, our situation was very difficult. The hygienic conditions were completely substandard. We didn't have any mattresses or straw. There was no bedding at all.

Social composition of POWs, prisoners, exiles:

In the camp in Kozelsk, there were over 2,000 rank-and-file policemen, about 1,000 rank-and-file military policemen and border guards, several dozen civilians – civil servants – and about 1,500 officers. About 5,000 people in total.

All of them were Polish. There were no criminals. The intellectual level was normal, good mutual relations.

Life in the camp:

In Kozelsk we worked mostly within the campground. On rare occasions we did some work outside, clearing roads of snow and dragging wood out of the bushes to heat the buildings in which we were lodged. Fuel was supplied very rarely and there was always very little of it. We weren't paid for our work and the food they gave us was very poor. It lacked fat and people had to live on 800 grams of bread a day. Our clothes were in a very bad state. We patched them on our own in effort to survive. Our mutual relations were good, but we were deprived of any form of cultural life. All the movies and newspapers to which we were given access were designed to spread communist propaganda, as were the lectures organized by the NKVD. The lectures were also used to curse the English whom the Soviets blamed for the outbreak of both wars, in 1914 and in 1939. The Germans, by contrast, were praised for the policy they pursued.

Attitude of the NKVD towards Poles:

Within the campgrounds the NKVD functionaries were quite civil in their treatment of Poles, but their conduct during interrogations, held outside the camp, in the buildings in which they were quartered and which were enclosed by high, impenetrable walls, was brutal. They behaved violently, pounding the table and yelling threats and abuse at interrogatees. Those who refused to testify the way they wanted weren't given the letters their families had sent them, although prisoners were sometimes shown that such letters actually existed. People who still had their families in Poland were threatened to have their relatives deported to Siberia if they failed to testify the way the interrogators expected them to. The Soviets ridiculed our country, repeating with contempt that there was no point in thinking about Poland because it would never exist again. We were called "the bourgeois" and accused of exploiting the working class.

Right upon our arrival in the camps in Murmansk and in the Kola Peninsula we were told that we were prisoners and that we were required to comply with the regulations they had given us. We were treated quite harshly, like prisoners. The food in the Kola Peninsula was very poor and irregular. Sometimes they gave us soup and 85 grams of bread a day. On such occasions we were told that food provisions couldn't be supplied to the camp because of the outbreak of the war.

Medical assistance, hospitals, mortality rate:

In Kozelsk there was a camp hospital and the medical assistance we received there was satisfactory. There were some deaths but I didn't know those who died. In the camp in Kozelsk two people committed suicide – a captain and a policeman. The names of neither of them are known to me. In the camps in Murmansk and in the Kola Peninsula, medical care was very poor. There were no medicines, although there were some Polish doctors.

Was it at all possible to get in contact with one's home country and family?

From November 1940 to April 1941, we were allowed to write one letter a month. Special vouchers were issued for this purpose. Every month I made use of the voucher, writing a letter to my family, but throughout the time I spent in the camps I didn't receive a single letter from my loved ones. My family was deported to Kazakhstan. They are still there. I had no contact with my family who remained in Poland, although I once wrote a letter to my mother in Poznań Voivodeship.

When were you released and how did you manage to join the Polish Army?

On 4 September 1941, I was released from the camp in Suzdal; all of the inmates were sent to the train station in Vladimir and transported to Tatishchevo where the 5th Infantry Division was being formed. There I joined the 14th Infantry Regiment of the 5th Infantry Division, and I have been in the army ever since.

Collection of the Hoover Institution Library & Archives at the disposal of the Central Archives of Modern Records, Władysław Anders Collection. Reports, 800/1/0/-/48, account no. 1687.

ANTONI POCZOBUTT-ODLANICKI

Personal data:

Antoni Poczobutt-Odlanicki, second lieutenant, born in 1904, [illegible], married.

Date and circumstances of arrest:

Interned by Lithuanians in Mejszagoła on 10 February [?] 1939; stayed in the Palanga and Vilkaviškis camps, from which he was deported to the USSR on 12 July 1940.

Names of the camps:

In the USRR: Kozelsk, Yukhnov, Murmansk, Kola Peninsula, Arkhangelsk, Vyazniki.

Description of the camps:

Kozelsk – part of the city with former monastery. It was once a large tsarist monastery. Destroyed, not renovated buildings, up to three levels of bunks each, on which (as indicated by the inscriptions left by others), many people of various nationalities, including Poles, had already slept, or rather struggled to sleep. Bedbugs and dirt were everywhere.

Yukhnov – there was a huge manor house with palaces of a tsarist count. The more acceptable buildings were housed by the NKVD, Poles lived in dilapidated stables, partly in outbuildings, most often they built mud huts or renovated old hovels. The residents were accompanied by bedbugs and lice at all times.

Murmansk – a camp of prisoners of any nationality – forced resting location (!) on the way to the Arctic Ocean islands.

Kola Peninsula – forced labor site. Tundra, with no buildings at all. Three shifts, about 1,000 people sleeping in several large tents 20 by 6 meters, on two-tiered bunks; walls were mostly made of moss and turf for protection against wind – we slept in the open air. As the works progressed (construction of a road through the tundra), groups of workers did not return to their stopping location, they quartered in the area of works.

Arkhangelsk – special barracks for all types of prisoners. Transitional stay. Conditions were the worst possible. Polish soldiers slept, stood, sat on every patch of land, even next to overfilled and spilling latrines. Dysentery spread rapidly.

Vyazniki – a huge camp for prisoners. Numerous barracks, in acceptable condition. Housing conditions – satisfactory (as for a prison).

Social composition of POWs:

Kozelsk – officers, ensigns, officer cadets and privates of the Border Protection Corps, police and gendarmerie. In the remaining camps, there were mainly privates and Polish officers who were hiding their true ranks.

Intellectual standing of those detained in Kozelsk was very high, but moral standing was unsatisfactory, in many cases even very low. Relations between inmates were terrible. In other camps, intellectual standing – average, moral standing – good. Relations between inmates were correct. Privates passed their life exam.

Life in the camps:

On the Kola Peninsula, everybody worked in tundra; works were performed uninterruptedly, 24 hours a day, in two shifts. Food was less than insufficient (daily ration consisted of 200 grams of bread, two pieces of sugar, half a liter of soup and boiling water), no remuneration. The "quotas" were not met, even in exchange for the promised improved food. Clothing (jackets) and underwear was provided. No fresh water. In the remaining camps, no one – with a few exceptions – was persuaded to work.

Cultural life was at a high level. We studied various languages, diverse training courses were very popular. Relations between inmates were good.

Attitude of the NKVD towards Poles:

During the interrogations, no physical tortures were applied (only moral). They tried to convince us and prove that their communist teaching was superior, but in vain. The effects of all propaganda activities were quite the opposite. Simple Polish soldiers could not only refute the Soviets, but also ridicule the doctrine representatives themselves. In a word, Polish soldiers behaved heroically and edifying. They toughened up morally and physically.

Medical assistance:

The doctors tried to treat us with all the available measures. Those more severely sick where transported to hospitals, where they received good treatment. The mortality rate was very low. Jews were the group of prisoners who died most often, mainly due to exhaustion. Among those who died in Kozelsk were Second Lieutenant Jerzy Dłuski (drainage technician from the Nowogródek Voivodeship) and one captain whose surname I don't know.

In the Yukhnov camp died Officer Cadet Wojciechowicz and several privates whose surnames I don't remember.

Communication with the home country:

We were allowed to send one letter to our home country every few months. Around 2% of prisoners kept in touch with their family and country.

Joining the Polish Army:

On 25 August 1941, a colonel arrived at the Yukhnov camp, and called up all Poles staying the camp, including me, to the Polish Army.

Miscellaneous:

Recalling the period between 19 September 1939 and 25 August 1941, I must admit that Poles, with a few exceptions, saved their honor as soldiers. They showed great fortitude in both physical and moral terms, and praised Poland throughout the Soviet Union.

Encampment, 24 February 1943

Collection of the Hoover Institution Library & Archives at the disposal of the Central Archives of Modern Records, Władysław Anders Collection. Reports, 800/1/0/-/47, account no. 620.

EDWARD GIELWERT

Personal data:

Edward Gielwert, sergeant major, born in 1899, chief of the State Police, married.

Date and circumstances of arrest:

I was interned by the Lithuanian authorities along with the military and police units after crossing the Polish-Lithuanian border on 19 September 1939, whereupon I was transported to the internment camp in Palanga. I was last in the internment camp in Vilkaviškis.

On 12 July 1940, I was arrested at the internment camp in Vilkaviškis by the NKVD and transported along with the other inmates to the USSR.

Name of the camp:

Kozelsk from 15 July 1940 to 15 May 1941; Murmansk; Kola Peninsula, Ponoy; Arkhangelsk; Suzdal.

Description of the camp:

Kozelsk: hilly terrain, forests on the northern side, Zhizdra River to the south, brick buildings, atrocious living conditions – divided into blocks in Orthodox monasteries, churches and church buildings. Each block housed 200 to 1,000 inmates on two- or three-level bunks. Walls were filthy, interiors damp, there were masses of bedbugs. Hygiene: weekly washing and decontamination of floors, bunks and bathhouse with a special fluid, change of underwear.

Murmansk: rocky terrain on the Barents Sea 4 kilometers from Murmansk, in barracks. Muddy area, fenced off with barbed wire, alongside Russian criminals. Housing conditions: 200 people in each of the barracks. Cesspools and filth around the tents.

Kola Peninsula, Ponoy: initially in the open air, later in tents. The camp situated on a rocky terrain, surrounded by tundra. Housing conditions: on bare ground, with no bunks.

Arkhangelsk: muddy terrain, tents with bunkbeds. Cesspools and slurries around the tents. Unbearable conditions.

Suzdal: dry hills, brick buildings, surrounded by a high brick wall (monastery and church). Housing conditions fairly good. Hygiene observed.

Social composition of POWs:

Polish nationals, officers of the army and police, non-commissioned officers of the army and police, judges, civilian officials, district heads, priests. Moral standing – we were generally depressed. Mutual relationships – sympathetic.

Life in the camp:

Kozelsk. Average day: forced labor twice a week, in blocks, in and outside the camp, no quotas and no wages. Food: 700–800 grams of bread, 20 grams of sugar per person per day, breakfast: tea. Lunch: potato soup on plant oil or cabbage soup, beetroot soup – rarely, with beef or mutton offal or with old mutton suet with a peculiar smell. Supper: tea and one herring or small fish. Own clothing, underwear – whoever did not have any was given two pairs, two blankets, two bedsheets and straw mattresses. Social life: intrapersonal kindness and uplifting patriotic spirit. Reading patriotic Polish books from a mobile library brought by the inmates from Poland and Lithuania (Reymont, Sienkiewicz, Mickiewicz, etc.). We were also shown Soviet propaganda films and given Soviet books.

Murmansk. 500 grams of bread for breakfast and fish or meat soup for lunch. Work in the camp – cleaning. Padded clothing and rubber boots. Good social life, reading own books.

Kola Peninsula, Ponoy. Forced labor building roads, airbases and the port, eight hours in two shifts, day and night. Work tough, no quotas and no wage. Food: 85–250 grams of bread and soup made from wheat flour and potatoes once a day. Padded clothing. Social life good, with a patriotic spirit. Cultural life cheerless.

Arkhangelsk. Temporary internment.

Suzdal. Work in the camp. Food: 500 grams of bread, 20 grams of sugar; breakfast: tea; lunch: fish soup, potatoes, beetroots; supper: tea. Camaraderie good, hope to be set free. Reading own books and Russian newspapers (Polish-Soviet agreement).

Attitude of the NKVD towards Poles:

Hostile attitude until the Polish-Soviet agreement was reached, whereupon it improved so drastically that the hostile treatment of inmates was stopped.

Interrogation methods: I was interrogated twice in Kozelsk. Neither torture nor repression was used on me.

Communist propaganda: implemented using films during my time in Kozelsk until 15 May 1941. The political commissars held lectures to this end and were often unable to answer any of the questions posed by the inmates. They were mocked and consequently their propaganda did not have any effect.

I will add that, during my time at the internment camp in Kozelsk, the NKVD would sometimes deport individual people to an unknown destination. They deported Lieutenant Colonel Dąbrowski, a resident of Wilno; the head of the Investigative Division Woronco, a resident of Wilno; Colonel Wiater from the Border Protection Corps, from Wilejka; a chief of the State Police August Milczewski, from Mołodeczno; and many others whose names I do not remember.

Medical assistance, hospitals, mortality rate (provide the names of the deceased):

Doctors: interned Polish officers.

Deaths: Tkacz, mayor of the Miżewicze Commune, Słonim District; Captain Wasilewski from the Baranowicze District could not stand the conditions and took their own lives by hanging. Four people whose names I did not note down died of natural causes. Senior sergeant major of the gendarmerie Waskiszewski from the Sokółka station, constable Jewtuszenko from Commissariat no. 4 in Wilno, as well as a lieutenant and an officer cadet whose names I do not know, all lost their minds. This happened in Kozelsk, although this also happened to a senior chief in Murmansk. I do not recall his name. These people were all taken away in an unknown direction.

Was it at all possible to get in contact with one's home country and family?

Throughout my whole stay in the USSR, I only had contact with Poland via mail in Kozelsk, between 1 September 1940 and May 1941. We were permitted to write one letter a month. Out of the nine letters that were written I received only three postcards from my wife in Wilno and one postcard from my parents from the Radom area.

When were you released and how did you manage to join the Polish Army?

On 19 August 1941, and representative of the NKVD announced that we had been freed by the stipulations of the Polish-Soviet agreement, but that we would remain in the camp in accordance with the orders of the Polish authorities in Moscow. On 23 August, the USSR authorities paid all of the inmates a one-time donation of 500 rubles.

Colonel Sulik-Sarnowski came from Moscow to the internment camp in Suzdal on 24 August and for the first time the Polish flag was hung beside the Soviet flag to welcome him. He announced to a general audience that we were free and that we remained Polish soldiers. The was a medical inspection for all of the inmates on the same day and I was accepted into the Polish Army. On 4 September 1941, I went with the others to join the 5th Infantry Division in Tatishchevo and was assigned to the 4th Police Health Services Battalion. I was then assigned to a security company on 4 October 1941 and finally to the gendarmerie in Yangiyul in March 1942.

Collection of the Hoover Institution Library & Archives at the disposal of the Central Archives of Modern Records, Władysław Anders Collection. Reports, 800/1/0/-/46, account no. 214.

WACŁAW OŁDAK

Wacław Ołdak, cadet artillery sergeant, 37 years old, married.

I was interned in Lithuania in July 1940, transported to Russia, to the camp in Yukhnov, and in May 1941 to the Kola Peninsula for work.

The camp in Yukhnov – located about 40 kilometers away from the railway station was situated in a former residence of Prince Orlov, by the river, surrounded by a forest and a park. We, however, were separated from all of this by a wire fence. The buildings intended for us were dirty and cramped. With time, we built one more barrack from a ruined old stable. Then each person had 170 by 80 centimeters of space on a bunk bed. The levels of the bunks were so close together that we couldn't event sit on them, and in addition there was practically no light. The small windows of the building offered some light on the upper bunks only. The inscriptions [left by our predecessors] indicated that Poles and Finns had been quartered there before.

We were given a bath every several days, and washed our underwear ourselves. Many of us were lice-ridden.

The camp was only for military men: non-commissioned officers and privates – non-commissioned officers were separated from private soldiers, who were divided into groups (*sotnya*).

The spirit in the camp was very good. Only a few of approx. 44,000 [internees] belonged to a union which was supposed to build Communist Poland. The others didn't want to go voluntarily from Lithuania neither to Germany nor to the Soviets, and were prepared for everything. If a political commissar approached the privates and praised his political system, they would report it to us, and we knew how to explain it to them. For example, my gunners, i.e. those who were in the same battery during the war as me, saluted their non-commissioned officers and would continuously consult us, although the political commissars told them that we incited them to rebel.

Every morning, the NKVD conducted roll-calls counting us carefully. We performed works only within the camp, i.e. built barracks, roads, etc. As for entertainment, we organized a choir and an orchestra, but prior to each performance, a political commissar had to make a speech to praise the Communist system. As for living conditions, it was too little to live on, too much to die on: *payka* of undercooked bread (supposedly 700 grams) and soup twice a day, in the evening – tea and a few spoons of sugar – for 10 days. This was heaven compared to the conditions that started at the beginning of May 1941, when we were deported to the Kola Peninsula, where we worked

14 hours a day, received about 100 grams of bread and dry rations (a few potatoes and a handful of groats). Before we arrived at the workplace, we hadn't eaten for three days during the sea journey. Who didn't want to work was put under the light machine gun and so kept even three days, naked. The quota was as follows: to remove 75 meters of turf from the rock and take it 150 meters away. We weren't paid at all.

It was announced that an agreement had been concluded with England, which caused tears of joy come to our eyes, since the sailors had told us that they would never transport us back. The order to return was received. We were completely exhausted but strong in spirit, so resting every 0.5 kilometers, driven by some inner force and helping the weaker, we managed to reach the harbor. We boarded the ship which was to take us to Arkhangelsk. However, we were still hungry and during the travel the hunger was as severe as previously. On the ship, one of the political commissars read the English-Soviet agreement out loud. We couldn't help but cry joyfully. When we asked him what about Poland, he replied: "Poland is where Sikorski is. There is no one to whom we could talk. Your government does not exist." These words made us sad, but we were full of hope. They brought us to Arkhangelsk. We thought that they would finally give us something to eat. Unfortunately, we didn't eat anything for another three days. We were locked in a camp which was so overcrowded that even on the yard there was no place to lie down.

We cried out for food, but it didn't help. We began to sing our national songs. After three days of starvation, we received some soup and bread. We were ordered to travel further, segregated into various groups. They loaded us onto a train, as previously, 35–40 people per wagon.

Locked without air, we continued our journey back, which was torture. Admittedly, we were given 200 grams of bread, 8–10 herrings and about three-quarters of a liter of water every day, but this was very little considering the terrible heat. In the wagon, we tried to catch air through gaps in the floor, but had to wait in a line to do that.

We arrived in Vyazniki, but not all of us could get off the train on their own. Those who passed out were carried away, some people lost their senses. People wanted to exchange the best watches for a cup of water, but no one had water. During this journey, the commandant of our wagon was forced to lie with his face down to the wagon floor as a punishment for our crying for water. Despite that, he didn't give away the person who initiated the shouting.

Once we were unloaded, in two, maybe three hours, the commandant of the Yertsevo camp arrived. We had a 40-kilometer march ahead of us, so he ordered to bring water by cars. Then, following meticulous division, everyone was given about three-quarters of a liter, which allowed us to reach the camp after two days of marching. We travelled in similar conditions from Lithuania to Russia. In the camp, we received 400 grams of bread every day and soup (half a liter), presumably made of millet grouts, but it was difficult to tell. Only after the conclusion of the agreement with the Polish government, the conditions improved slightly. The soup remained similar, but they gave us more bread – 700 grams. On the Kola Peninsula, we received padded clothing and shoes, but only few could wear them, because they were too small.

There were many talks (*beseda*) in the camp in Yukhnov – especially at the beginning – concerning the Communist political system. They condemned capitalist states and called England an old prostitute. However, the internees were great patriots and didn't let the political commissars win them over. We started arguing with them about politics, shouting and whistling. At a later stage, these talks were less common and concerned the wartime situation. In March 1941, political commissars even started to claim that England would not lose the war. This time we were shouting for joy. When we were traveling to the Kola Peninsula and stayed in Murmansk for five days together with Soviet prisoners, they said they were told that we were bandits. The NKVD men often said we were not worth a bullet. As for Poland, the NKVD sometimes said that it would not exist again or that it would exist, but only as a Communist state. Several Poles in the camp – obviously those weaker in sprit – believed them; they even established a union which strived for Soviet Poland, but only were a few out of nearly 4,000 internees joined them.

Medical assistance would be satisfactory – because the doctors were Poles – if not for the lack of medicines. The doctors were unable to treat us properly and the health care in the North was very poor. The camp had a sick room, but it was too small to accommodate those who were weak. The mortality rate was low. Several people died, but I don't remember their surnames.

Despite being sent often, letters from our home country were rarely delivered. Half of the content of those that were received had been cut out.

From the collective camp in Yertsevo, I got through to the Polish Army together with thousands of other internees at the end of August.

Collection of the Hoover Institution Library & Archives at the disposal of the Central Archives of Modern Records, Władysław Anders Collection. Reports, 800/1/0/-/46, account no. 112.

ALEKSANDER GOŁOST

Aleksander Gołost, platoon-leader, born on 5 December 1902, assigned to the 1st Supply Company.

I was arrested after crossing the Lithuanian border on 19 September 1939 together with my unit, stationed at Commissary Materials Depot No. 12 in Wilno. I was then moved between various internee camps in Lithuania until 12 July 1940.

On 12 July 1940, while I was in the internee camp in Vilkaviškis, the Bolsheviks, having replaced the Lithuanian camp guards with their own soldiers a few days earlier, took over the internees and immediately set about organizing us into companies. Under a strong escort, comprising soldiers on foot and horseback, aided by dogs, and having been warned that if any one of us stepped out of line they would be fired upon without forewarning, we were led to the train station, where they loaded us onto goods wagons destined for Russia. The voyage: the wagons were terribly overcrowded and the heat stifling. We had our own food, but no one touched it because we were completely deprived of water; worse still, the Soviets didn't give us any water during stops – even though we asked them to. We passed through Wilno and arrived in Mołodeczno, where in the evening the Bolsheviks carried out a selection: they took the officers, priests, policemen and functionaries of the Border Protection Corps, while we – the rank and file – were loaded onto a different train, which set off on its way in the morning. Our thirst was so great that when it started raining further along the route in the USSR, we all tried to catch a few droplets so as to moisten our lips. Some of us tried to catch the rain running down the dirty wagon walls with spoons, and those who succeeded in gathering even half a spoon of the precious liquid were happy indeed.

Having reached our destination, we were driven on foot from the train station for over 30 kilometers to the camp of Yukhnovo, which we reached on 16 July 1940. There we met a small group of Polish soldiers who had arrived earlier. After a body search, we were let into the camp, where we received hot meal and boiled water. We slept in the open, in the square. The next day we were sent to buildings, which were equipped with plank beds.

At this point the NKVD took over, writing down our personal details, inquiring as to who we were in Poland, where we worked, and to what social organizations we belonged. They were particularly interested in finding members of the Camp of National Unity.

The political indoctrinators implemented a strong propaganda campaign, talking about the political system of the USSR, the country's power, etc., on every occasion, and stressing that Poland had ceased to exist for good. The attitude of Bolsheviks from the camp administration towards the internees was, I would say, courteous to the extreme, while the guards were ruthless and, indeed, savage. A day room was set up, and we also had a cinema, although this was used solely to disseminate propaganda. The library contained only Soviet newspapers and books on politics.

Our work consisted in building new barracks around the camp, cleaning the sewer ditches, digging sewage pits, and constructing a larger building, which was supposed to house a second day room. Some of the internees organized a string orchestra and a choir. In the summer of 1941 (I do not remember the month) I was sent through Murmansk to the Far North, right up to the Kola Peninsula.

The train journey was very difficult. In the main, we were fed with salty fish and herrings, and were given very little water. The wagons were searched frequently. Our escort was despicable – brutal and pitiless. The journey by ship was terrible, we literally lay one on top of the other in the cargo hold. It lasted for a week or so. During the last few days we were not given any food, for there was a storm and they found it difficult to unload us. Exhausted and famished, we got out onto the shore. The Soviets drove us on foot to the camp, which was already staffed with police. There were no tents – we had to set them up ourselves. There was a shortage of food, and especially bread, of which we received no more than 100–150 grams. We were taken to work in the port, and thereafter some 20 kilometers further, deep into the desert, were an airfield was being built. The work was hard, and we had absolutely no bread. The living conditions were simply atrocious, seeing as we were forced to sleep on the bare ground, which was cold and wet. The Bolsheviks treated us mercilessly and brutally. We did not stay there long, for only 10–12 days after our arrival we were sent back to the shore and loaded onto another ship, which took us across the White Sea to Arkhangelsk. From there we traveled by train to the camp in Vyazniki, where we were visited by Colonel Sulik-Sarnowski, and the Soviet guard was finally removed. After enlisting in the Polish Army, I left for Tatishchevo, where I served in the field bakery of the 5th Infantry Division. I arrived in Persia on 5 April 1942.

Encampment, 17 March 1943

Collection of the Hoover Institution Library & Archives at the disposal of the Central Archives of Modern Records, Władysław Anders Collection. Reports, 800/1/0/-/48, account no. 1383.

SYLWESTER MARTENKA

Sylwester Martenka, senior rifleman, son of Feliks and Augustyna, born 14 December 1890 in Rzadkowo, Chodzież District, Poznań Voivodeship, State Police officer (senior constable), Roman Catholic, married, residing in Wilno at Filarecka Street 23, flat 2.

After crossing the Polish-Lithuanian border on 19 September 1939, I was interned and imprisoned in the Vilkaviškis camp. After Lithuania was seized by Russian troops on 10 July 1940, the camp was taken over by the Russian army, and on 12 July I was transported to Kozelsk, USSR, together with other internees.

There were about 300 people in the transport. Between 45 and 60 people were put into one 15-tonne train car, the doors were tightly sealed and only two iron-barred windows were open. The route led from Vilkaviškis through Kaunas, Wilno, Mołodeczno, Minsk, and Smolensk, to Kozelsk. The railway cars were jam-packed and there was little air inside. More than 10 people passed out on the way; they were not given any medical assistance. There were policemen, soldiers, and officers in the transport. In Mołodeczno, the transport was loaded onto a broad-gauge train. During transport we were not allowed to get out to relieve ourselves; we did that in the train cars, through a small hole in the door. The food during transport consisted of bread, dried salted fish, and an insufficient amount of water. Water was provided twice a day, two buckets per car. During transport the heat was enormous, so the lack of water was acutely felt.

On the way, the transport was divided: military men were directed to the camp in Yukhnov, while military and police officers, as well as police, Border Guard, gendarmerie, and Border Protection Corps personnel were sent to Kozelsk. I stayed in Kozelsk from 15 July 1940 to 15 May 1941. Investigations continued all the time; each person was interrogated more than ten times; they demanded that we disclose the names of people who collaborated with the police in Poland, threatening that we would be deported to Siberia, etc. The food in the camp was sufficient; each day we received 800 grams of bread, soup in the morning, soup and thick groats porridge with oil, as well as small quantities of meat for lunch. The sanitary conditions were good, the place was clean, we had a bath once a week. Medical assistance was good, it was usually provided by Polish doctors; there was a well-maintained hospital in the camp, but there was a shortage of medicines.

From December 1940 we were allowed to write one letter a month to our families in Poland. After receiving a reply from the family, everyone was individually summoned to the office of the camp authorities, where they showed you the letter and demanded the disclosure of the identity of informants. If you refused, they drove you out of the office and didn't give you the letter.

In March 1941, I received a letter from my wife, from Wilno, which contained a photograph of my wife and children. When I came to the office, an NKVD officer showed me the letter and the photograph, but didn't give them to me, demanding that I disclose the names of informants; when I refused, I was thrown out of the office and never received the letter at all.

In Kozelsk, we lived in buildings that were sufficiently heated during wintertime.

On 15 May 1941, with a thousand of my colleagues, I was deported from Kozelsk to Murmansk, and then, on 5 June 1941, placed on board a ship called "Stalingrad" and taken to the Kola Peninsula, where on 19 June 1941 I was put to work at the port, unloading barges. The work was very hard and there was no shelter, so we spent the nights under an open sky; it rained heavily for a few days at that time. Work lasted 12 hours a day. There was a shortage of fresh water to drink and use for cooking. On 4 July 1941, after we had finished unloading a ship, we were sent to a camp located 10 kilometers into the Kola Peninsula, where we were given 200 grams of bread a day and one tin of peas every five days. On 13 July 1941 we were placed on board the "Uzbekistan" passenger ship and transported to Arkhangelsk; from there, on 22 July, we left for Vladimir; next, we were placed in the camp in Suzdal, where on 24 August I was transferred together with the others to the Polish authorities and, on 8 September 1941, sent in a transport to the Polish Army – 5th Infantry Division in Tatishchevo.

Encampment, 9 March 1943

Collection of the Hoover Institution Library & Archives at the disposal of the Central Archives of Modern Records, Władysław Anders Collection. Reports, 800/1/0/-/48, account no. 1755.

STANISŁAW GORCZYCA

Personal data (name, surname, rank, age, occupation and marital status):
Stanisław Gorczyca, corporal, born on 6 May 1900, State Police officer, married, with two children.

Date and circumstances of arrest:

On 19 September 1939, I crossed the Lithuanian border together with all the policemen from the Nowogródek District, and we were placed in the internment camp in Ukmergė, in military barracks. Once the Soviet army had occupied Lithuania we were transferred from the barracks to the Vaitkuškis estate, Ukmergė District. On the night of 15/16 July 1940, the camp was surrounded by Russian soldiers, the so-called NKVD. On 16 July in the morning, we were all arrested – about 2,000 people – and taken to Russia in sealed freight cars, as enemies of the people.

Name of the camp, prison or forced labor site:

Our first camp in Russia, after we had left Lithuania, was called Kozelsk, Smolensk District – we stayed there until 15 May 1941. The second forced labor camp was located on the Kola Peninsula on the White Sea coast near the Ponoy River. We were transferred there from Kozelsk in June 1941.

Description of the camp or prison (grounds, buildings, housing conditions, hygiene):

In Kozelsk, we lived in an Orthodox church building and slept on bunk beds made of raw wood and built on a wet concrete floor. Water from the ceiling dripped onto our beds. The building was poorly heated in winter. In the space intended for 200 people, there were 490 of us living there. Every two weeks, we had a change of underwear and had a bath in a temporary bathhouse that we had built by ourselves.

On the Kola Peninsula we lived outside for a few days, on the frozen ground of the tundra. Finally after a few days, we had constructed tents, but we still slept on wet ground, warmed up by our bodies. We washed our underwear by ourselves in salty water, which we also drank and bathed in.

Social composition of POWs, prisoners, exiles (nationality, type of crimes, intellectual and moral standing, mutual relations, etc.):

In Kozelsk there were 2,700 people, including 780 military and police officers. The rest were from the Border Protection Corps, Border Guard, gendarmerie, police, and regular non-commissioned officers. We were all Poles and we were accused of being counter-revolutionaries and enemies of the people, who fought against Communism.

On the Kola Peninsula, there were about 3,000 of us, mostly police and Border Protection Corps officers, and some regular non-commissioned officers, members of the Border Guard, gendarmerie, and officer cadets of Polish nationality. We were accused of the same crimes, but had already been sentenced, in absentia, to permanent exile.

Life in the camp or prison (daily routine, working conditions, quotas, wages, food, clothes, social and cultural life, etc.):

Camp life in Kozelsk, despite threats by the NKVD, was buoyant because of our spirit, because we were all convinced that it would all end soon and we would return to Poland. Daily routine: after we'd been woken up and had eaten a morning meal, we were summoned for interrogation and did some work within the camp. There were no quotas, but there was also no remuneration. Meager food – herring, fish, and [illegible]. Clothes – everyone wore the clothes they had brought from home.

On the Kola Peninsula, we were as hopeful as in Kozelsk, but the daily routine was different: we worked on the construction of an airfield and roads, 16 to 18 hours a day, the quotas were impossible to meet, and we were not paid. Food: 200 grams of bread, soup twice a day, meager and thin. We wore our own clothes and short padded jackets distributed by the NKVD.

Attitude of the NKVD towards Poles (interrogation methods, torture and other forms of punishment, communist propaganda, information about Poland, etc.):

The attitude of the NKVD towards Poles was unbelievable, simply mean. They mocked everything that was Polish. They mocked Polish authorities in all sorts of ways and they were vulgar in many respects.

Manner of interrogation: the NKVD summoned us usually at night, and every few hours by day. During interrogations, the NKVD pulled the prisoner's hair and beat his head against the wall, or placed him facing the wall and then they shot a gun over his head to extort testimony. They also hit people in the stomach and kidneys, or took them outside the camp to the forest, allegedly for execution; then they were brought back, pale of fright. This resulted in several people falling mentally ill, and they were taken away in an unknown direction. Following such interrogations we had a few days off, during which we were forced to attend communist meetings, where propaganda speeches were given and propaganda films were screened. Types of punishment: locking in dark cells, placing people naked in cold water, without any food. We received almost no news concerning Poland, except for what we managed to understand from letters, although we did not receive many of them.

Medical assistance, hospitals, mortality rate (provide the names of the deceased):

Medical assistance was very poor. Despite the fact that we had our own doctors, they were not able to treat us due to the lack of medications and to close supervision of the NKVD. Eight of the 2,700 thousand people died in Kozelsk and three people committed suicide by hanging, but I do not remember their names – they were mostly officers and we, privates, were not allowed to go to their blocks.

Was it at all possible to get in contact with one's home country and family?

We had little contact with the home country and our families. In Kozelsk, some people received letters every few months, but on the Kola Peninsula we received none.

When were you released and how did you manage to join the Polish Army?

Two weeks after the Germans declared war on Russia, all the Poles were taken away from the Kola Peninsula, loaded on ships, and transferred to Arkhangelsk, and from there to Suzdal, Moscow Oblast, where we met Colonel Sulik-Sarnowski. On 24 August 1941, having appeared before a medical committee, we were all enlisted into the 5th Infantry Division that was being formed in Tatishchevo.

Collection of the Hoover Institution Library & Archives at the disposal of the Central Archives of Modern Records, Władysław Anders Collection. Reports, 800/1/0/-/47, account no. 1286.

PIOTR ŁUCEK

Piotr Łucek, corporal, son of Jan and Agnieszka, born on 4 November 1893 in the village of Bełcząc, Lubartów District, lately he served in Poland in the police in the Stołpce District, Derewno police station, married, four children at school age; gendarmerie station of the 2nd echelon of the Gendarmerie Department [?].

On 17 September 1939, together with other policemen, I went by bicycle towards Nowogródek, Lida and Wilno, then from Wilno to Lithuania; I crossed the border on 19 September 1939 and stayed in the camp as an internee in Palanga, and subsequently in Vilkaviškis for 10 months.

After the occupation of Lithuania by the USRR, I was deported to the camp in Kozelsk (Russia) together with other policemen. There were officers, gendarmes, Border Guard and police, about 3,000 people in total. The buildings were made of brick, former Orthodox churches; the bunks were old, infested with bedbugs, which made our life a misery. We slept three months on bare bunks, without straw. The food was acceptable; however, we were not served any fat. Works within the camp were not heavy, outside the camp work was performed rarely. Relations between inmates were good.

The NKVD carried out communist propaganda, but all internees despised it and ridiculed their reign. There were two idiots who praised the Bolshevik rule, which made them being spit and pointed at by everyone. The displayed films were mostly propaganda, and as for books – we borrowed and lend those brought from Lithuania amongst ourselves. After three months, the Soviet authorities allowed us to write letters to our families, and every month, we received a coupon to write one letter. I was interrogated in terms of property held, family and my police service, but I was not tortured; they only threatened and admonished us to learn Russian, because Poland would not exist anymore, and when I replied that this was not certain, he laughed sneeringly, called me a fool, and threw me out of the room.

Following 10 months in Kozelsk, in May 1941, we were transported to Murmansk, where we were declared prisoners and were treated as such. Next, from Murmansk we were deported on a ship to the Kola Peninsula for forced labor, i.e. to build roads and an airfield. In this camp, there were no officers – only privates, i.e. policemen, gendarmes, Border Guard and soldiers from the camp in Yukhnov. The conditions were poor, we slept in the open air, in the rain, in a word we suffered hunger and cold. 12 hours of hard work a day, such as digging trenches, carrying stones to provide a passage through marshes, pulling blocks from the Ponoy River and other works; food was scarce – 80, 100, 150, no more than 300 grams of bread and soup once, sometimes twice a day.

However, also here a glimmer of hope appeared. When we found out about the war between Germany and Soviets, we were all cheered up. Large tents for 150 people were built, which allowed us to rest a little; we slept on the ground, but were provided with padded clothing, which we placed underneath us while laying. Hygienic conditions were miserable, the camp was cramped, everyone would relieve themselves next to the place where they lived and ate.

There were two doctors, Polish and Soviet officers, but no medicines were available.

On 13 July 1941, we left the Kola Peninsula for Arkhangelsk on a ship, where we were starving. On 17 July 1941, we got off the ship and here in the camp located at the Arkhangelsk harbor, were starving again. On 22 July 1941, we left for Suzdal on a train. In this camp, the conditions were better, since a recruitment board arrived on 24 August 1941, which admitted me to the Polish Army. On 4 September 1941, we set off on a journey to the 5th Infantry Division in Tatishchevo, which I left for Kazakhstan on 31 October 1941. On 2 March 1942, I arrived at the 7th Division of the 22nd Infantry Regiment in Kermine, and I am in the army to this day.

Encampment, 19 January 1943

Collection of the Hoover Institution Library & Archives at the disposal of the Central Archives of Modern Records, Władysław Anders Collection. Reports, 800/1/0/-/48, account no. 1743.

WACŁAW GRZELAK

Personal data (name and surname, rank, age, profession and marital status):
Wacław Grzelak, senior sergeant, 42 years old, regular non-commissioned officer, married.

Date and circumstances of arrest:

On 19 September 1939 at the order of the commandant of the Wilno garrison, along with his men, while crossing the Lithuanian border (Zawiasy-Jewie).

Name of the camp:

Lithuania: Palanga, Vilkaviškis; USSR: Yukhnovo, Mumansk, Kola Peninsula, Arkhangelsk, Talitsy (Yuzha).

Description of the camp:

Palanga: seaside villas, wooden buildings, single-story, damp and cold; hygiene inadequate; food good.

Vilkaviškis: Russian barracks (Tsarist), damp and cold, located in town.

Yukhnovo: wooden barracks constructed by internees, damp and very cold, terrain fenced off by three rows of barbed wire, 35 kilometers from the train station, barracks set up in a field.

Murmansk: tents in a valley, surrounded on all sides by rocky mountains, terrain very limited, fenced off with barbed wire; food very bad; hygiene inadequate; dirt (huge amounts of bedbugs).

Kola Peninsula: taiga, muddy terrain (mires); people crammed into tents (45 centimeters of space per person), living conditions very bad; hygiene inadequate; lack of drinking water (only seawater); atmospheric conditions very difficult.

Some people were sent to build the airfield and float trees on the Ponoy River, others were detained in a seaport labor camp (loading and unloading of goods for war and food). The people sent to build the airfield and float the trees had the worst possible living conditions: they lived in the open air. They made tents out of bark and sheets (whoever had one), slept on the bare ground (there was no undergrowth suitable for bedding in the taiga), they were literally lying in the mud. The food was no better. We received provisions in small quantities, the official rations were very small (food was provided by Poles specially selected for this purpose), a special transport company was created in the camp whose task was to carry food for the fellow inmates on their shoulders (manual transport was the only one that could reach its destination). Those carrying the food, like all the Poles, were very exhausted from their marches, train journeys, and especially poor nutrition and either ate the food on the way or simply left it on the roadside, wanting to relieve themselves of the burden (one person had to carry 35 kilograms by himself, and the food was often in hard packaging such as a chest). The Poles working at the airfield were starving as a result.

Arkhangelsk: wooden barracks, very limited and muddy terrain.

Talitsy-Yuzha: wooden buildings in camp – single-story, cold and damp, quarters poor, people slept on the floor, bunks were made near the end of my stay at the camp. Insufficient kitchens to cook meals (the kitchen cooked each meal several times, 24 hours a day). The camp included more than 12,000 people. Hunger was rife, as were the consequent illnesses. Hygiene inadequate, terrible lice infestation.

Social composition of POWs:

There were Poles, Belarusians, Ukrainians and Jews at the camp. Criminal category: service in the Polish army and organizations. Intrapersonal relations good.

Life in the camp:

6.00 a.m. – wake-up call, 7.00 a.m. – roll-call, 7.30 a.m. – breakfast, 1.00 p.m. – lunch, 7.00 p.m. – supper. Lights out and sleep at 11.00 p.m. The current condition of the work companies was checked by calling off names every few days, general inspection in the rooms every now and then: they searched mainly for tools like hammers, saws, etc. – various kinds of material. Polish books were also confiscated; anything written in Polish was taken away. The labor consisted primarily of cleaning works, next, living quarters were built strictly in the area of the camp from wood supplied by NKVD soldiers. In exceptional cases, Poles were sent beyond the wire fence to collect wood or to remove the snow from the roads, but they were under a tight guard and those sent out were verified by name before being permitted to leave.

Attitude of the NKVD towards Poles:

Very poor. Communist propaganda vigorously disseminated and applied at every possible opportunity in addition to the constant communist and atheistic lectures. Interrogations were mainly used to catch out officers and non-commissioned officers working in the 2nd Division as well as both uniformed and investigative policemen.

Medical assistance, hospitals, mortality rate:

There were no hospitals in the camp, there were so-called sick wards with a very limited number of beds and inadequate equipment. There were also sanitary ambulances which functioned very poorly. Medical advice was generally given by nurses and our sanitary non-commissioned officers. The lack of medicine made treatment difficult. Mortality was generally low. Retired sergeant Czesław Krupski died suddenly at 7.30 a.m. on 18 November 1940 in the Yukhnovo camp. His last place of residence in Poland was in Baranowicze. There was one more death, but I don't remember the name of the deceased. I know he was a sergeant major serving in the cavalry.

Was it at all possible to get in contact with one's home country and family?

There was contact with Poland, but it was inadequate. Letters from families took very long – two or three months – to be delivered. The letters we sent also took a very long time to reach their destination. Of course, the letters from our families were kept at the camp headquarters and later used against us during interrogation. I maintained contact with my wife in Poland through our children.

When were you released and how did you manage to join the Polish Army?

I was released from the camp on 25 August 1941 following the English-Polish-Soviet agreement. I was sent to the 5th Infantry Division in Tatishchevo, USSR, along with the other prisoners.

Encampment, 19 February 1943

Collection of the Hoover Institution Library & Archives at the disposal of the Central Archives of Modern Records, Władysław Anders Collection. Reports, 800/1/0/-/46, account no. 161.

JOACHIM JAKUBOWSKI

Joachim Jakubowski, born in 1897, State Police officer, married, with two children; platoon of the 1st company of the guard battalion, temporarily attending training for car drivers with the 104th transport company.

I was interned and deported on 12 July 1940 from the internee camp in Lithuania to the internee camp in Kozelsk, USSR. I was detained in the camp in Kozelsk from 14 July 1940 to May 1941.

The camp was set up in former monastery buildings. We lived in monastery rooms, a few hundred or more men to each. For the first few weeks we slept on bare boards, and later we received a kilogram of rotten straw per person, which was to serve us as bedding. The rooms were damp, unheated and murky. The hygiene was in a deplorable state.

As for the composition of the internees, there were over 2,500 people: officers of all ranks from the Polish Army and the police, non-commissioned officers from the Border Protection Corps, gendarmerie and Border Guard, and State Police officers, both young and older, up to 60 years of age, the majority being of Polish nationality, representing a higher intellectual level, and having held various state positions back in Poland. The majority of the inmates of the Kozelsk camp were sent there from Lithuanian camps. The rest were prisoners of war or civilians arrested by the Soviet authorities in the eastern regions of Poland after September 1939. They were arrested or interned because, as loyal citizens of the Polish Republic, they had occupied various state positions. I myself was interned for being a criminal investigation police officer.

At first our life in the camp – considering the living conditions of Soviet citizens – was bearable, although still far below par. Our food consisted of black bread, half a liter of soup and a few spoons of groats seasoned with oil. During my ten months' stay in the Kozelsk camp I was under investigation by the NKVD, during which I was subjected to moral torture, as they tried all possible means to break the spirit of Polishness in me. During interrogations, the NKVD functionaries, whose surnames I didn't catch, often tried to convince me that Poland had been a temporary state, that it would never be reborn and that Communism would rule the world. The NKVD also carried out propaganda activities to the same effect, through talks and lectures delivered in the clubs and through the literature that we had access to in the camp. When the investigation was closed, we were separated from the officers and deported for forced labor to Far North, that is, to the Kola Peninsula.

It was only there that I experienced real camp life. I received clothing consisting of valenki boots, padded pants, shoes and a cap. These clothes were meant to last me through the freezing winter in those parts, where temperatures fell to about 70 degrees below zero. We were transported in sealed boxcars to Murmansk, and from there by ship to the desolate Kola Peninsula. Our food rations consisted of 80–120 grams of bread per day, dried fish and twice some soup made of rye flour. We carried out earthworks at the airfield and road construction sites. I lived in the open air and toiled for 12 hours a day.

The supervising NKVD soldiers were very brutal, and those who couldn't go to work had dogs set on them.

There was neither a bathhouse nor a hospital, and the sick lay on their pallets. The living conditions were unbearable. Had it not been for the German-Soviet war, I wouldn't have endured it.

Following the amnesty we were transported from there first to Arkhangelsk, and then to Suzdal, where after some time I joined the Polish Army.

During the entire period of my stay in the Soviet territory I received only one letter from my wife, who lived in the German-occupied territory, although – as she mentioned – she wrote numerous letters.

In general, my stay in the Soviet Union left me with the worst impression imaginable.

Encampment, 14 March 1943

Collection of the Hoover Institution Library & Archives at the disposal of the Central Archives of Modern Records, Władysław Anders Collection. Reports 800/1/0/-/48, account no. 1710.

TADEUSZ KOBYLARZ

Personal data (name, surname, rank, age, occupation and marital status):
Tadeusz Kobylarz, cadet sergeant, 30 years old, senior border guard, bachelor.

Date and circumstances of arrest:

On 22 August 1940 I was taken from the Ulbroka internee camp in Latvia by the Bolsheviks.

The Name of the camp, prison or forced labor site:

Kozelsk.

Description of the camp or prison (grounds, buildings, housing conditions, hygiene):

The camp in Kozelsk was located in a former monastery. Housing conditions were generally good.

Social composition of POWs, prisoners, exiles (nationality, type of crimes, intellectual and moral standing, mutual relations, etc.):

Those detained in the camp were army and police officers, border guards, and civilians – mostly those whom the Bolsheviks regarded as a threat.

Life in the camp or prison (daily routine, working conditions, quotas, wages, food, clothes, social and cultural life, etc.):

Life in the camp was very monotonous. We spent our time learning foreign languages and playing chess. The food was fairly decent. No clothes were provided for us. As regards cultural life, there was a cinema in the camp, but every film was a very naive and foolish piece of propaganda. Apart from that, there was a Polish choir and an orchestra.

Attitude of the NKVD towards Poles (interrogation methods, torture and other forms of punishment, communist propaganda, information about Poland, etc.):

I was interrogated three times. They asked me about my service as a border guard and the situation on the German border. I was not beaten during the interrogation. Political officers who spread communist propaganda were always ridiculed by the Poles.

Medical assistance, hospitals, mortality rate (provide the names of the deceased):

There was a hospital on the camp grounds, but I was never a patient there. Several deathsoccurred among the internees and two people committed suicide by hanging.

Was it at all possible to get in contact with one's home country and family?

I received no letters from home during my entire stay at the camp. Three letters from my family back home were handed to me only a few days before I was transported to the Kola Peninsula. Other internees received letters quite often, some even got food parcels.

When were you released and how did you manage to join the Polish Army?

In June 1941, I was transported to the Kola Peninsula. From that moment on, we were treated like prisoners and dealt with in a brutal manner. We were transported on board the "Klara Zetkin" ship in terrible, cramped conditions. We received very little food and when we arrived – having had trouble anchoring on account of the stormy seas – we were not fed at all for three days. There were no accommodations on this peninsula apart from several tents. Some of us had to sleep in the open air. There was no bedding or furniture inside the tents. Our task on the peninsula consisted in building a road and working at the port. Food was insufficient, we were given soup, foul-smelling fish, and very little bread – sometimes as little as 75 grams per day. If it were not for the war, 80% of us would not have survived the first winter. People started swelling up due to hunger and the local climate. We stayed on the peninsula about two weeks. They treated us brutally and said that we were going to die there. We were then transported from the Kola Peninsula to Arkhangelsk, and later to the camp in Suzdal. Showing no change in their attitude during our journey back, they beat some of us with rifle butts. Conditions in Suzdal were better. This was where we learned about the treaty with Poland. I joined the Polish army there in August 1941, when Colonel Sulik-Sarnowski visited the camp. No longer under escort, we made our way from Suzdal to Tatishchevo.

Collection of the Hoover Institution Library & Archives at the disposal of the Central Archives of Modern Records, Władysław Anders Collection. Reports, 800/1/0/-/48, account no. 2112.

WALENTY KASPRZYK

Personal data (name, surname, rank, age, occupation and marital status):
Walenty Kasprzyk, cadet platoon-leader, 38 years old, school principal, married.

Date and circumstances of arrest:

Interned in Lithuania in July 1940; deported to the Yukhnov camp in Russia, then sent to work at an airfield construction site on the Kola Peninsula.

Name of the camp, prison or forced labor site:

Ponoy Port, Kola Peninsula.

Description of the camp or prison (grounds, buildings, housing conditions, hygiene):

The main camp consisted of tents. The labor camp, where working groups were sent from the main camp, was a clearing by the river, with no tents. We dug ditches in the ground and covered them with sheets for shelter. It wasn't until later when the tents were sent in, and more and more groups would be placed there. It went on for over a dozen days. There was no medical care at all. Tents in the main camp were infested with bedbugs.

Social composition of POWs, prisoners, exiles (nationality, type of crimes, intellectual and moral standing, mutual relations, etc.):

About 90% of POWs were Poles of Roman Catholic denomination, the rest being Orthodox or unaffiliated. Both reserve soldiers drafted in September 1939 in [illegible] an non-commissioned officers, farmers, craftsmen, and police officers.

Life in the camp or prison (daily routine, working conditions, quotas, wages, food, clothes, social and cultural life, etc.):

We worked two shifts building an airport, 12 hours a day. The quotas were so high that literally nobody was able to fulfill them. We didn't receive any remuneration. The food rations we got were absolutely insufficient even for an idling person. There were days when we were given 80 [sic!] grams of bread and soup once a day. In the initial days, dry provisions were allotted. After returning from work, we had to cook food, but a lack of firewood made it extremely difficult. The ones who were weaker physically were carried back from the airfield. Any kind of cultural life was out of question. One shift never met the other. The shift which arrived at work was held at the side of the airfield until the previous shift went out of sight.

Attitude of the NKVD towards Poles (interrogation methods, torture and other forms of punishment, communist propaganda, information about Poland, etc.):

They tried to induce a conflict between us in the Yukhnov camp. They appealed to the working-class solidarity – they agitated at meetings, in the common-room, through screenings, and at individual talks. A striking demeanor of craftsmen and workers should be noted. There were 41 people who attended the alluring propaganda meetings, mostly the intelligentsia, and they created a cell commonly referred to as Jewish commune. Most people mocked the speakers and made fun of their ignorance. Their [illegible] efforts and creativity were astonishing. They picked on Poland, claiming it would never exist again. On the Kola Peninsula, we were told clearly: "This land is your grave."

Medical assistance, hospitals, mortality rate (provide the names of the deceased):

Medical assistance in Yukhnov was at quite a good level. There were four or five cases of death. On the Kola Peninsula, there was no such care at all. There were medical assistants who didn't even have a thermometer.

Was it at all possible to get in contact with one's home country and family?

The letters would get through to us, but not everybody received them.

When were you released and how did you manage to join the Polish Army?

Following the Polish-Soviet agreement, we were deported from Kola [Peninsula] via Arkhangelsk to a camp outside Vyazniki [Talitsy], where recruitment for the Polish army was held.

Collection of the Hoover Institution Library & Archives at the disposal of the Central Archives of Modern Records, Władysław Anders Collection. Reports, 800/1/0/-/47, account no. 650.

ANTONI PYZEL

Personal data:
Antoni Pyzel, sergeant major, 40 years old, regular non-commissioned officer, married.

Date and circumstances of arrest:

On 11 July 1940 I was deported by the NKVD from an internment camp in Vaitkuškis/Ukmergė in Lithuania. I had been interned on 25 September 1939 in Lithuania, and sent to a camp in the township of Birštonas.

Name of the camp, prison or forced labor site:

Yukhnov camp (Pavlishchev Bor).

Description of the camp or prison:

Pleasant woodlands, ordinary buildings – former stables. In winter the place was damp, the walls were all wet and we had water and mud on the floor.

Housing conditions: cramped, dark and stuffy rooms, three-story bunks, plenty of bugs, rats and mice.

Maintaining hygiene was possible, as we were issued soap; underwear was washed in the general laundry by the internees, who took turns doing it. There was bath once a week and checking for lice; cutting hair and shaving were for free, by ticket; the barbers were from among the internees, but they had pitiful haircutting utensils at their disposal.

Social composition of POWs, prisoners, exiles:

There were about 2,800 internees; 85% were of Polish nationality, and 14% were Belarusians and 1% Jews. Categories of crimes: almost exclusively internees, of average intellectual level, a lot of non-commissioned officers and officer cadets on active duty or in the reserve; privates in the reserve – teachers, public and private clerks, specialists and owners of various enterprises. Moral standing: about 1.5% supported the Soviet system and attended lectures on the history of Lenin, Stalin, Engels and Marx which were held in the "synagogue" as we called it, and they also started the so-called "Impiety Club" for combatting religion; in February 1941, the same people sent a congratulatory card to Stalin on behalf of Soviet Poland.

Once – availing myself of an opportunity – I entered this club and saw a banner on the wall; I don't remember what it said, but my hair stood on end when I read it. It was usually non-commissioned officers on active duty and officer cadets who were proponents of all of this; it all happened in the evenings behind closed doors.

Life in the camp, prison:

The course of an average day: wake-up at 6.00 a.m., dressing, washing, cleaning the area and the barracks; 7.00 a.m. – roll-call, checking numbers by an NKVD political commissar; 7.30 a.m. – breakfast; 8.00 a.m. – a gathering of those who volunteered for work or worked in the brigades of the internal camp service (peeling potatoes, carting and chopping wood etc.). Others had time off, so they walked around the camp, read books and newspapers. Dinner at 1.00 p.m., supper at 7.00 p.m., curfew at 9.00 p.m.

Work was done on a volunteer basis – there were no work quotas, but you received an additional ration of 400 grams of bread and hot meal. We didn't receive any remuneration except for bread and soup. Food rations: 800 grams of bread. Breakfast: potato soup or a soup of millet groats; dinner: soup and dry oat or millet groats; supper: tea. We received 600 grams of sugar and five packages of shag tobacco per month. At times they fed us decently, taking into account the situation of their economy, and at times it was the other way round. At first, soon after our arrival, they gave us rotten meat, so-called green carrion; the cooks told us that the meat would fall apart in their hands, and when they cooked it, they could barely stand the stench in the kitchen. They made goulash from this meat and served it with groats; those who were hungry had to eat it.

As for clothes, the majority had their own military clothing, well-groomed and mended personally and with great care; the privileged ones received padded jackets and warm trousers, and those who didn't have blankets were issued some.

As for social life, it was good. People usually formed small groups, as we were afraid of those who liked to repeat to the NKVD what we were saying among ourselves, and it was difficult to find out who did so.

Cultural life: our own Polish books brought from Lithuania, Russian books from the camp library, various weekly and daily newspapers, always old ones. There was a radio, but it was difficult to understand anything – it was a piece of old junk. We watched films very often, but they were nothing but propaganda. Before we left for the Kola Peninsula, that is, in May 1941, they screened a film that was shot in Poland by Wanda Wasilewska, entitled "Wiatr od wschodu" [The Eastern Wind]. This film is based on lies and slanders Polish authorities, such as the army, the judiciary and the police. Suffice it to say that during the screening, the audience began to whistle and stomp, and someone was heard saying, "If you think yourself a Pole, please leave and don't watch these lies."

Before the film, there would be some Polish and Russian singing or sometimes a short performance, always arranged by the camp commandant.

Attitude of the NKVD towards Poles:

In our camp, the interrogation methods were mild. You would come to an interrogation, and the NKVD political commissar would tell you to sit down and offer you a cigarette; then he would begin the cant. I was interrogated three times, but I didn't tell them the truth as regards military matters, though I did as regards my personal details and that of my family.

They would wake you up at night for an interrogation. They also deported us to other camps: then a political commissar from the NKVD would come at night and read out a surname. "Is so-and-so present? Take all your stuff, you're going to the I Corps." He wouldn't leave until the man in question was ready; those who went away never returned, and it was a puzzle for the rest of us where and for what reason he had gone. The time has come, we have met again. Torture wasn't used at our camp. There were disciplinary penalties for slandering one another, since when the NKVD learned of it, they never failed to make some use of it. For disobedience you were put in jail.

Communist propaganda was very widespread; everything down to the smallest detail was red. In the first days after our arrival at the camp, we were subjected to agitprop; there were many meetings which we attended because we had been told that they were obligatory, but as soon as people realized how weak and stupid the Russians were, they began to ignore the meetings and the attendance dropped. I will now give a brief summary of a speech delivered by a captain, NKVD commissar Lavrenko, to the internees gathered at a meeting. He said that England was a prostitute, that it suffered from "syphilitic decay," that it was stupid and that it caused the outbreak of the war, and that we Poles made a mistake in siding with them, that it was because of England that our officers had fled abroad, and that we lost the war because our officers did nothing but partied and were poorly educated. After such a meeting there was time for *voprosy*; when one of the internees said something about the Germans, the captain yelled like a wounded animal, "All lies, what's your name?" And a few days later this person was deported to another camp.

Information about Poland was scant, mostly from daily and weekly newspapers, and critical of everything that was Polish – everything was bad, Poles rode on mules, peasants didn't have axes and cultivated land with wooden plows. "Poland has disappeared for good. They had liberated us from oppression of the landowners, Belarus and Ukraine would rule forever, and then other countries would also fall." In short, according to their propaganda – which was based on what Jews said – everything that was Polish had ceased to exist.

Medical assistance, hospitals, mortality rate:

The doctors were from among the internees and provided very good medical care, but a large number of patients led to a shortage of medicaments; also, there was no dental care. The hospital at the site was small, with some 40 beds, but it was quite decently equipped and clean. It was run by the internees, but the post of the chief doctor was occupied by a Soviet doctor.

Mortality in the period from 14 July 1940 to 6 June 1941 – five people. Cavalry Captain Gabriel Sierdziukow from the 1st Uhlan Regiment fell ill on 3 May and died on 5 May 1941. He was my friend from the garrison back in Poland and my companion in misery – we shared one pallet at the camp. I don't remember other surnames.

One of the internees committed suicide – he drowned himself in a latrine that was up to 3 meters deep. Reason: on 1 June 1941, 1,000 people from the camp were deported in an unknown direction. He must have thought that they had been taken for forced labor or even execution, and the poor man's nerves gave way. It happened on 4 June 1941 at 3.00 a.m. He was taken out with pike-poles by the NKVD. He came from the Wilno region; he had repatriated from America. I don't remember his surname; I made some notes, but they took them away from me.

Was it at all possible to get in contact with one's home country and family?

I got three letters and a small food parcel from my wife. The letters had been sent by mail from Białystok, and the parcel was sent from Baranowicze. Probably it was forbidden to send food parcels from Białystok. I also got a letter from my friend in Warsaw, sent by mail. I would like to emphasize that I learned virtually nothing from my wife's letters, as they had been cut up by the Soviet censors. I had the opportunity to see my files, the so-called *Uchotnoye Delo* [register], known as the black book – it contained some 12 letters, which I never received despite my pleas.

When were you released and how did you manage to join the Polish Army?

On 6 June 1941, we were deported from the Yukhnov camp to Murmansk; it was the second transport and comprised 1,000 people. On 22 June we were loaded onto the "Klara Zetkin" ship in the Murmansk harbor and taken by a circuitous route to the Kola Peninsula.

During the journey we didn't get anything to eat for three days, but nevertheless we were all in a good mood in that big coffin. We sang patriotic songs, such as *Boże, coś Polskę* [God save Poland], *Rota* [The Oath], *Mazurek Dąbrowskiego* [the Polish national anthem], *Polonia* and many others.

On 27 June we gave our best wishes to all those named Władysław and on 29 June to all those named Piotr and Paweł. On 1 July we reached solid ground and were unloaded. We were marched 5 kilometers away from the sea, and when we stopped they said that this was the place where we had to live and work.

It is difficult to describe it all. Dense forest, swamps; you wouldn't even spot a bird. It was July, but when the sun disappeared, we had to put on our coats. They told us about thc outbreak of the war with the Germans, but we had learned about it earlier – reporting for work on board the ship was a chance to find out about something and share the news.

All this time we had to work for 12 hours, in two shifts: one during the day and the other at night. They needed a road from the Ponoy harbor to a makeshift airport situated 17 kilometers inland, where half of our friends worked, suffering cold and hunger.

On 11 July they ordered us to abandon work and take our things, and when we were all gathered they marched us to the harbor. They loaded us onto the "Aldan" and transported us to the Arkhangelsk harbor. In Arkhangelsk we were locked behind the wires of a labor camp. We were impossibly cramped – they must have crammed 100 people where there was room for 10 – and they began to starve us. We stormed the gate, singing patriotic songs. We succeeded, they gave us food, although very little.

I don't remember the date, but one day they loaded us into a train at the station in Arkhangelsk and brought us to Vyazniki. From there we covered 40 kilometers on foot to reach the Yuzha camp, where we were placed behind wires. There we met over 10,000 of our companions in misery from various camps. Everyone looked for his friends, colleagues etc. We spent a few days there. Food was very scant. Finally a day came when they announced to us that we – former internees, POWs, inmates and exiles – had become free citizens of an independent Polish state and that the Polish Army was being raised in the USSR. We rejoiced and cheered, and they told us that we would be paid damages. We were given 500 rubles each.

Finally a day came when they told us that a delegate from Poland would come to see us. On the morning of 27 August I peeked through the wires; we couldn't believe our own eyes: there was a stand decorated with greenery and Polish flags next to it. Thousands of hearts trembled with joy; it was a great holiday at the camp. We formed into squadrons, companies and batteries; we went outside the wires for the first time without our guards, as free citizens, in serried ranks – a great celebration was to be held.

We arrived at the square and waited for our savior with our hearts pounding and our eyes fixed in the direction from which the guest was expected to come. There was silence, deep silence; we were curious: who is he? Finally, some silhouettes emerged from the building; someone in the ranks recognized his old commander – recognized him despite the fact that he wore civilian clothes and looked haggard after all the time he had spent in prison.

The man in plain clothes was Colonel Sulik-Sarnowski, who had been released from prison a few days earlier. He gave a short but impassioned speech, addressing us in soldierly words. Many of us cried like babies, picturing themselves already in Poland, with their dearest ones, their family. There was a parade, the old brothers-in-arms did not forget their trade, and marched before the tribune with such vigor as if they had just secured a most beautiful victory; we marched with our heads up to the throbbing of our hearts, which beat out the rhythm in place of a march played by a band. On that day we all marched with an appearance so solemn that, without knowing who we were, one might have taken us for guard units rather than people deprived of everything, harried by more than two years of camps, prisons and exile into the unknown, people who had no right to live. People, who – according to Hitler and Stalin's norms – were to disappear from the face of the earth.

On that festive day the soldiers received passes to kolkhozes and hamlets to get food. We began a new life, and cows, sheep, hens etc. were brought from the kolkhozes.

At the same time, we appeared before the medical board. We were all in good health; everybody wanted to join the army and made plans for the future, and we simply couldn't wait to finally put on the uniform of a Polish soldier. It didn't come easy, as we had to wait a long time for our beautiful uniforms, but finally that moment also came.

Towards the end of August, we were loaded as the Polish Army onto trains at the station in Vyazniki. We left for Tatishchevo, Saratov area, where we were assigned to the 5th Infantry Division.

Collection of the Hoover Institution Library & Archives at the disposal of the Central Archives of Modern Records, Władysław Anders Collection. Reports, 800/1/0/-/48, account no. 2338.

GLOSSARY

A-D

amnesty – here: the release of citizens of the Second Polish Republic who had been arrested, deported or detained in the USSR in the years 1939–1941. Pursuant to the Sikorski-Mayski Agreement of 30 July 1941, the Presidium of the Supreme Soviet of the USSR issued a decree granting amnesty to the Polish citizens on 12 August 1941. The amnesty was a chance for survival for thousands of detainees.

beseda (Russian for 'a talk') – in the context of labor camps, a *beseda* was a propaganda talk delivered by an official from the political department of the NKVD, who usually praised Communism and life in the Soviet Union, while criticizing Poland and claiming that it would never be restored.

"Clara Zetkin" – one of the cargo ships used for transporting Polish internees for labor to the Ponoy camp. The ship was named after Clara Zetkin (1857–1933), a German Communist activist who emigrated to the USSR after Hitler came to power.

death marches – eastbound transports of prisoners and POWs from the detention sites in the western oblasts of the USSR that followed the outbreak of the German-Soviet War. During the evacuations carried out by the NKVD, prisoners and POWs were forced to march at an extremely strenuous pace or were transported in overcrowded cattle wagons. Some of them died of exhaustion and many were shot by the escort.

dezokamera (Russian for 'delousing facility') – a facility used for exterminating lice and disinfecting clothes, which was set up in every prison and labor camp, and where the prisoners were obligated to hand in their clothes upon arrival to the detention site and later at specific intervals. Despite the existence of such facilities, there were frequent instances of typhus epidemics.

detskyi dom (Russian for 'orphanage') – a high mortality rate among the exiles in 1940 resulted in a large number of Polish orphans, who were put up in Soviet orphanages. After diplomatic relations were established

GLOSSARY

between the Polish and Soviet governments, Polish orphanages also began operating.

dopros (Russian for 'interrogation', used synonymously with **voprosy** ('questions')) – the POWs were usually interrogated at night and often beaten and threatened in the process.

Gulag (Russian: *Glavnoe Upravleniye ispravitelno-trudovykh lagerey* – Main Administration of Corrective Labor Camps) – an agency operating in the years 1930–1960 with the objective of managing unpaid labor of prisoners in the territory of the USSR. The Gulag comprised approximately 30,000 detention sites.

internees – civilian and military persons forcibly deported to a detention site. When soldiers from countries engaged in a military conflict enter the territory of a neutral state, they can be disarmed and interned by the said state. This policy was used by the neutral Baltic states, Hungary and Romania with regards to the Polish Army soldiers who crossed their borders in September 1939.

ITL (Russian: *Ispravitelno-trudovoy lager* – corrective labor camp) – the system of Communist repressions was based on forced labor of political prisoners. Their slave labor was a substantial element of many key branches of centrally planned economy, e.g. forestry and construction. Deportation to such camps was carried out pursuant to a court ruling.

NKVD (Russian: *Narodnyi komissaryat vnutrennikh del* – The People's Commissariat for Internal Affairs) – in the years 1934–1946, the NKVD combined the competences of the Ministry of Internal Affairs and a secret service. It was also in charge of the criminal police and special court martials (*NKVD troikas*) and the entire network of forced labor camps.

northern camps – a collective term for forced labor camps in the Far North of the USSR, which included camps in the Komi Republic, Murmansk Oblast, Arkhangelsk Oblast and Kolyma, located partially in the subarctic zone. Harsh climate and heavy labor caused high mortality among the prisoners.

oblast – a unit of administrative division in the Soviet Union and modern-day Russia. The USSR was divided into union republics, autonomous republics, autonomous oblasts, national okrugs, krais and oblasts. Unfamiliar with this complex administrative structure, the exiles often used the term *oblast* with reference to all areas of the USSR in which they were detained.

Osoboye soveshchaniye NKVD (**Special Council of the NKVD** or **Special troika**) – an organ operating in the years 1924–1953, comprised of three members: representative of the NKVD for the Russian Soviet Federative Socialist Republic, head of the main command of the police, and commissar of the union republic in which the crime was committed. The majority of sentences were passed in absentia – without calling the defendant.

otkaznik – a person who refused to work. Everyone in forced labor camps had to work and fulfill quotas. *Otkaz* (Russian for 'refusal') was punished with solitary confinement, withdrawal of food rations and deportation to camps with harsher conditions. Refusing to work allowed prisoners to save some strength and was often their only chance for survival.

payok, payka – receiving a full food ration was practically impossible in the camps, so the prisoners often used their daily bread ration (*payka*) to measure their actual food rations. The rest, i.e. soup, groats, fat, fish and sugar was commonly referred to as *payok* ('food ration'). The quantity of the food was determined by climate conditions (e.g. an arctic *payok* was increased), percentage of the quota that was fulfilled or by the prisoner's status.

pomeshchik (Russian for 'landlord') – after the revolution of 1917, all estates belonging to landlords were nationalized. A *pomeshchik* – just like "the bourgeois" and "counter-revolutionaries" – was considered an enemy of the people. The term was applied in criminal law and used as an insult.

prembludo (Russian for 'bonus meal') – an additional food ration, e.g. a piece of bread or fish. In most cases it consisted of a *pirozhok* (a type of bun) with peas, potatoes or cabbage. A bonus ration was awarded only for exceeding the quota, which meant that it was available solely to the Stakhanovites.

sabotazhnik (Russian for 'saboteur') – pursuant to Article 58 of the RSFSR Penal Code, put in force in 1927, sabotage was a crime punishable by death in the Stalinist period. The definition of the term was very broad and had a political character.

Solovki – a common name for the Solovki Special Camp located on the Solovetsky Islands in the White Sea. It was the first concentration camp in the Soviet Union, which operated in the years 1923–1933. Presently, Solovki is an important site commemorating the victims of Soviet repressions, which has been added to UNESCO's World Heritage List.

sotnya – a group of one hundred; work in the camps lasted 24 hours a day, so prisoners worked shifts – when one group numbering 100 people worked, another remained in the barracks.

Stakhanovites – members of the movement promoting exceptional work productivity in the Soviet Union, named after its official initiator, miner Alexey Stakhanov. The Stakhanovites in the camps received e.g. larger and better food rations.

taiga – coniferous forests in the cold and temperate climate in the Northern Hemisphere. The internees from the Second Polish Republic often mixed up the taiga with the tundra, and used both terms when referring simply to the northern parts of the USSR.

tundra – a treeless vegetation zone in the cold climate of the arctic and subarctic regions of the Northern Hemisphere, characterized by harsher climate conditions than the taiga.

INDEX OF PERSONS

A-J

INDEX OF PERSONS

INDEX OF PERSONS W-Ż

INDEX OF LOCATIONS

Index includes countries, regions, towns, cities, residential districts, streets, and other common toponyms appearing in the witness interview reports. It reflects pre-war administrative division to which the witnesses usually referred. In an administrative area was subsequently incorporated into a given city of if a street name was changed, the appropriate information is given in brackets.

INDEX OF LOCATIONS

INDEX OF LOCATIONS

INDEX OF LOCATIONS

SHARE YOUR MEMORY

In Chronicles of Terror, it is the voice of witnesses and victims of totalitarianism that is heard. But we would also like to see their faces. Join us in making our portal as complete as possible.

We are continually adding photographs, documents, letters, and accounts as well as other mementos linked to those testifying and to those whose names appear in the testimonies to the digital database (**ChroniclesofTerror.pl**). We are also interested in any material related to the places and events described in the testimonies. Whether you live in Poland or abroad, we would be delighted to include your mementos in our portal in digitized form.

If the names of your ancestors, relatives, friends, or neighbors appear in the testimonies, and if you have any additional information or material pertaining to their fate, please get in touch with us and share your memory!

podzielsiepamiecia@instytutpileckiego.pl

CHRONICLES OF TERROR VOL. 8

Concept of the series: Anna Gutkowska, Wojciech Kozłowski, Tomasz Stefanek
Concept of the volume: Bartosz Gralicki
Managing Editor: Iwona Jabłońska
Translators: Aleksandra Arumińska, Natalia Charitonow, Piotr Czyżewski, Edyta Grabowska, Joanna Jodłowska, Jagoda Lembicz, Katarzyna Makulec, Artur Mękarski, Paulina Monczak-Mancewicz, Julia Niedzielko, Ian Stephenson, Maciej Szwarc, Maciej Zakrzewski
Copy Editors: John Cornell, Dominika Gajewska, Michael Miskiel, Julia Niedzielko, Patryk Roczon, Jonathan Weber
Glossary: Olga Lebedeva
Rewievers: Prof. Daniel Boćkowski, Dr. Jerzy Rohoziński
Indexes: Małgorzata Ziemińska
Graphic Design: Kasper Skirgajłło-Krajewski
Typesetting: Maciej Sawicki
Printed by: Mariusz Rajski Soft Vision

On the cover: photograph of the officers of the Ceremonial Squadron boarding a train, 1919–1923, taken by Narcyz Witczak-Witaczyński, ensign of the cavalry of the Polish Army (source: National Digital Archives).

The testimonies of victims of Soviet crimes gathered under the "Chronicles of Terror" project come from the Hoover Institution Archives. The microfilms which are held by the Archives of Modern Records were digitalized by the National Digital Archives.

Published by: Witold Pilecki Institute of Solidarity and Valor
ul. Foksal 17, 00-372 Warsaw, Poland
www.instytutpileckiego.pl

Ministry of Culture and National Heritage of the Republic of Poland.

ISBN: 978-83-66340-16-9
Warszawa 2020